John Watts De Peyster

An Inquiry into the Career and Character of Mary Stuart

John Watts De Peyster

An Inquiry into the Career and Character of Mary Stuart

ISBN/EAN: 9783337064082

Printed in Europe, USA, Canada, Australia, Japan

Cover: Foto ©ninafisch / pixelio.de

More available books at **www.hansebooks.com**

AN INQUIRY

INTO THE

CAREER AND CHARACTER

OF

MARY STUART

("CRUX CRITICORUM.")
("The puzzle of critics.")

AND A

JUSTIFICATION

OF

BOTHWELL

("AUDIRE EST OPERÆ PRETIUM.")
("What is herein disclosed is worthy of attention.")

BY

★ J. WATTS DE PEYSTER, ★

"Anchor."

New York:
CHARLES H. LUDWIG, PRINTER, 10 & 12 READE STREET.
1883.

To the Original of this Pen Portrait.

"The prettiest, tiniest little head
That ever sat on an ivory neck—
So smooth and so rounded—without a fleck—
That jewels were wasted such throat to deck—
In its muslin frill, like pearl in its bed;
With a flood of soft, rippling nut-brown hair,
Reflecting in gold the kiss of the air;
Ears small and so perfect—but by him seen,
Praxiteles models they might have been,
To complete his statue of Beauty's queen:
And eyes like turquoise and sapphire mingled;
A voice as when silver bells are tingled—
And withal so saucy! There's not a grace
But finds a fit home in that charming face!"

TO WHOSE SUGGESTION

THE AUTHOR'S

STUDIES ON MARY STUART AND BOTHWELL

ARE DUE,

This Work is Gratefully Dedicated.

Bothwell.

"And wrought fell deeds the troubled world along,
For he was fierce as brave, and pitiless as strong."
SIR WALTER SCOTT's *Vision of Don Roderick,*" xxx.

LADY BUCCLEUGH.—" And loves she Bothwell?"
LADY KERES.—   " Yes, indeed she does:
  And she hath found in him a nobler mate
  Than any yet on whom she's fix'd her choice:
  The rest were boys. In him she's found a MAN;
  A rough one it is true, but still a MAN:
  A diamond but half polish'd, but a MAN:
  HEPBURN's a jewel meet for MARY STUART.
  They greet at him, but such as he can scorn
  The calculating, hypocritic guile
  Of foxy MORTON, KNOX's fav'rite MURRAY,
  Who leaves to baser instruments the deed,
  And looks at evil through, betwixt, his fingers;
  Ready to pluck the fruit when it's matur'd
  Upon the muck heap fully fed its growth;
  And if *for him* cares not how 't grew or grows.
  James Hepburn, with his mail'd and stalwart hand
  Plucks the ripe ear at once, with fearless front;
  He is no coward. 'Mid false, sordid ' Bonds'
  That rule this Scotland, HE *alone* is true.
  Poor he has been, despite his lofty birth,
  So poor he's lack'd a single golden piece
  To pay his score: yet never took a bribe
  To wrong his country for a foreign quean;—
  He never sold his honor to Queen Bess,
  As other nobles flout at faithfulness
  So that their jerkins gleam at Tudor cost.
  His creed he's clung to spite of ev'ry wile,
  Nor ever made, like Murray, creed the cloak
  To hide intent, and set the kiln on fire
  That burn'd our land, aye, to the very bone,
  So that it prov'd alembic whence t' extract
  Gain, influence, power, for selfish ends.
  Hepburn's no hypocrite! He loves MARY
  For Mary Stuart's sake, and will not yield
  A single inch to foreign lure or price,

>   Content to risk the loss of all he seeks
>   Rather than sacrifice the faith is his.
>   Sin! he may sin against his own brave soul,
>   But never 'gainst what he deems great and true
>   To foster his ambition. The people,
>   They know that in his soul, there burns the fire
>   For Scotland's Independence flaming high.
>   The nobles love him not. He scorns their lies,
>   Their moral weakness and their selfish strength,
>   However brave in brawl and shedding blood.
>   Among the nobles, Hepburn's not a friend;
>   But 'mid the people, duly weigh'd 's the man,
>   There's not a lord is held in such content
>   And honest admiration. This makes MARY,
>   Despising such a coward thing as DARNLEY,
>   Seek to break loose from brilliant toy she once,
>   With love begotten through the eye, not reason,
>   So madly wed, and long to link her fate
>   With one who, once beside her on the throne,
>   Fit mate would be for a queen to mate with:
>   And brave as she, throw banner to the winds,
>   And say to England, 'Come what storm come may,
>   I and my husband will affront it boldly!'"
>
>   "JAMES HEPBURN, Earl of Bothwell," *a Tragedy*.

HE world judges by results. Admiration, even if accompanied with discontent or heart-burning irritation, follows those men who, by audacious craft, succeed in attaining the highest power. He, however, who just before reaching his objective, has a fall, perhaps richly merited, may be certain that not merely hate, but also ridicule and even contempt, will sit in judgment on him; and, at the same time that his chief characteristics are denied to him, the decision will be so distorted as to be irrecognizable. If, again, the individual, on trial, has sought to elevate himself by crime, no enemy will let the opportunity escape for throwing the full weight of moral vengeance upon him, and, in

this way, win, in turn, for himself the appearance of being a defender of the innocent and a champion of the right. Not such should be the judgment of history: and, if the hate of contemporaries has, as it were, stoned a prominent man, then the duty of the Muse, as difficult as it is necessary, is to trace back the causes and sift the evidence on which the verdict was founded,—a labor often long deferred by passions, aroused and successful—for the time being—to what clearness is possible, and to extricate the *truth*, so to speak, from the ruins.

A fate of this sort, tragical not only by reason of rapid elevation and sudden fall, but also of the undeservedly severe verdict of posterity, has been the portion of JAMES HEPBURN, EARL OF BOTHWELL, the third husband of Mary Stuart. In his case, if nothing more is regarded than the intimate relations into which he came with the unfortunate queen, this alone should furnish the strongest incentive for historians to investigate his true character thoroughly, in order to derive therefrom important historical data to form a correct judgment of the whole period. Unhappily, calumny grows luxuriantly over the fallen. It springs up, partly, from wickedness originating in design, and, partly, from blind moral anger, multiplied and recorded by scandalous, and yet more by thoughtless, persons, without proof. It climbs like poisonous ivy, thick and disorderly over Bothwell, and so conceals his true form that this can only, at last and with great labor, be, as it were, stripped of the rank investure. One writer only has as yet, properly speaking, taken his part, Dr. PHIL. A. PETRICK, who, in his Pamphlet, about 50 pages, "*Zur Geschichte des Grafen Bothwell,*" Berlin—St. Petersburg, 1874—a wonderfully clear and honest production, has striven to show to what lengths falsehood, calumny, enmity, jealousy, and a host of other meaner characteristics, crowned with success, can go to blacken the life and memory of an honest opponent after he had lost the game and stakes in a contest with the vilest sharpers.

A defence, and counsel, by the principles of a wise justice, among civilized peoples, is allowed even to the manifestly guilty. How much more is it a duty to accord it to one whose guilt is at least *not* certain, and whose motives may be clearly traced. Yes, it is an unavoidable duty. The object of this little work, confined within the narrowest limits, is not intended to be, properly speaking, a defence, but it inevitably becomes such. This is a consequence of the facts drawn from trustworthy sources. It is especially intended to fulfill a task which should long ago have been performed, and which is indispensable as a preparatory study to any impartial inquisition into that period of history. This is so not only because it will clearly show what accusations have been heaped upon him justly; what others without proof, and what others from sheer calumny. This is the more necessary on account of the short time during which he influenced the fate of Scotland, not only greatly but decisively (1566 and 1567). During this period he was the central figure of the crisis—a crisis replete with results. This investigation will especially clear up, with the aid of all the means at the command of the critic, the facts of his previous career, as well as of its termination, and seek to obtain a judgment on him and of his character and motives, from both of those periods. When even great writers of history, examining those years alone, however closely, let him, so to speak, rise out of the darkness and then leave him to sink back into the same darkness, such an examination as is proposed herein is a wonderful satisfaction, if nothing else. It is not only from interest in the man, but much more for the purpose of understanding the times in which he so prominently figured, that the complete comprehension of his characteristics are indispensably requisite. And if we are unable to determine scarcely more than approximately the date of his death and the day of his birth, it is yet an absolute duty to piece together, with all possible exactness, whatever facts of his life may yet be discovered. To quarry them out of the original sources is indeed a difficult, but not a thankless toil, since the most fruitful revelations for the whole period become the rewards of the difficult labor—and the more that the authorities consulted, to a greater or less degree, immediately obscure the image, the more does it become evident that only a very close investigation and comparison can reveal with clearness, the true form, its proportions, peculiarities and excellencies.

The judgments pronounced on Bothwell are almost unanimous, and yet they do not hang together. They are unanimous in that all, to a certain extent, condemn him. They are all inconsequent, because they are founded on statements which not only differ from, but contradict each other. Suspicion as to these verdicts is thus only too fully justified.

First in order, his contemporaries, among his accusers, require consideration. Buchanan never styles him otherwise than "a wicked and perfidious man." The "pirate" is with him the regular epithet. In the same way, in Murray's Diary for the 20th July, the "pirates" are Bothwell and his friends. Buchanan, in his " Detection of Mary and Action against Mary" the Queen, is full of the lowest abuse of him. Certainly the skillfully planned design of throwing back the implied reflection on Mary herself shows through only too clearly, and yet calumny always attains its object, in so far that a part of it invariably seems to impress itself indelibly upon the recollection. "Calumniate boldly," says the Proverb, "some will stick." The English Ambassadors in Scotland, Throckmorton, Randolph, Bedford, next join in. Throckmorton, November, 1560, calls him "a vain-glorious, rash and hazardous young man." This is a forced translation ; "GLORIOUS" (*gloriosus*) has for its primary meaning "illustrious."

Randolph to Cecil, 3d June, 1563, styles him "a naked, good for nothing beggar; the same, 31st March, 1562, "The Earl of Bothwell (tried to) waylay Ormiston twice;" 6th April, 1566, "I assure (you) Bothwell is as naughty a man as liveth, and much given to the detestable vices." Bedford to Cecil, 12th August, 1566, "Bothwell has grown of late so hated that he cannot long continue." Yet sharper is the official letter of James VI. (that is of his guardian, the Earl of Murray, for James was then evidently only two years old) concerning the delivering up of Bothwell by King Frederick II. of Denmark, of the date 21st August, 1568. It reads, "An assassin of well known cruelty;" "A robber condemned by divine and human judgment." Elizabeth to Frederick II., 1569. 26th August, 1568, "the parricidal murderer of his king." She seems to believe that he was related to Darnley. Remark that in this letter Elizabeth styles Darnley "King," to whom in his lifetime she always denied that title, even at the christening of his son. Buchanan to Frederick II. of Denmark, 19th March, 1591, "An incorrigible traitor," All this is outdone by Thomas Buchanan, Ambassador of James VI., to Denmark, in his letter to Frederick II., 1571, "A monstrous beast, and of all men who exist, or ever will, the most wicked."

That all the accusers of Mary Stuart sound loudly the same notes is the more easily explained that these contemporaries were simply accomplices of Bothwell, as will be demonstrated. Those who especially followed the tactics of painting Bothwell in the blackest colors felt the more compelled to do so in order, by this means, to destroy the character of Mary Stuart. But when a Hume will concede nothing good of Bothwell, and says, " without being distinguished by a single talent, whether for politics or war, he had obtained for himself a certain amount of reputation; perfectly immoral, overwhelmed by debts which were greater than his property, he had plunged himself into absolute need by his dissoluteness, and appeared to have no other resources than desperate undertakings "—it is notably unintelligible how such a man, " without a single talent," could attain to so great a preponderance that he even, by the admission of his enemies, governed Mary Stuart, and got rid of Darnley by murdering him, without any one daring to rise against him; forced even the Parliament to acquit him; compelled the assent of the whole nobility to his marriage with Mary; and could be eventually overthrown only by cunning, surprise and treachery, such as transcended the cold-blooded calculation of a Machiavelli, the sensual cruelty of a Borgia, and the conscienceless fiendishness of a Visconti.

"Italy has been commonly regarded as the country where, in the Middle Ages, the art of political perfidy reached the highest degree of perfection; but we may search the annals of Rome or Venice in vain for the details of any plot which, for depth or villainy, can match with that of which the murder of Rizzio was only the first act. What were the consequences to be anticipated from that outrage? Probably the miscarriage, perhaps the death * of the Queen; and failing these contingencies, her deposition and imprisonment. What was to follow next? The elevation to the throne of a prince who was an object of hatred and contempt of every one of his associates, and whose incorrigible folly would speedily afford them an opportunity and a pretext for depriving him of his authority. Then, and not till then, would the true objects of Rizzio's murder be disclosed—namely, the usurpation of the government, with the certain support of the more fanatical section of the Scottish Protestants and the hardly less certain support of the Queen of England. Machiavelli never conceived—he has certainly never described—a plot more devilish in its designs than that which was devised by the more knowing of the conspirators, ostensibly for the death of Rizzio, but in reality for the destruction of both Mary Stuart and her husband." (Hosack I., 142-3.)

On the other hand, it might be reasonably supposed that the champions of Mary Stuart would also defend him (Bothwell). Not at all; they abandon him entirely. Camden styles him "a weak man." Melvil, the trusted

---

* Melville, who was at Holyrood at the time, says: "For she being big with child, it appeared to be done to destroy both her and her child; for they might have killed the said Rizzio in any other part at any time they pleased."—"Memoirs," 66.

counsellor of Mary, who, however, quickly changed into her persecutor, describes him as making, continually, attempts on the life of the Queen (!), of Arran, of Murray, of Darnley, of Melville, and of whom else who knows; and he entirely denies to Bothwell the possession of courage. The following abuse is applied to him: "Heart failed him, his arm was not so valiant as his tongue;" so also the "*Histoire Tragique*," "his cowardice." Herrera, "wherefore being very ambitious and given to self-indulgence." Blackwood, in his "Martyrdom of Mary Stuart," calls him "audacious, proud, easy to be influenced." Brantome, the devoted worshipper of ladies, thinks to annihilate him: "For this Bothwell was the most ugly man and the most ungraceful that could be seen." Blackwood, however, energetically contradicts this, and cites Bothwell "For his beauty." Furthermore, as a pattern of disconnected, self-contradicting judgment, may stand a passage from Buchanan, his embittered enemy (Action against Mary, Jebb I., 255): "What is there in him that would be attractive to a woman who was at all particular? Does any one see in him any dignity of speech, or figure, or strength of mind? But there is no need to say much of eloquence or form, when no one who heard him could doubt the puerility and dullness of the man. He was prudent in the business he undertook, resolute in facing danger, munificent in giving, temperate in his pleasures! Not even those most devoted to him ventured to credit him with prudence!! [Note the absolute irreconcilableness of these last two sentences.] He secured a reputation for bravery; but surrounded by horsemen, mounted upon a fierce horse, personally safe, looking at the fighting of others, now and then he pursued a flying enemy. He never could endure to look upon the threatening countenance of a foeman at close quarters."

This would be killing judgment if it only possessed either sense or connection, but does it not seem exactly as if a writer were credulous enough to put together, without examination or comparison, a mosaic of scraps picked up blindly from promiscuous sources of information? What is more, the whole of these* do not agree together, and it

---

* Rapin, acknowledged by all but ultras—Papists and Mariolotrists—as a standard and trustworthy authority, makes some remarks upon the the history of this period which must be conclusive to every reader not cased in the stiff panoply of religious prejudice, and wrapped, as to the mental vision, with the bandage of bigoted dogmatism. In his folio edition (London, 1733; Vol. II., pp. 76, 77): "Three historians, who may be considered as originals, have related what passed in Scotland during the reign of Elizabeth; namely, George Buchanan, William Camden and James Melvil." He then goes on to dissect the character and expose the motives of the three. While doing justice to Buchanan's narrative, in many respects, he says, "[As to motive] he was Murray's creature, and deem'd revengeful." In other words, he was the enemy of Mary and Bothwell and all who sustained either. As to Camden, Rapin actually styles his account a "forged story." "Many believe *Camden* writ nothing in his Annals about Scotland but what was dictated to him, or enjoined by James I." Osborn says, "that Camden's lines were directed by King James." "In short, it may be said of these three historians, in regard to Queen *Mary*, that *Camden* had *scarce said one word of Truth*, that *Buchanan* has said *all*

is this very diversity which condemns their otherwise striking unanimity in and of malice.

But if the defenders of Mary Stuart abandon Bothwell, is not that a decisive argument against him, her third husband? By no means; for if those accusers painted him as odious as possible, in order in this way to dishonor her, the others might have adopted the same tactics from a belief that there was no other way of saving her than by rejecting him; of denying every connecting link between them, and indeed maintaining the impossibility of any inclination on her part for him. Since, however, certain traces of such an inclination could not be got rid of by denying them, this was always the weakest point of the defence; but it is decidedly an illogical conclusion to believe that Mary, even if she loved Bothwell, must necessarily have been an accomplice in the murder of Darnley. He could very well have arranged it without her knowledge, behind her back; yes, carried it out, and yet have taken his measures so skillfully that she noticed nothing, and honestly believed him innocent. But why was it that Bothwell found no friend, no defender? Are not interested motives for the general hatred against him to be discovered everywhere? He had no party, he belonged to no party—he was a party in himself. This, this was his damning sin, his condemnation.

the Truth, and *more than the Truth,* and that *Melvil* has said the Truth, *but not the whole Truth.*"—(Rapin, Fol. II., p. 77, Note 2.)

Although the author has presented so much that is original, and arrived at so many opinions diametrically opposite to the vast majority who have undertaken to write upon the subject of Bothwell, but have simply slipped into the rut of vituperation without being able to extricate themselves from it, he finds that in a foreign land, and in a foreign tongue, James Hepburn has found an advocate who used in some instances the very same terms, or words, in vindication of the Scottish Earl. Consequently, in this, his third pamphlet on the subject, the writer determined to follow closely, but not obsequiously, Dr. Petrick, and present a translation of what might be termed the able German's brief. The only absolute error discovered in the whole presentment of Dr. Petrick in respect to Bothwell—differences of opinion between the doctor and the author as to Mary do constantly occur — is contained in the following paragraph, and it would not be allowed to appear were it not to show how a critic, right in ninety-nine points, may err on the hundreth simply from an oversight; viz.: that he confounds two men, both created Earls of Bothwell; Ramsay—of low birth, who had previously neither position nor land—by James III., and Patrick Hepburn of Hales—who belonged to one of the most ancient, honorable and influential families in Scotland, who (these Hepburns) held in their "fast grip" the lands constituting the Lordship of Bothwell—by James IV. Our James Hepburn was the great-grandson of this Patrick, first Earl of Bothwell, and there was no more connection of either with the *titular* Bothwell, Ramsay, than a clear mountain stream, glorious in every attribute, has with an artificial muddy ditch.

Family feuds and the pride of noble blood are nowhere else so strong as in Scotland. Ancient blood and the bonds of race which, to some extent, went back to the blood of the Pharaohs, are the final determining "factors of the parties." Bothwell's race [a complete error] could not boast itself of the same antiquity carried far back. They were upstarts, and that not from the first ranks. It is incomprehensible [but still correct] that Robinson (I., 317) should call him the head of an old family. He was only the fourth Earl of the name, and the title seems not to have been in existence previously to 1484. [But he *was* one of the noble, ancient Hepburns.] He must, therefore, have appeared to the nobility as very mean, and have been hated as an intruder. In fact, the first Earl of Bothwell had been too much such a one for Scottish family pride to digest or ever to pardon it in his great grandson. King James III., who, in 1485, was beaten at Bannockburn by a coalition under his own son, James IV., and killed in the fight, was hated both for his love for the fine arts and for his democratic penchant for favorites from the lower classes. Robertson mentions among them, Cochran, a mason; Hammil, a tailor; Leonard, a smith; Rogers, an English musician, and the sword or dancing master, Torfisan or Torphicen. Among these was a James Ramsay of Balmain. At the time that the higher nobility, exasperated by this, and because James III. had caused his brother, the Earl of Mar, to be murdered—a fate which the other brother, the Duke of Albany, escaped only with great difficulty—they fell upon the King in the camp at Lawdor (Lauder) Bridge, 1483, and in his own chamber hanged all but one of the favorites before his eyes. Only Ramsay escaped, because James covered the young man with his own body, whom the King afterwards raised to the command of hisLife-Guards, and to be the first [titular] Earl of Bothwell. He appears to have fallen with his King at Bannockburn. [Another error, he lived to be favored by James IV., but the Hepburns were too strong for him, and he showed his bad blood by turning out an accomplished spy for the English king, Henry VII.] To his descendants, [all wrong again] however, remained the title and dignity and deep-rooted hatred, coming, indeed, from this unforgotten circumstance."

To the hatred of the Hepburns of Hales, become so mighty through their own merits and the confidence of their sovereign, must be added the religious quarrel which aroused the spirits of all. Bothwell was a Protestant. He refused to hear mass with the Queen. He was married to his first wife after the Protestant form only; but the next time, to Mary, after both rites, the Protestant, to satisfy his own convictions, and the Catholic to gratify her. He was not, however, a zealot, and by no means a fanatic, as, in those times of excitement in regard to religious belief, was demanded among such a hot-headed people as the Scotch. That he did not make common cause with the "Lords of the Congregation," 1559-'60, in opposition to the government, *i. e.*, against the Queen-mother-Dowager, Mary of Guise, and had not sustained their revolt, so thoroughly justified according to their ideas, his loyalty was in their eyes, of itself, an unpardonable treachery in a Protestant to the cause of religion.

But why did Bothwell separate himself from his comrades in creed? Purely from loyalty to the monarch,—a peculiarity certainly which made him appear as a WHITE CROW in Scotland, where the mighty "Bonds" of the nobles had for centuries kept down every attempt to elevate the power of the sovereign. This simply confirms the historical fact that the Feudal nobility always made "Bonds" against the royal power; the nobility by Patent always with it, sustaining the sovereign. The latter must take this course, and it was only a pity that, there (in Scotland), and at this time, the nobility by Patent (!) was represented by only a single example of unvarying loyalty—Bothwell.

"While these important changes [in the relative influence of the feudal nobility] were taking place among her neighbors, the condition of Scotland remained unaltered. Her nobles had never been weakened, like those of England, by the wars of a disputed succession, and her towns had as yet acquired no political importance. It was in vain that, during this and the succeeding century, the most strenuous efforts were made by the Scottish kings to break down the overgrown power of these great vassals. In all these struggles the latter proved victorious; and, of the first five Jameses, no fewer than three perished the victims of aristocratic anarchy. The division of nearly the whole of the Church lands among a body of men already too powerful was a necessary result of the Reformation; and, from the death of James V. until the union of the two crowns, *Scotland was oppressed by a nobility the most rapacious and corrupt that probably ever existed."* [*This was the period of Mary Stuart's short reign and long misfortunes.*] ("Mary Queen of Scots and her Accusers," by John Hosack. Edinburgh and London, 1870.)

"With remarkable fidelity he (Bothwell) stood by the royal house; throughout life he had been the deeply attached servant of the dynasty." (Jebb, "The Innocence of the Queen," I., 463.) Blackwood confirms this: "At every period of his life a very faithful servant of the crown; * * * his constancy and fidelity in being almost the only one among all the nobles of her kingdom who has never varied nor failed in the duties of a good subject, &c."—Herrera: "This man was always very loyal and faithful to the crown." To this he adds: "A generous man, and one of worth, but at the same time bold, proud and prompt to execute whatever action fell to his part." Even Robertson calls him "remarkably true to duty,"—"extraordinarily so" in fact. It is yet more worthy of notice that no one has drawn from all those admissions the inevitably correct conclusion as to his character. Was he faithful to duty from selfishness? No! for the only thanks he got often consisted in banishment. He was faithful as from a sense of duty. Loyalty and constancy, however, are certainly not the accompanying characteristics of an abandoned character; and, if the other rebel lords were greater politically than he, as men, morally, they certainly were inferior to him. What must appear a merit to the unprejudiced, was the worst of crimes to the interested; and, when it becomes apparent that it was just his faithfulness to duty which drew down upon Bothwell the greatest hatred, this must throw a great weight, in his favor, into the scale. There were at this epoch only two parties. Catholics and French and Royalists appear to be identical. So, on the other hand, with Protestants and Republicans, the English party. Bothwell was the only Protestant who supported the Royalist party, yet without yielding the first place to the French; and he did this not simply from loyalty, but also from a ripened conviction that the modern State stands above parties (!), and should not be made to depend on religious fluctuations (!) Thus he occupied an important but isolated position; and along with his loyalty and his liberal ideas, it may have been to the Scottish nobles the most unpardonable sin, that he was powerful and determined enough to attempt to check or control them by the power of the State. His efforts only failed because he had no party behind him, since the Catholics regarded him with mistrust and did not comprehend his motives, and of these he was himself perhaps unconscious. He dreamed of being in himself a separate party, and that idea hastened his fall. Consequently, since only Catholics and Protestants, English or French, wrote his history, he could only have had his enemies for judges; and it was precisely his undeniable virtues as a governor, his statesmanlike ideas, which procured for him the measureless hate of those aristocratic tyrants. Bothwell was a Bismark, but appeared too soon.

If any one wishes to obtain a general view of the varied life of this remarkable man, it becomes necessary, and especially so, first, to seek for information in the only full contemporary account, that of Buchanan; but it is striking that this author nowhere mentions Bothwell's age. If this be carelessness, the Index to his book will assist us. There stands correctly "James Hepburn, Earl of Bothwell, given into custody, p. 513; Banished to France and England, 523; Rival of the Earl of Lennox, 542; Recalled from France by the Queen, 641:" When was that? The Earl of Bothwell was imprisoned, together with Robert Maxwell, Walter Scott, Mark Carr, in the year 1530, by James V.;—and, in 1537, banished. The *Comes Leviniæ* is the Earl of Lennox, the father of Darnley, and father-in-law to Mary. In what was he a rival to this nobleman? In suing for the hand of the widow of James V., the Queen Dowager, Mary (of Guise). This is in the year 1545, but

Mary Stuart was born in 1542; so Bothwell, when he was imprisoned 1530, must have been about twenty years, and at the time of his wooing Mary, fifty-seven years old. In fact, an otherwise very painstaking and skillful writer, Keralio, depends on these dates and facts in order to show the impossibility of a love affair between the two—Bothwell and Mary Stuart. If the figures were only correct! How? Cannot one trust Buchanan, who, as a contemporary, knew well the persons in question? Yes, *if he had not confounded* our James Bothwell with his father, Earl Patrick Bothwell, and ascribed the whole story of the latter to the former. This seems incredible, and yet it is undeniable. Robert Douglass' "Peerage of Scotland," I., 228, says "James, Fourth Earl of Bothwell, was served heir to his father, 3d November, 1556; his father died five weeks, or thereabouts, preceding. Queen Mary describes him (James) as in his very youth at his first entry into this realm, immediately after the decease of his father." What opinion, after this, can any critic entertain of the credibility of Buchanan? Yet many have fallen victims to his error; for example, Robertson, (I., 50, 87,) speaks of an Earl Bothwell without saying that it is the father, not the son.

The grandfather of our Earl James, that is Adam, Second Earl of Bothwell, fell on Flodden-field, the 13th August, 1513, at an early age, for he was married only in August, 1511. Thus the third Earl of Bothwell, Patrick, must have been born in 1512 or 1513, and at the time of his death, in 1556, forty-four years old. The life of this man seems to have been, if possible, more full of mutations than that of his son. Even in regard to his education there was a contest. This could not have occasioned the best results. A lawless time prevailed. At eighteen years he (Patrick, the father) was already a prisoner. At twenty-three years of age he was banished for twenty years. This, however, did not last long, and he was speedily back again, since, 1st August, 1539, he was again banished for an indefinite time from Scotland, England and France! This drove him into the arms of England. In 1549, he (Patrick, the father, not James, the son) received an English pension of three thousand crowns. Hosack, Mary's advocate, demonstrates such a charge cannot be brought against Patrick's son, James, the champion of the Maries, mother and daughter, and the lover and husband of the latter. He pronounces, (I., 296,) Bothwell "a stranger to fear," but "not proof against remorse." A man who knows no fear, and yet can repent, is better than most men. The widowed Queen, Mary of Guise, called Patrick back to Scotland about 1545, when he came forward, together with Lennox, as a suitor for her hand, and was an enemy of the English party. Then again, a third time banished, he, Patrick, was yet again recalled in 1553. His amnesty, on the 26th March, 1554, is noticed in the Privy Seal Record. He faithfully served her (the Queen); was one of the Lords who handed the Regency over to her in place of the incapable Duke of Chatelherault; sat in the Parliament of 1554-5, which ratified it, and was her Lord Lieutenant of the Borders, in which capacity he is often mentioned; and, as has been said, died 1556. Whether this changeful life was only a consequence of the disorderly times and an ungoverned spirit, or of a dangerous character, is not evident. Baseness, at least, does not appear to be proved against Patrick, third Earl of Bothwell. Chalmers (II., 202) indeed calls him "one of the most profligate men of a most corrupt age," yet without giving any reasons or proofs. In no case is this to be attributed to the son, James, whose life might be called monstrous if one commingle it with that of the father. One thing, however, must have kindled the inextinguishable hate of the Protestants toward the father, Patrick. George Wishart, the teacher of the renowned Knox, and one of the foremost of the revered, prophet-like Reformers, was set upon by Earl Patrick, in the house of Lord Ormiston, and, in spite of a promise to take Wishart to his own castle, Earl Patrick surrendered Wishart to his enemies. This was in 1546. Bothwell delivered him to Cardinal Beaton, who caused him to be burned at the stake, 1st March, 1546. The verdict on Earl Patrick's conduct may be divided. Knox and Mac Crie maintain that Earl Patrick broke his word of honor. Hetherington (46) assures us to the contrary, that the Cardinal compelled him to act as he did; but all seem to overlook the fact that he was Sheriff of the county in which it happened, and, thus obligated, he was imperatively bound to undertake the arrest. In no way, however, can any blame attach to James, as Rudloff (I., 54) maintains, who, if he were present, Rudloff charges, could have been only thirteen years old at the time, since the marriage of his father, Patrick, with Agnes Sinclair, daughter of Henry, Lord Sinclair, cannot well be placed before 1532. Chalmers makes it two years earlier, 1530. This, however, is incredible, on account of the extreme youth of Earl Patrick, and because at this very time he was in prison for a length of time.

Robert Douglas assigns these events to about 1535. Accordingly, even the year of Earl James' birth is very uncertain, and has also been the object of violent controversy. It cannot well have been before 1532, nor after 1536 (?), as his father was then in exile. Whether James Earl Bothwell's sister Jane, who, in 1562, married the Prior of Coldinghame (bastard son of James V., who died in 1563), and, in 1566, John of Caithness (who died in 1577), and, finally, Archibald Douglass—was older or younger than her brother, is not evident. It seems the least inaccurate to assume 1535 as the year of Bothwell's birth, and thus at the death of his father he was twenty-one years old; "he was in his very youth." Schiern (3 and 7) says he was born in 1536 or 1537, and in his nineteenth or twentieth year when his father died.

The education of the fourth Earl, James, was conducted under his grand-uncle, the Bishop of Murray. Buchanan denounces this man as "ignorant and without conscience, and given up to all kinds of lust." "What virtues, forsooth, were to be expected in a man brought up in the very palace of a Bishop of Murray, that is in by far the most corrupt centre of all—amid wine and loose women, among the vilest managers of their (*i. e.*, the Papists) dissolute discipline." How far the measureless passion of Buchanan distorts things in this connection it is hard to say. Bishop Murray was not worse nor better than most of his peers. Pleasure loving, fond of pomp, and certainly not without cultivation, he surely would not have withheld the latter from his nephew, and the documents from Bothwell's hand prove this. The Scottish letter, which is still preserved in the Register Office at Edinburgh, is as well composed and published as any other of the time. Teulet prints, as his, a letter to Charles IX. of France, of the 27th May, 1567, and one of 12th November, 1567, to the same from Denmark; besides two memorials of his to Frederick II., King of Denmark, of the 5th of January and the 13th of January, 1568; justifying himself. The sense and clearness of both are as marked as the excellent French in which they are written. These papers, since Earl James was in prison (under restraint?), are in his own hand. Undoubtedly his education would be nothing more than that probably appropriate to a gentleman and knight.

Yet in this he surpassed most of his contemporaries, and he had, by repeated sojourns in France, sufficient opportunity to cultivate his original inclination for the polish of that nation. When and where he, in his youth, "roamed about as a pirate," as Buchanan says, is not perceptible. Subsequent to the restoration of his father, 1554, he seems to have been with the latter, and to have received his education, with the further advantage of practical lessons in statesmanship afforded by the influential position occupied by his parent. Moreover, as he had an inclination for hand-to-hand encounters, there was no want of opportunity to gratify his inclination in this respect amid the anarchical condition of the "Borderers," whom, properly speaking, only he and his father brought into anything like order, and whom it was impossible for any chief to manage except he was manifestly endowed with courage and personal bravery. Thus James, the Fourth Earl of Bothwell, was already a prominent person at the time of his father's death, by which he not only inherited rich feudal fiefs, but the hereditary dignities of Sheriff of Berwick, Haddington and Edinburgh; of Baillie of Lauderdale, with the Castles of Hales and Crichtoun, and especially, in addition, with the office of Lord High Admiral of Scotland, which was granted as hereditary to his grandfather, Adam, in 1511, by James IV. Undoubtedly he would not, if circumstances permitted, delay to distinguish himself at sea in this capacity, perhaps in combats with pirates; but to call an hereditary High Admiral "a pirate," is what could only be done by a Buchanan.

Thus born and endowed, he was early in life the richest man in the south of Scotland after the Duke of Chatelherault, the head of the Hamiltons, and no doubt lived accordingly, not without show, folly, frivolity and dissipation; but, when Buchanan declares "he grew up there with dice and loose women, and so wasted the most ample patrimony that, in his penury, he had not a brass farthing, the price of a halter," such assertions are more than spiteful—they are untrue.

The largest part of his (Bothwell's) hereditary estates could not have been alienated from him, and we find him, up to the time of his banishment, in unbroken possession of his properties, without its being necessary for the Queen to reinstate him in possession of them. Banished he was several times, but never deprived of his dignities. May not this allusion be, like others, to his father Patrick, third Earl, whose possessions *were confiscated* up to 1554. Still Randolph also chimes in with the expression, "a naked, good-for-nothing beggar, whose property has been eaten up, even to a Portugal piece;" very funny! but unfounded. Something like envy appears to crop out here. Bothwell retained his jewels to the last; until he lost them in his flight to Denmark, in August-September, 1567.

That he was not only the richest man, but one, in the south of Scotland, by inheritance, but also early in life distinguished by efficiency and ability as a ruler, is shown by the Queen Dowager's naming him, at twenty-three years old, her Lord Lieutenant of the Borders, and Keeper of the very important castle "Hermitage," one of the most material and responsible positions, for which especial abilities were needed. Knox, Robertson, Laing are in error when they put Bothwell's first appearance in the Privy Council, and as Lord Lieutenant, in 1565 or 1566. He was appointed to these positions, for the first time, as early as 1558, during the violent War of the Protestant Lords of the Congregation against the Queen Dowager; secondly, during Murray's Rebellion, 1565, and, also, afterwards, several times. Under him served Lord Hume, or Home, as Warden of the Eastern Borders, Kerr of Cessford, of the Middle Borders, and Sir John Maxwell of the Western. His position was that of an almost irresponsible ALTER EGO of the Queen Regent.

He had already, and previously, taken his seat in the Parliament, and, on the 14th December, 1557, signed the Commission for the marriage of Mary Stuart with the Dauphin (Francis II.) The second time, 29th November, 1558, he officiated in opening the Parliament as Sheriff of Edinburghshire.

He was not undeserving of the trust put in him.

"In some of the wild Border troubles, the too famous Bothwell," according to Sir Walter Scott, "is said to have given proofs of his courage, which was at other times very questionable." He was Lord of Liddesdale, and Keeper of the Hermitage Castle. "About this time the Scottish Borderers seem to have acquired some ascendancy over their southern neighbors." (Strype, Vol. III.) * * * In 1559 peace was again restored."

Holinshed's popular Chronicle contains an account of a dangerous and successful cavalry incursion made by him, 1558, into England. In this instance he was supported by the "Congregation."

The unfortunate Mary, in her famous "Apology," says "that in the weiris against Ingland, he gaif proof of his valyentnes, courage, and gude conduct;" and praises him especially for subjugating "the rebellious subjectis inhabiting the cuntreis lying ewest the marches of Ingland." (*Keith*, p. 388.) "He appears actually to have defeated Sir Henry Percy in a skirmish, called the Raid of Haltwellswire."

At the time of the Peace Negotiations at Chateau Cambresis, April, 1559, he had a conference with the Earl of Northumberland on quieting the Border conflicts, and, in August, 1559, he sat as one of the Commissioners with Sir Richard Maitland and Sir Walter Kerr. The English Wardens did not like him. The Earl of Bedford and others allow the ugliness of their own personal enmity to show itself in their remarks. This, however, does him no discredit, for his energetic representation of his own country was the cause of it.*

---

* " It is worthy of note that Darnley should never, so far as we know, have exhibited any jealousy or even dislike of Bothwell. That nobleman had not acquired so great an ascendancy at Court, and

The Protestant (English) party (even after peace, England secretly supported the Scottish "Congregation") was especially embittered by a decidedly lucky stroke of Bothwell. When, in October, 1559, Elizabeth sent to the Rebel Lords, 4000 crowns, by John Cockburn of Ormiston, a very essential and much desired subsidy, it was Bothwell who snatched it away and handed over the money to the Queen Dowager. Great was the wrath of the "Congregation." The Earl of Arran and Lord James Stuart (the Earl of Murray) seized, as indemnity for the money,

---

was so much hated on that account, that a plot had been already formed for his overthrow. Mary has been much blamed for the favor which she now showed for this celebrated person, but the explanation is simple and obvious. BOTHWELL *was the only one of the great nobles of Scotland who, from first to last, had remained faithful both to her mother and herself.* We have no proof of the charge made against him by the unhappy Arran ; and, *whatever may have been his follies or his crimes, no man could say that* JAMES HEPBURN *was either a hypocrite or a traitor. Though staunch to the religion which he professed, he never made it a cloak for his ambition ; though driven into exile and reduced to extreme poverty by the malice of his enemies, he never,* so far as we know, *accepted of a foreign bribe. In an age when political fidelity was the rarest of virtues,* we need not be surprised that *his sovereign,* at this time, *trusted and rewarded him.* We may add, that although the common people admired his liberality and courage, Bothwell, among his brother nobles, had no friends. His chief reliance, next to the favor of the Queen, was placed upon his Border vassals and dependants—men whose lawless habits rendered them impatient of repose, and who were ever ready, at the bidding of their lord, to embark in any enterprise, however dangerous or desperate."—" Mary, Queen of Scots, and her Accusers," by John Hosack. Edinburgh and London, 1870. Vol. I., pp. 155, 156.

Bothwell's castle at Crichtoun while he was with the Queen Regent, but they did not hold it long. They, however, never forgave him for this "lucky hit." That they hated him for it is easily to be conceived, but that it should be used as a reproach against him, and as such recorded by serious writers, arises from inexcusable maliciousness or ignorance. Even if he had taken the money without authority in the course of a Civil War, it was simply by the "Right of War." Should he, the Lord Lieutenant of the Queen Dowager, have allowed the contribution of an enemy to pass into the hands of her rebellious foes. This, indeed, would have shown a want of fidelity to his position. Posterity must consider as faithful service that which contemporaries attributed to him as robbery. He was indeed a Protestant, but he set his Loyality above his Creed. It is a pity that it is not known when and where he became a Protestant, since his father— possibly in his presence—had at a former date taken Wishart, the Reformer, prisoner and turned him over to the Cardinal Primate, by whom he was cruelly executed at the stake. Our Bothwell was by no means a zealot. Buchanan says, "and who between the factions of different religions, a despiser of both, pretended to be in favor of either." This is false in many particulars. He did not feign Roman Catholicism, not even in France. He would not even do the Queen—whom he so ardently loved—the pleasure of hearing the Mass with her; yet, by no means, from fear of the Protestants, whom he was always disposed to snub.

It is not necessary to consider him a Freethinker, still less an Atheist: only there was too much disputation for him, and it is often the mark of an energetic, vigorous, practical character to undervalue mere distinctions [of form] in religion. That he, as an avowed Protestant, steadily, sometimes singly and alone, supported the royal, Catholic cause, must win for him respect for his loyalty, for his liberality of ideas and for his statesmanlike views.

In December, 1559, he marched at the head of eight hundred French and Scottish troops of the Queen from Edinburgh to Sterling. He received more important commissions when, in the middle of May, 1560, the Queen Dowager—while the Civil War was at its most dangerous crisis—sent him over to France, for assistance. That he was not forced to flee the country on this occasion is demonstrated by his letter from his reconquered castle, Crichtoun. But, before his arrival, the Queen Dowager died, and the Duke of Chatelherault assumed the Regency. Bothwell appeared at the Court at Paris as a faithful adherent of the Scottish Crown and a most influential nobleman of the first rank in the kingdom, and likewise as a fiery, yet merry youngster, whom probably only a Brantome would style "the most ugly"—one who was already much talked about and was graciously received at the French Court. The King, Charles IX., appointed Bothwell as his Chamberlain. Mary Stuart certainly called upon him frequently for advice, because she could find no other counsellor so experienced in Scottish affairs.

Important businesses of state were the subjects discussed between them, so carefully concealed as to escape the eyes of the astute English envoy, Throckmorton, who was nevertheless sharply watching Bothwell. Mary sent by his advice four Commissioners, the Lairds Craigmillar, Ogilvie, Leslie and Lumsden, to Scotland. Bothwell himself hastened thither also, unexpectedly, in November, 1560, by way of Flanders, probably to escape the English spies. This movement was made in order to form a legally constituted government composed of Seven of the most powerful Magnates, selected from different parties, of whom any three together, could assemble the Parliament. This was an attempt at a compromise, but the attempt was wrecked. The Duke of Chatelherault and James Stuart [Murray] were not willing to let slip from their grasp the power they had already obtained. Moreover the eldest son of the former, the Earl of Arran, was an implacable enemy of Bothwell. This condition of things decided Bothwell to go back again to France and to return only with the Queen, August, 1561. This fact is important!

Although after her return to Scotland, Lord James Stuart [Murray], the Queen's brother, was the chief director of the government, she raised—almost in exact accordance with the above plan of Bothwell, by an ordinance of 6th

September, 1561—all the nobles previously designated to be Members of the Privy Council. The first point was to restore peace. This the Queen had very much at heart. Bothwell allowed himself to become reconciled with the Catholic Lord Seaton. At the same time Lord James and Cockburn of Ormistoun, his old enemies, became friends with Bothwell. It was only with Arran he could not succeed in effecting an amicable arrangement. Arran, like his father, as incapable as he was ambitious, weak, vain and boastful—since he stood next to the crown through birth and position—flattered himself that he might win the hand of the Queen. He had the fantastical folly—although he was the only person in the kingdom who did so—to set himself up in opposition, by an open protest, to Mary's free exercise of her religion. If he afterwards became deranged, a predisposition to loss of mind had, thus, showed itself at an earlier date. No sensible person would make this, Arran's enmity, a subject of reproach to Bothwell. The Queen took all possible pains to induce Arran to become reconciled with him; and Randolph, himself, allows that Bothwell was placable, but Arran "showed a refractory spirite and obstinately resisted the efforts of the Queen and Council to produce peace." On the 2d February, 1562, Mary compelled peace. It did not last for any length of time. By the end of March, Arran all at once, through Knox, charged Bothwell and his (Arran's) own youngest brother, Gawin Hamilton, Prior

of Kilwinning, with having conspired along with himself
to carry off the Queen to Dumbarton Castle (which belonged to his father Lennox) and to kill her, likewise
Lord James [Murray] and the influential Secretary of
State, Maitland.* All agree that, immediately after this,

---

* "JAMES STUART, being now regarded as a Person who had pre-
serv'd his Sister from a Surprise which might have been fatal to her,
usurped, by this Reputation, and the Assistance of that Faction, of
which he was the Chief, an Authority over her little differing from that
of a Tyrant—he assumed the disposal of all Posts and offices of Trust;
and, under the pretence of serving her, left her not the power to serve
herself—She could, she must, in fine, do nothing now without consult-
ing him—her Guards were Creatures of his own, whom he had placed
about her, not so much for her Safety, as to be so many spies on her
Actions.

"THE first Use he made of his sudden Change of Fortune, was this:
The County of *Murray*, which had been in the possession of the Earl
of HUNTLEY ever since the Death of a Prince to whom the Queen was
immediate Heiress, he got into his Hands, and took upon him the
Name of it; therefore we shall thenceforwards call him Earl of
MURRAY. But the Earl of HUNTLEY, who had held the County, by the
Queen's Courtesy, for a considerable time, could not bear the taking it
away without great Resentment. As he was not the only Person who
felt the Effects of this new made Earl's Covetousness and Desire of
Power, he had a great number of Confederates against him. The Earl
of HAMILTON, who, being a Prince of the Blood, cou'd not choose but
think a larger share of the Government ought to have been invested in
his hands, rather than in the others; and, for that reason, as well as
the difference of Parties, conceiv'd a deadly Hate to him: joining
therefore with the Earl of HUNTLEY, a Plot was lain between them to
ruin MURRAY, and then seize on the Queen, and compel her to marry
young GORDON or ARRAN, leaving her the choice which of them she
would take. Both these Earls vowing to each other, that all thought
of Animosity or Rivalship should be laid by, and each should afford

Arran became insane. Whether he perpetrated the act from derangment or from malice, or with the design of advancing himself, nothing is proved. The accused denied

his utmost power to the destruction of their common Enemy. In this Conspiracy soon entered himself, JAMES HEPBURN, Earl of BOTHWELL, who, by his Extravagancies and Debaucheries, having spent his Estate, which had been very large, had no way of recruiting himself but by Change of Government and publick Disturbances. He had once offer'd MURRAY to kill the Earl of HAMILTON with his own Hand; but MURRAY, whether he mistrusted the Event, or did not believe it practicable, would not hearken to it: HUNTLEY, being a Man of much more POLICY than HAMILTON, would not appear openly in the Affair, but, knowing the Disposition and Principles of BOTHWELL, said to him one day, when they were alone, that if he would make the same Proposal to HAMILTON as he had done to MURRAY, he would not find him so hard to be worked upon. BOTHWELL, who was glad of an opportunity of doing mischief any way, readily embraced the Proposal; and, going immediately to HAMILTON, represented to him the Injuries he had received from MURRAY, who had aimed at setting aside the Succession; that there was nothing that he might not in time bring about, having in his hands the greatest part of the Queen's Authority, which, with the Assistance of the Protestants, and the favor of the *English* Queen, might enable him to subvert a Government much better settled than that of *Scotland:* He alledg'd that the Design which MURRAY had in preventing the Queen from marrying, was, that if she died without Issue, he was confident of succeeding her. In a word, he told him the only Way toward this Blow was to kill him; and proffer'd himself to be the Executioner of what he proposed.

"The Earl of HAMILTON gave into this immediately: He knew, that on the Ruin or Death of MURRAY, not only his Right of Succession, *but his Son's Marriage with the Queen depended.* He had been often heard to boast, that the Family of the STUARTS, whether legitimate or not, ought to be preferr'd to the *Hamiltons;* and this was sufficient to stir up the Revenge of a man less ambitious than the Earl. He con-the charge and nothing indicates their guilt. Nevertheless Lord James seized the opportunity to throw the objects of his personal enmity, among them Bothwell, into prison. Bothwell asked for a hearing. He received none. After being six weeks confined in the Castle of St. Andrews (which belonged to Lord James), and then in Edinburgh Castle, he escaped from the latter on the 28th of August to his own strong mountain Castle of Hermitage, in Liddesdale, on the borders of England. Here he kept quiet until the fall of Huntley, in October of the same year, made it dangerous for him to remain there any longer. He put to sea from North Berwick—his enemies say, un-

---

sulted with BOTHWELL, therefore, on such Measures for his Death, as he could not possibly have escaped the Stroke, had not the Design been discovered by the most unguess'd at means. The Plot was laid to destroy him [Murray] when he went a Buck-hunting with the Queen in a Forest near *Faulkland Castle*, in which he then resided. Nothing could be more Easy than the Execution of the Project, because that part of the Country were all entirely devoted to the Family of the HAMILTONS; and would be so far from revenging the Death of a Man so hated by them, that they would readily take up arms to oppose whatever might be attempted by his Friends against the Authors of it. But Providence, for the punishment of others, who, if not equally guilty, were not also without their share of Crimes, had yet work for this consummate villain [Murray], which was, as yet, unfinish'd, and screened from the impending Blow this Minister of Vengeance."— "Mary Stuart, Queen of Scots: Being the Secret History of her Life, and the Real Causes of all her Misfortunes. Containing a Relation of many Transactions in her Reign; never yet Published in any Collection. Translated from the French. [Rare.] The Second Edition. London: Printed for D. Browne, Jr., at The Black Swan, without Temple Bar; S. Chapman, at the Angel in Pall Mall, and J. Woodman and D. Lyon, in Russel-Street, Convent Garden, 1726." pp. 27-31.

doubtedly as a "pirate," but forgot in their malice that he was Lord High Admiral of the realm, and got under sail in that capacity. Having been driven on to Holy Island* formerly Lindesfarne, a peninsula insulated at high water, nine miles S. S. E. of Berwick-on-Tweed—he was arrested by English officers, brought to London, and, without any reasons shown, detained there as a prisoner until January, 1564 (Sir Randolph to Cecil, 22d January, 1563, in which the British Agent confesses that "Murray (Lord James) and others *intrigued* with him to have Bothwell detained in England, of which he is a determined enemy." There is no trace of proof that any one reproached him, at this time, with "piracy." If they had

---

* "Lindisfarne, an isle on the coast of Northumberland, was called *Holy Island* from the sanctity of its ancient monastery, and from its having been the episcopal seat of the See of Durham during the early ages of British Christianity. A succession of holy men held that office, but their merits were swallowed up in the superior fame of St. Cuthbert, who was sixth Bishop of Durham, and who bestowed the name of his 'patrimony' upon the extensive property of the see. The ruins of the monastery upon Holy Island betoken great antiquity. The arches are, in general, strictly Saxon; and the pillars which support them short, strong and massy. In some places, however, there are pointed windows, which indicate that the building has been repaired at a period long subsequent to the original foundation. The exterior ornaments of the building, being of a light, sandy stone, have been wasted as described in the text. Lindisfarne is not properly an island, but rather, as the venerable Bede has termed it, a semi-island; for, although surrounded by the sea at full tide, the ebb leaves the sands dry between it and the opposite coast of Northumberland, from which it is about three miles distant."—Scott's Poetry, Vol. VII., p. 94. "Marmion," Canto II., 1, Note 1.

found the slightest shadow of proof to sustain such a charge they would more than willingly have brought it forward. Finally, January, 1564, (the Scottish Government) yielded to the pressing reclamations of his mother, Agnes Sinclair—who separated from Earl Patrick (father of James) Bothwell, March, 1554, possessed up to her death, 1573, the Barony of Moreham, and thence was known as the "Lady of Moreham," and retained the liveliest affection for her only son, James—and, through Mary Stuart, compelled the liberation of Bothwell. He now went directly to France, where he experienced, to say the very least, the most friendly reception, for he was appointed, by Charles IX., Captain of the Scottish Body-Guard which had the peculiar care of the persons of the Kings of France. The Castle "Hermitage," of which he (Bothwell) was Castellan, was handed over to Robert Elliot; nothing else belonging to him was confiscated. (Consult J. W. de P.'s "JAMES HEPBURN, Earl of Bothwell," *United Service*, September, 1882, 328–332.)

From this story, as well as others, even an enemy, if he is honest, can extract nothing criminal against Bothwell: whom unjust calumniations, founded on the declaration—afterwards recalled—of a weak-minded person, drove for more than two years into exile, into prison, and into banishment, and even out of the favor of his royal mistress. This occurrence is distorted, more than all others, by Raumer, who bases his statement, however, on the invariably always self-contradictions of the unreliable and prejudiced Randall, miscalled Randolph. It is false, when the latter writes to Cecil, on the 31st March, 1562, "this day the Earl of Bothwell, with three others, waylaid, for the second time, Lord Ormistoun. In the first place, how could Randolph note down what was occurring on the very same day, when it was taking place at a distance—miles away. Secondly, Bothwell was at this very date already in prison at St. Andrews. Thus it appears that this waylaying of any person, existed solely in Randolph's wicked imagination. Furthermore, it is false that, three days later, Bothwell (2d April) wrote in the way of reconciliation to Arran, and it is false that they lived on the best terms with each other; for, at the very time, they both were in confinement. They were, however, unwillingly reconciled on the 20th February, and when, at a later period, Randolph declares "Arran assures me that the whole (*i. e.*, the conspiracy) was *imaginary*." What else than "imaginary" can any suppose it to have been, and in what way was Bothwell's behavior in regard to it improper. At length Bothwell's sojourn in France became too protracted for his feelings, and he petitioned for liberty to return home, or else for the means to live abroad, which, it appears, were not allowed to reach him. Even if it were true—as David Pringle, his servant, wished to prove—that he "has spoken dishonorably of the Queen, and threatened to kill Murray and Maitland" (this again is only on the doubtful witness of Randolph, 15th March, 1565); and such words are not inevitably subject to an evil construction for a man of his times, under such circumstances of aggravation. Gross injuries had been done him, and every justice was denied him. When, finally, in March, 1565, after three years, without permission, but in open day, he returned to Scotland, this action on his part speaks sufficiently both for his boldness and consciousness of innocence. He openly visited his mother. Although Murray laid snares for him, Bothwell maintained himself in the Castle of Hermitage, retaken by him, where he kept up a large retinue and force. However, he promised the Queen to present himself before the Tribunal in Edinburgh on the 4th of May; but his enemies, Argyle and Murray, appeared on the spot, on the 1st of May, with 4,000 men, and the Queen was obliged to put a stop to his coming, far more from anxiety *for her own personal safety* than fear for that of Bothwell. As Bothwell was in even more danger than she, it is no wonder that he did not appear, and, being absent, had to allow himself to be outlawed. Even in this case, however, he was not entirely deprived of his estates. No one made this conduct on his part a reproach to him, except his enemies and those ignorant of the customs of the country. Nor should it be forgotten that the same unrelenting enemies who persecuted him throughout life—who on this occasion, hindered him by force from appearing before the court, and profited by his keeping away, were ready, at once, to accuse him of the most flagrant contempt of the laws when he himself did the same in April, 1567—when he was accused of the murder of Darnley—and he came before a similar tribunal accompanied by several thousand adherents simply to protect himself. Bothwell, in order to escape the snares laid for him, again put to sea towards the end of April, 1565. But, by the 4th July, 1565, Randolph writes to Cecil, "it is said that the Earl of Bothwell and Lord Seton are sent for, which has the appearance of truth." Trustworthy friends were now needed by Mary. Her public union with Darnley was preceded, nearly four months, by a custom peculiar to Scotland, termed "handfasting," which permitted the familiarities and personal rights of espousals without a definite tie. The marriage itself, with Darnley, which was at first proposed and then opposed by Elizabeth's—in this case, at least—insidious state policy, was celebrated on the 29th of July, 1565, against the will of Murray, who at once began to organize an insurrection. At last—at this crisis—the Queen called to mind the faithful services of Bothwell and his fearless and experienced leadership. On the 5th August, 1565, leave to return home was granted to the Earls of Sutherland and Bothwell, together with an assurance of amnesty as regarded the escape from confinement in Edinburgh Castle. This proved, in addition, that the Queen saw into the groundlessness of that accusation, and that his estates had not been forfeited.

On the 6th August, 1565, next day, the Earl of Murray was, in turn, declared a rebel. Huntley and Bothwell became Mary's counsellors. The 10th August, only four days later, shows us Bothwell present at the Council at Castle-Hill, before Dumfries. He led a part of the army under the (*nominal*) chief command of King (?) Darnley. If we are to believe Randolph, a quarrel broke out between Mary and Darnley concerning him. The latter wished to make his father, the Earl of Lennox, Lieutenant-General; Mary desired to create Bothwell such. Mary carried her point, and rightly; for Bothwell had given the best proofs of his fidelity, steadfastness, statesmanship and military capacity. In any case, he was, on the 22d October, named by both of them, expressly, "Lieutenant-General of all the Marches." In this Randolph may be right. "*My Lord Bothwell, for his great virtue, doth now all.*" After the banishment of Murray, he was appointed, on the 29th January, 1566, to confer concerning peace with his old enemy, the Earl of Bedford, and, on the 8th of February, 1566, this latter writes to Cecil, "I despair of justice on the Borders while Bothwell is Warden." What sort of justice did he (Bedford) desire, who, for eight years, had fanned up every insurrection on the Marches? This should seem to any unbiassed critic the very best proof of Bothwell's energy and patriotism.

The Queen now stood higher than ever, and if it is asked by means of whom, *only through the influence and action of* Bothwell. If she, as many maintain, thought at that time of a forcible reinstatement of the Catholic religion, this conception of hers must have been in the fullest agreement with the relative possession of real proportions of power, recently acquired, in her favor ; all due to Bothwell.

Meanwhile, Bothwell espoused the sister of the Earl of Huntley, Jane Gordon, in the Chapel at Holyrood, 22d February, 1566. This marriage had also a collateral political object—that of reinstating the Earl of Huntley (son of the Earl killed in 1562) in the possessions of his race, of which he had been stripped. It is of importance for the character of Bothwell, for his liberal ideas, for his independence, that he decidedly refused the request of the Queen, and of his bride, to have the marriage performed according to the Roman Catholic rites.*

---

* The most curious fact in connection with the relations of Mary with Bothwell is that Bothwell,—about the time that policy impelled him to the marriage of Jane Gordon, 24th February, 1566,—advised and induced Mary to restore the Consistorial Court for the trial of cases of divorce which had been abolished in 1560. Is not this a sure indication that, as soon as Darnley's baseness manifested itself, he was looking forward to an event—his marriage with Mary—when such a court might be of efficient service to him in getting rid of the wife he did not want and who stood in the way of his plans.

Froude, (VIII., 190), sometimes comes in emphatically, with corroborations, the force of which none but a careful critic can perceive. At her marriage with Darnley, or Darley (names were not always written correctly at this date, witness Randolph or Randall), Mary wore "a mourning dress of black velvet," "*whether simply for a great political purpose*," to show "she was *doing an act which in itself she*

The scenes of peace, of such short continuance, were as vanishing sunbeams amid the increasing accumulation of the storm clouds of the excited parties or factions. The ground was already undermined. The 9th March, 1566, brought in the assassination of Rizzio. Circumstances became continually more and more involved. Morton, the

LOATHED, *it is impossible to tell.*" Secretly living as man and wife, or mistress and lover, with Darnley, since early in April—meanwhile learning more and more to esteem and love, passionately, Bothwell—she had arrived at the stage of "LOATHING" the "long lad"—the silly, debauched young fool; what can demonstrate the truth of this but the event—the union with Bothwell and the catastrophe.

"Darnley's death being resolved, Bothwell began to consider how he was to act after it had taken place. He probably made arrangements for various contingencies, and trusted to the chapter of accidents, or his own ingenuity, to assist him in others. But there was one thing certain, that he never could become the legal husband of Mary, so long as he continued united to his own wife, the Lady Jane Gordon. Anticipating, therefore, the necessity of a divorce; and aware that the emergency of the occasion might not permit of his waiting for all the ordinary forms of law, he used his interest with the Queen at a time when his real motives were little suspected, to revive the ancient jurisdiction of the Catholic Consistorial Courts, which had been abolished by the Reformed Parliament of 1560, and the ordinary civil judges of commissary courts established in their place. In accordance with his request, Mary restored the Archbishop of St. Andrews, the Primate of Scotland, to the ancient consistorial jurisdiction granted him by the canon laws, and discharged the commissaries from the further exercise of their offices. Thus Bothwell not only won the friendship of the Archbishop, but secured for himself a court where the Catholic plea of consanguinity might be advanced, the only plausible pretext he could make use of for annulling his former marriage. This proceeding, however, in favor of the archbishop and the old faith, gave great offence to the Reformed party, and, when the Primate came from St. Andrews to Edinburgh, at the beginning of January, for the purpose of holding his court, his authority was very strenuously resisted. The Earl of Murray took up the subject, and represented to Mary the injury she had done to the true religion. Bothwell, of course, used every effort to counteract the force of such a representation; but he was unsuccessful (?). By a letter which the Earl of Bedford wrote to Cecil, from Berwick, on the 9th of January, 1567, we learn that the archbishop was not allowed to proceed to the hearing of cases, and that, 'because it was found to be contrary to the true religion, and therefore not liked of by the townsmen; *at the suit of my Lord Murray*, the Queen was pleased to revoke what she had before granted to the said bishop.' Probably the grant of jurisdiction was NOT 'revoked' but only suspended, as Bothwell subsequently availed himself of it; but even its suspension sufficiently testifies that Mary, at this period, listened implicitly (?) neither to one nor the other of her counsellors." [Still Bothwell carried his point and profited by it. Mark that!]—HENRY GLAUFORD BELL's "Life of Mary, Queen of Scots," I., 22, 23.

friend of the banished Murray, and the most unprincipled expression of an unprincipled era, together with other Hotspurs, had found means to persuade the weak-minded Darnley that Rizzio was intimate with the Queen, and without proof he believed it, and made himself the tool in a frightful political murder. The consequences of such a deed must have been as inevitable as they were almost—as they proved—illimitable,—perceptible two centuries afterward.

"It almost seems as if there had been a purpose of killing the Queen" through terror; the table fell upon her; "but Ruthven, with his complices cast down our table upon ourself." Rizzio was stabbed over the Queen's shoulder; [they] "struck him over our shoulder with whinyards;" [he was] "killed upon the threshold of the chamber," "at the entry of the cabinet" [they] "gave him 56 (!) strokes with whinyards and swords, one part standing before our face, with bended [aimed] daggs" [pistols]. (Mary, to the Archbishop of Glasgow. Labanoff I., 345). "The King (Darnley) held her; the King constrained and embraced her, holding her in such a way that she could not move." (Despatch to Cosmo de Medici, 8th October, 1566. Labanoff, VII., 93.)

Bothwell was taken unawares by this occurrence. Doubtless the attempt was also aimed at him. He and Huntley saved themselves with difficulty through a window. They hurriedly, amid the confusion and darkness of the bloody night, collected together a few troops for the defence of the Queen; but, anticipated by Morton, who was all prepared, they were forced to retire. It was not simply the killing of a favorite. Certainly some had designs on the life of the Queen. In any case, she was to be held as a prisoner. Let those bear this in mind who see in the occurrences of the following year only the consequences of her guilt in consenting to the murder of Darnley and espousal of Bothwell. The Murray party (the "Lords of the Congregation") were with the pliable Darnley to take the rudder of government. It was again Bothwell who, at this juncture brought help. The whole following plan seems to have come from his head. Darnley—who here played a fool's role, which made him utterly contemptible—was persuaded by the Queen *to escape with her from his friends*, and yet worse from his accomplices. Huntley and Bothwell guided the flight and brought them to Dunbar Castle. There Bothwell quickly assembled such a large army that the Queen, within nine days, as early as the 18th March, was able to march in triumph against Edinburgh. The conspirators fled; the mostly guilty even to Elizabeth, who protected them. A few blows sufficed to settle everything. Bothwell was installed in place of the Provost of Edinburgh Castle, and as Castellan of Dunbar Castle, since the previous commander of the latter had been an accessory to the Rizzio crime. *This was the only reward Bothwell as yet had received from Mary for his invaluable services.* No man in Scotland could win a victory so rapidly as Bothwell, for the one side, or, for the other side, as Murray. His native capacities for command, not without harshness, appear here in the right light. *Mary was*, politically speaking, *thrust more and more into his arms*. This must have made him yet more hated by those who had the habit of looking on legal order in the light of a fetter. It is, however, the essential cause of his increasing and finally all-powerful influence. No other man gave peace to the state, although it was with a severe and heavy hand. Was Mary Stuart in love with him? It is very probable that among so many unfaithful or weak specimens about her, this "REAL MAN," her only help, may have appeared very deserving of respect. Yes, she must, at least, have given esteem and trust to this *pithy*, strongly-marked character. That the impulse of the heart joined is not less demonstrable. It may not appear, clearly, that this swelled up into a sweeping all-forgetting passion. But it did. It is true, it might not follow that the heart should inevitably chime in where the urgencies of the state imperiously forced her into the arms of the Earl! In this case, her passions did so. Bothwell, the *only representative of modern political ideas of order and duty*, was at the same time the sole man who possessed the power of curbing the recalcitrants. This quality, however, least of all contented the Scottish nobility; and, in proportion as his power grew, silently, but the more dangerously for that reason, the general hatred of the nobility augmented toward him. Simultaneously, in him, qualities acquired additional force which were even more pregnant with fate to himself. These were his self-reliance and superlative confidence in himself. It was indeed exactly these, his inborn qualities as a ruler, which, as they multiplied enemies for him, ripened in him, as in Macbeth, what Dargaud styles the "Hell-born" qualities—ambition to make himself the head-ruler and grasp the helm of the state, even if to do so it was necessary to commit a crime.

Meantime arrangements were to be made for the safe lying-in of the Queen, whose death would have been acceptable to many. Edinburgh Castle was determined on as the safest place for this occurrence, and, moreover, she desired to enjoy a little tranquillity. It does great honor to the Queen's heart that she pardoned Darnley, was herself reconciled with her brother Murray, and his brother-in-law Argyle, and also persuaded Huntley and Bothwell to a like course. Bothwell's acquiescence is the best and most honorable testimony to his readiness to restore concord. Murray and Argyle lived in the castle; Huntley and Bothwell did not. The latter, soon after, set off for the Borders for the purpose of watching the movements of Morton, who, without hindrance from any one, was threatening them from England. Affairs of state were principally in the hands of the Bishop of Ross.

The difficult period of Mary's lying-in passed away happily. James VI. was born on the 19th June, 1566.

Four weeks later the Queen's excursion took place. This was by water over the Forth to Alloa House, under the escort of Murray, of Mar, and, as was natural, of the Lord High Admiral of Scotland, Bothwell. What, however, do the calumniators of Mary Stuart make out of this trip. Listen to the Journal of Murray. On the 20th July (" or thereby "), " she fled the company of the King (?) and past with boythis (vessels) to Alloa house with the pyrattes; and the King came also and was repulsed." "With the pyrattes!" as if Bothwell and his companions were sea-robbers, and as if the Queen could know that these four would be concerned in the murder of Darnley. How? Were Murray and Mar likewise sea-robbers? "And the King was repulsed." Darnley, on the contrary, landed, and was reconciled with the Queen, as the French Ambassador, Castelnau affirms. Lethington, the Secretary of State, then and there received pardon. Of Bothwell, however, Bedford informs us, August 2d, to Cecil, " he is generally hated, and is more insolent than even Rizzio was," that is to say, *he kept every one in check, and maintained peace and order in the country.* Only on the Borders things were yet in a disquieted condition, and this was due to the underhand intrigues of England.

On this account it was determined by the " pirates " in Alloa to hold solemn Courts of Justice (*Justiciairs!*) at Jedburgh, on the English Border, for the restoration of the peace and order. So many things, however, intervened, that they were put off until October. On the 7th September, Bothwell was in the Secret Council. Here the first combination of Bothwell and Murray against Darnley seems to have occurred. What followed is made better known, and will be described in as short a space as possible, so as not to exceed the limits assigned to the discussion. It cannot, however, be omitted, for then a gap would appear in the general exposition. The points on which the views of the case herein presented are based on the most substantial grounds. Wherein they differ from others can only be indicated and summarily established.

Peace at this time, as has been stated, had been established and was temporarily maintained. A few such years of tranquillity under the government of Bothwell, now that he was reconciled with Murray, and perfect order might have been permanently assured to Scotland. The folly, the unsteady character of Darnley, however, did not allow of the long continuance of quiet. His haughtiness without strength, his disposition, vaccillating without amiability, made him hateful to all, and finally so to himself. Serious differences between Darnley and Mary could not fail to arise. Still, to find matter of reproach against Mary on this account can only be attributable to ill will, or spring from a want of acquaintance with the circumstances. Darnley wanted to obtain the crown-matrimonial of Scotland. For Mary to concede it to him was to put folly on the throne, to make all parties her enemies, and to deliver over the state to insurrection. Mary was obliged to refuse the crown-matrimonial to him. The refusal called forth such a childish display of petulance that he became despicable to all, and when, entirely without reason, he wished to flee to France (as he informed the French Ambassador du Croc, on the 25th September, and on the 29th September), his father wrote to the Queen, that his son had inflicted upon himself the most damaging blow possible. The Members of the Council of September 29th, 1566, were unanimous in a decision adverse to him, and he was obliged to confess he had no good reason whatever for his conduct.

Doubtless Murray's idea of getting rid of Darnley now took more solid form; only how to do so was undecided. Here it should be particularly noticed that the whole Council of the 8th of October, formally declared that, "so far as facts had come to their knowledge, Darnley had no ground of complaint."

Bothwell was not present at this "sitting," but only at those of the 3d and 6th October, which were held to discuss the same subject. * * * *

On the 17th December, 1566, the baptism of the infant prince, James VI., took place. If we choose to believe Buchanan and Murray's Dairy, the attention of the Queen was especially taken up in having Bothwell's dress particularly handsome and even in supplying him with money. It is of greater consequence to know that, although it was a Roman Catholic baptism, he himself a Protestant, conducted it—was complete Master of the Ceremonies. The other Protestant Lords were so intolerant that they would not even enter the church. As their action in the National Council—wherein, at that time, there was no Roman Catholic—was essential, it is highly to the credit of Bothwell that he alone, as ever, was unprejudiced enough to afford his hearty co-operation to the Queen. His influence had already reached its full height, and certainly rightly so. Even his old enemies coveted his favor and he put faith in them. This was assuredly a sign of his openheartedness and nobility of character. He was all-powerful and surrounded the Queen with his creatures. Thus he was entirely master of the situation. This, and the consciousness of inborn power to rule, unfortunately made him too sure of enduring triumph, and carried him—*a nobleman who, as it can be proved, had hitherto been guilty of nothing dishonorable*—beyond the restraints of virtue and determined him to set about compassing the death of the King, Darnley, despised on all sides—a result which everybody desired, but from the execution of which all, except Bothwell, shrunk back from fear. *Their* (not his) hesitation was based neither upon pity nor virtue, but simply upon interested personal or political motives.

Let it here be distinctly noticed that, despite the general assumption, *Bothwell's participation in the murder of Darnley has not been* strictly proved—that is undeniably and completely beyond the power of reasonable denial. In opposition to the allegations of his enemies, stands his being pronounced not guilty by *them;* the unscrupulous acquittal of himself and condemnations of others by the Parliament; his own denial; and the subsequent probable falsifications of the testimony and of the dying declarations of witnesses. It would not be impossible, that some, at least, formally sought to pronounce him fully exonerated. Petrick, however, follows the general opinion; firstly, because he shared it; secondly, because, according to the morals of the times when it occurred, *it is certainly not dishonoring for Bothwell.* Petrick concludes by observing he does not acquit him, but in all things he desires if he is compelled to condemn Bothwell, if, and when, it must be done, he seeks to do so justly, not otherwise.

Darnley was always in discredit with Murray's party; he had lost the favor of the Queen, on account of his personal conduct and his participation in the murder of Rizzio and his denial of his falsehood and treacherous acts. To Morton and the other conspirators he had become contemptible from his credulity and hateful for his treachery to their cause. Foreign powers did not recognize him as king; nevertheless, he who could not rule himself demanded the Crown Matrimonial with childish vehemence. "A young fool and 'crank'" (Martyre de Marie, Jebb II., 211), he threatened with death, every instant, one or another of the magnates. Still Mary openly seemed unwilling—or played her part so—to be separated from him. On these accounts, the state was in danger of being precipitated from one crisis into another. What wonder is there that people thought of some method of getting him out of the way, and that Bothwell, the boldest and most powerful, undertook it. Thus the subsequent fatal deed is not excused—it is explained.

One fact should be clearly brought to the light. All parties supported Bothwell in his action; all desired the result, but each shunned the deed—especially Murray, who has steadfastly denied it, and Morton, upon whom, during his trial, it was proved. Both were in the plot. In the preparation, the following coincidences can be distinctly noted: at Edinburgh, 29th September; at Craigmillar, 5th December, and at Whittingham, 20th January.

When Darnley, on the 29th of September, played that deplorable role at Craigmillar, all came to the conclusion that he was impracticable. How far the consultation went, cannot be exactly determined. To a certainty, the idea first of making way with him originated with the Secretary Maitland (Lethington), who at once won over his friend Murray to it, and, on the 30th September and 3d of October, they had two interviews with Bothwell on the subject. The latter did not require much persuasion.

The mutual good understanding which appears between the two ancient enemies, Murray and Bothwell, until after the murder, is the best token of this. The plot advanced to a new stage when all came to Craigmillar Castle on the 23d November, where they remained until the 5th December. On the 3d December they presented themselves, together, before the Queen—Murray, Bothwell, Argyle, Huntley and Lethington. The last was spokesman, and proposed a matrimonial separation. Mary did not agree to this, but wished, herself, to withdraw to France and to leave Darnley behind as Regent. This at once brought matters to a crisis. Threats against Darnley were let fall. Nevertheless, publicly, *whatever may have been her private views and feelings*, the Queen refused energetically to have anything to do with the affair.

The peaceful means of adjusting matters was wrecked. Doubtless a "Bond" was at once drawn up by Sir James Balfour (who at a later date abandoned Bothwell) and signed by Bothwell, Huntley, Argyle and Lethington, with the final intention of killing Darnley. Murray did not sign it; yet any one must be blind who holds him guiltless because he did not actually affix his signature. He was astute enough not to compromise himself by his handwriting; but without his knowledge and approval what followed could not well have occurred. Lethington himself says, "*I am assurit he will look through his fingeris thairto,*" and, in addition, it is proved by the protest of the Earls of Huntley and Argyle. His friend Lethington, his brother-in-law Argyle, were present, and the price or consideration of that "Bond" was the recall of

Morton, Murray's friend, which was obtained at the time of the Baptism, at the request of Bothwell and the others. The plan of Murray was laid in a masterly manner to kill the King, to recall his friends, to throw the whole responsibility upon Bothwell, and, then, on the overthrow of this latter, to come out as the champion of morals. Bothwell certainly overlooked, or was blinded to, the fact that he was nothing but a tool. He believed in the honor of the others and this trustfulness of his was a co-operating cause of his fall. As a usurper he failed in not possessing the ignoble characteristic of mistrust and a contempt of his fellow men, as well as, likewise, the ever intently-listening-ear of a bad conscience, which, after some experience of treachery, hears in anticipation what in coming. *He was a master in power, but not in cunning.* His unprincipled, cold blooded, co-conspirators were exactly the reverse of this.

When Mary apparently sought a reconciliation with her sick husband, then the Confederates concluded there was no more time to lose and the conspiracy became ripe on the 20th January, 1567, at Whittingham, the Castle of Murray's brother. Maitland, Morton and Bothwell were the three who executed everything. On the following day, the 21st, Bothwell accompanied the Queen on her journey to Glasgow, whence she wished to bring away her consort as far as Callendar. Then Bothwell turned about, so as to arrive in Edinburgh on the 23d of January, and on the following day to leave for Hermitage in Liddesdale. His intention was no doubt to raise support among his clansmen.

Mary's ignorance of the preparations for the removal of her husband, Darnley, even if she did love Bothwell, cannot be clearly proved, even by her most ardent champions and advocates.

In the night of 9th–10th February, the blow was struck. About two o'clock, the house in which Darnley resided was blown into the air. Nevertheless, although this much is certain, the mode of his death is still an unsolved riddle. The proclamation of the 26th June, 1567, accuses Bothwell of having murdered Darnley "with his own hands," but in flat contradiction to this is the testimony of his enemy, Buchanan. "Especially when on the whole body nothing appeared broken, contused or livid." Consequently it may be at least doubtful whether or not Bothwell, in person, was present at the murder. Nevertheless it must not be forgotten that the whole nobility, then and at a later period, sympathized with the deed, and that the wild ideas of that time and of the Scottish people made little account of a murder. Consequently it is inconsistent with common sense to believe that the bold Bothwell, any more than the hypocrite Murray, rose above his time. If, later, Bothwell's actual accomplices—Morton among them, who was subsequently executed for his participation in the crime—pretended to avenge the murder of the King—

whom they never had acknowledged as such, whom they persecuted during his lifetime, and whose death they procured—and set no bounds to their outraged morality; all this was only the culminating zeal of accomplices who, in fevered haste, strove by so doing to clear their own skirts, fouled with so many crimes. Immediately after the murder they showed no exasperation; they associated intimately with Bothwell, and Murray invited him to his house to a formal banquet, perhaps from fear. At the time of the murder, Murray could have immediately got together an army, driven Bothwell away and punished the murderers, but that was contrary to the Agreement or "Bond" and its consummation, at which he had "looked through his fingers."

MURDER OF DARNLEY.—"The narrative contained in the third part of the poem will be found to correspond closely with the account of the murder given by Bothwell's accomplices, Ormiston, Hay of Talla, and Hepburn of Bolton, in their examinations and confessions, which are printed at full length in Pitcairn's *Criminal Trials*. Yet over some parts of this frightful tragedy there still hangs a cloud of mystery; in particular, it appears impossible to ascertain whether Darnley perished by the explosion, or whether he was strangled in bed, or in the orchard, when attempting to escape. [By Douglas and his Scids, not by, or with, the knowledge of Bothwell or his subordinates. What is more, the house had been mined and the mines charged before Bothwell's men brought a grain of powder into the building.] *There is strong evidence to support the latter view.* On the following morning his body, and that of his servant Taylor, were found lying under a tree, in an orchard, about eighty yards from the ruins. There were no marks of fire or of actual injury on his person: and what is most remarkable, his furred pelisse [overcoat] and pantoufles [slippers] were found close by. The bodies of four men, members of Darnley's household, were found crushed among the ruins. The only survivor, Thomas Nelson, was asleep when the explosion took place. Buchanan says that on that night there were three distinct bands of conspirators watching the house. Drury, writing not very long after to Cecil, makes an averment to the same effect, and specifies Ker of Fawdonside, the ruffian who, at the murder of Riccio, levelled a pistol at the Queen, as having been on horseback near the place, to aid in case of necessity. Drury further uses these significant words, "the King was long of dying, and to his strength made debate for his life." Melville says, "it was spoken that the King was taken forth, and brought down to a stable, where a napkin was stopped in his mouth and he therewith suffocated." Herries' account is different, but very circumstantial. He says that Bothwell, after leaving Holyrood, "went straight to the Kirk-of-Field, up Robloch's Wind, where he met with William Parris and John Hamilton (a servant to the Archbishop of St. Andrews), who had stolen the keys of the gates. They entered softly the King's chamber, and found him asleep, where they both strangled him and his man, William Taylor, that lay by him on a pallet bed. [*This is utterly impossible, Bothwell was far off in another direction.*] Those assassins that are named to be with Bothwell, and actors, were those two above named, Parris and Hamilton, John Hay of Talla, John Hepburn of Bolton, George Dalgleish, and one Powrie, Bothwell's men all; James Ormiston of that Ilk (called Black Ormiston), Hob Ormiston, and Patrick Wilson. After they had strangled the King and his man dead, they carried them both out at a back gate of the town-wall, which opened at the back of the house, and laid them down carelessly, one from another, and then fired some barrels of powder which they had put in the room below the King's chamber; which, with a great noise, blew up the house. They imagined the people would conceive the house to be blown up by accident, and the corpse of the King and his man to be blown over the wall by the force of the powder. But neither were their shirts singet, nor their clothes burned (which were likeways laid by them), nor their skins anything touched by fire: which gave easie satisfaction to all that looked upon them."

☞ My own conviction (W. Edmonstoune Aytoun) is that Darnley

was strangled in the orchard while attempting to escape; that he had been awakened either by the sound of the locking of the door, or by the smell of the burning fuse, which, Bolton says, was lighted for a quarter of an hour before the explosion took place; and that, in his haste, he had caught up the garments which were found beside his corpse. I do not see how it is possible to account otherwise for the appearance of the bodies and the scattering of the dress. For let it be supposed possible that the bodies could be blown through the roof, and cast such a distance into the orchard, without presenting any visible marks, still no one can believe that loose articles of dress could be carried there by the explosion. I think that the real details of the murder, from whatsoever source they might have come, were known to Drury; for the accuracy of the information obtained by the agents of Elizabeth, with regard to every important event in Scotland, is truly wonderful. But if Darnley was murdered in the orchard, and not in the house, *I must also conclude that other actors, unknown to Bothwell and his men, were engaged in the villianous work.* [This is so; proved.]

Bolton and Talla, who confessed to having put the powder in the house, fired the match, and locked the door behind them, averred, both in their depositions when examined and in their confessions before execution, that there were but nine of their company, and that they neither saw nor knew of any others. The nine were Bothwell, two Ormistons, Bolton, Talla, Dalgleish, Wilson, Powrie, and French Paris. And the confession of Bolton, corroborated by that of Talla, bears, "He knows no others, but that he (Darnley) was blown in the air; for he was handled with no man's hands as he saw; and if he was, it was with others, and not with them." They both concur in saying that the two Ormistons went away after the powder was put in, the Queen being then in the house with Darnley, and that they did not return; which tallies perfectly with the account given by Ormiston in his confession, for he says that the clock struck ten as he returned to his lodging, "to avoid suspicion, that no man should say I was at the deed-doing; for I was an hour and more in my bed before the blast and crack was." Wilson and Powrie were mere servants, who brought the powder, by order of Bolton, and, having delivered it, returned to the Abbey, where they waited, until summoned by Bothwell to go with him to the Kirk-of-

Field. They were carrying back the mail and trunk in which the powder had been conveyed, when, "as they came up the Black Friar Wynd, the Queen's grace was going before them with light torches." This marks the time of their departure. Dalgleish, Bothwell's groom of the chamber, was not at the Kirk-of-Field in the earlier part of the night, and only witnessed the catastrophe. Paris went away at the same time as Ormiston, but he seems to have come back to witness the explosion. This man, whose real name was Nicholas Hubert, and who had previously been in Bothwell's service, was the party who furnished the keys. There is, however, trace of one other person, Archibald Betoun, who was Queen's usher, and the proper custodian of the room in which the powder was placed. Nelson, the sole survivor of the explosion, deponed that this Betoun had the keys; and Ormiston, in his confession, says, that "Archie Betoun" was along with Paris while they were preparing to lay down the fuse. But, apart from this, all the confederates and servants of Bothwell, who were executed for their share in the murder, declared that they knew of no others present at or concerned in the deed. Neither Ormiston, nor Bolton, nor Talla, could have any motive or interest in giving a false account; for they all three admitted that they were principal actors in causing the explosion, by which they evidently thought that Darnley perished. [He did not—he was strangled by Archibald Douglas.]

Powrie, however, stated in his deposition, that when he and Wilson brought the powder to the gate at the entrance of the Black Friars, there were with Bothwell two strangers, "who had cloaks about their faces;" and, upon being re-examined, he said that the Earl of Bothwell came to them at the gate, "accompanied with three more, who had their cloaks, and 'mules' upon their feet." Mules were large slippers, worn to prevent the tread of the feet from being heard. From evidence given at a much later trial, it appears extremely probable that one of these strangers was Archibald Douglass, Parson of Glasgow, a near relative of Morton. But, whoever they were, they had departed by ten o'clock; and both Hepburn of Bolton, and Hay of Talla, who were in the house "till after two hours after midnight," when the match was lighted, say positively in their deposition that they knew of no others concerned, save the nine in their company. It is quite possible that their depositions may have been *altered to suit the purposes of Murray and Morton*, before whom they were emitted; but there is no evidence to that effect, and we must take them as they stand. "[Why? Knowing those two men, should their frauds stand without the nicest critical investigation? Far from it."] If their depositions are entitled to credence, they establish this much, that these two men, as well as Bothwell, believed that Darnley was asleep in the house when the explosion took place, and that no other company was on the watch.

But, as Miss Strickland, who has taken great pains in the investigation of this point, has shown, it appears from depositions recently discovered in the General Register House of Edinburgh, that on that night two detachments of men, one of eight, and the other of eleven (two of whom were in armor), were seen hurrying from the Kirk-of-Field, immediately before and after the explosion. There is thus evidence that another party, besides that of Bothwell, was on the watch; and this circumstance strongly corroborates the account of the murder which was sent by Drury to Cecil. [See statement of Opitz, 1879, pp. 415-16, and of Bekker, 1881, pp. 417-23 (translated from the German), in the *United Service*, October, 1882].

These complications may appear to the casual reader unnatural and overstrained; for at first sight it seems extremely improbable that two bodies of conspirators should have been sent on the same errand, without the one being cognizant of the presence of the other. *But then it must be kept in view that the main object of the other conspirators was to implicate Bothwell,* and to avoid anything that might leave a trace of their participation in the deed. ☞ Murray found it convenient to go over to Fife on the morning before the murder, selecting Sunday as his travelling day, which assuredly was a great lapse in so rigid a professor of Calvinism. ☜ Morton was at St. Andrews. His kinsman, Archibald Douglass, was indeed in the plot, as the Earl long afterwards confessed on the eve of his execution, and had told him of the purpose; but then, as he said to the inquisitive [Presbyterian] ministers, "Mr. Archibald at that time was a depender of the Earl of Bothwell, making court for himself, rather than a depender of mine." In short, *the leading conspirators were desirous of two things—firstly, that Darnley should be effectually disposed of,* and, secondly, that *the whole blame should rest on the shoulders of Bothwell*—and they took their measures accordingly.

It seems very clear that they had not much faith in Bothwell's dexterity; for they made provision, unknown to him, that he should not blunder in the execution of his design. From Bolton's deposition and Ormiston's confession, it would appear that, until two days before the murder took place, Bothwell understood that Darnley was to be disposed of in a different manner—viz., that each conspiring nobleman was to send "two servants to the doing thereof, either in the fields or otherwise, as he may be apprehended." "But," said Bolton, "within two days before the murder, the said Earl changed purpose of the slaying of the King in the fields, because then it would be known; and showed to them (Ormiston, Bolton and Talla) what way it might be used better by the powder." Now, as to the quantity of powder used. That was contained in a trunk and a mail or portmanteau, and was brought by Powrie and Wilson from the Earl's lodging in Holyrood to the Black Friar's gate, where it was handed over to Bolton and Talla. It was in bags and was poured out loose on the floor of the room below Darnley's chamber. All this is distinctly proven. Bolton and Talla, after lighting the match—a soldier's fuse, "of half a fathom or thereby"—locked the door, and joined Bothwell outside; and so long was it until the explosion took place, that Bothwell could hardly be restrained from entering the house to ascertain whether the match had not failed. When it came, the explosion was awful. Not only the upper part of the house, but the whole fabric, from the foundation-stones, was heaved into the air. French Paris said, it was like a tempest or a thunder-peal, and that for fear thereof he fell to the ground, with every hair on his head standing up like awls! To use the language of the Privy Council, the house was "dung into dross." The same phrase is used in Mary's letter to Archbishop Betoun (Labanoff, Vol. II., p. 3). "The matter is so horrible and so strange, as we believe the like was never heard of in any country. This night past being the 9th February, a little after two hours after midnight, the house wherein the King was lodged was in an instant blown in the air, he lying sleeping in his bed, with such a vehemency, that of the whole lodging, walls and other, there is nothing remaining—no, not a stone above another, but all other carried far away, or dung in dross to the very ground-stone."

In the first volume of Chalmers' "*Life of Queen Mary*," there is a facsimile of a drawing, taken at the time, of the ruins, which entirely corroborates the statement that the house was blown up from the very foundations. I do not pretend to be a master of the theory of explosive forces, but I have asked the opinion of some competent judges, and I am assured, that if the facts above stated, regarding the quantity of powder deposited by Bothwell's people, are correct, it is absolutely impossible that the house could have been so demolished from the foundation. Here, then, is another mystery. Bothwell's only agents were the men specially named; and they did nothing more than bring to the Kirk-of-Field, on the night of the murder, a quantity of powder quite inadequate to produce the actual result. *The house had been previously undermined.* There was no difficulty in doing this, for the house of Kirk-of-Field belonged to Robert Balfour, brother of Sir James Balfour, who drew the original "Band" for the King's death, and he was entirely in the hands of [the utterly unprincipled but remarkably astute] Lethington. This is not a mere hypothesis, for the fact rests on undeniable evidence, and it is proved that both Sir James Balfour and Archibald Douglass sent powder for the purpose. Miss Strickland has the great merit of having brought together, in a little compass, all the evidence upon that point. That such were the operations of the conspirators is also evident from the terms of the indictment raised *against Morton* in 1581, in which it is set forth that he "most vilely, unmercifully, and treasonably, slew, and murdered him (Darnley), with William Taylor and Andrew MacKaig, his cubiculars (grooms), when as they, buried in sleep, were taking the night's rest, burned his hail lodging foresaid, and raised the same in the air by force of gunpowder, which, a little before was placed, and in put by him and his foresaids *under the ground, and angular stands, and within the vaults, laigh* [laig (?) cellars, foundation, or lowest parts] *and derne* [secret] *parts and places thereof, to that effect.*"

These operations, however, *seem to have been studiously concealed from Bothwell;* nor was the idea of blowing up the house suggested to him until two days before the period fixed for the murder. Like many other men of action, Bothwell was infirm of purpose, and liable to be imposed on, as indeed his whole history shows, and he fell at once into the snare. But he never was informed that the house was already undermined—for this reason, that the other conspirators calculated on his taking such steps as would avert suspicion from themselves. And so it proved; for the powder, conveyed to the Kirk-of-Field in the trunk and valise, was brought on the Saturday, by Bothwell's order, from the magazine at Dunbar, of which he was keeper, to his apartments in Holyrood—was carried by his own servants, and laid down by his own associates—things which could not be done so secretly as to defy detection. In consequence, he was looked upon as the sole deviser of the murder, which, however, there are strong grounds [incontrovertible proofs] for believing was not perpetrated by his means." "Bothwell," a Poem, in Six Parts, by W. Edmondstoune Aytoun. Boston. 1856. Note (page 220, &c., Appendix) to Part III., § xiii.

"About the middle of January the Queen returned from Stirling to Edinburgh, accompanied by the infant prince. The Earl of Morton had by this time returned to Scotland; and, even before he reached his own home, Bothwell and Maitland met him, and proposed that he should join in the conspiracy for the murder of the King [Darnley]. This remarkable interview took place at Whittingham Castle, in East Lothian, the residence of a kinsman of Morton's [? Archibald Douglas, who was the actual murderer of Darnley]; and, according to the confession of that nobleman, made before his execution, in the year 1581, he refused to take part in the enterprise unless it was approved by the Queen. The conspirators assured him that this was the case; but, as they failed to produce any evidence of her assent, he says that he declined to join them. This incident occurred about the 20th January, 1567.

Morton was thus, by his own confession, acquainted with the fact of the conspiracy; and there are strong reasons for believing that, notwithstanding his denial, he aided in the prosecution of the plot. Motives still more powerful than revenge urged him, as well as the other conspirators, to seek Darnley's death. Morton and Maitland, as well as Murray, had imposed upon the generous nature of the Queen in the disposal of the crown-lands, and they knew that Darnley had expressed his disapproval of the improvident bounty of his wife. They knew, moreover, that by the law of Scotland any such grants made without the sanction of Parliament might be revoked at any time before the queen attained the age of twenty-five. The fears of the conspirators were not imaginary, for, during the preceding reign, various grants which James V. had been induced to make to his nobles during his minority were cancelled before he arrived at the full age prescribed by law. Mary had now entered her twenty-fifth year, and it was of the utmost consequence to the conspirators to obtain a confirmation of their titles in the Parliament which was about to meet in the spring. If this opportunity were allowed to pass, the Queen might at any time, before December, 1567, resume the extensive grants of Crown and Church lands which she had made to the chief of the Protestant nobility before her marriage. The conspirators had good reason to fear that Darnley would exert all his influence to induce her to take this step; and as his illness might not improbably lead to a reconciliation between the royal pair—for they all knew her forgiving temper—the danger was obvious and imminent. Although *Bothwell had shared less* [!] in the bounty of the Queen than his associates, we know he had a motive no less powerful for seeking the death of Darnley [the hand of Mary]. Thus was formed the third plot [Bond] of the Protestant nobility for the destruction of Darnley and the Queen. Two had already failed, but the conspirators were at length to reap the fruits of their perseverance and audacity.

If it is asked why Maitland and Morton should have lent themselves to the daring schemes of Bothwell, the answer is plain. They knew that, if successful, they must prove fatal both to him and to the Queen. Bothwell had long been regarded as an enemy by the faction of which Murray was the chief. The reconciliation between them was recent, and it had never been sincere. The murder of Darnley, followed by the marriage of the Queen to Bothwell, could not fail to exasperate the people; and amid the general discontent the Protestant chiefs would have an excellent opportunity of carrying out their long meditated scheme of seizing on the government. Robertson seems to think it incredible that men should help to elevate a confederate whom they hated with a view to his ultimate ruin; yet we know that the same men had played the very same game with Darnley only a few months before. They had engaged to obtain for him the crown-matrimonial as the price of his adhesion to the conspiracy against Riccio; but who can doubt that, if Darnley had ever acquired that dignity, he would have been speedily hurled from it by the men to whom he was indebted for his elevation ? ☞ *The plot for the destruction of Darnley failed from causes already explained; the plot for the ruin of Bothwell was entirely successful."* 🙻 "Mary, Queen of Scots, and Her Accusers." By John Hosack. Edinburgh and London. 1870. Vol. I., pp. 178-181.

Thus far the author, with divergences—expressions of his own opinions and contrary to those of Dr. Petrick—has followed generally the learned German. The rest of Petrick's arguments constitute the basis of the author's Second Article on the Earl of Bothwell, in the October (1882) number of the *"United Service,"* pp. 423-437, —issued together with the First Article in the September number—in pamphlet form, and entitled "A Vindication of James Hepburn, Fourth Earl of Bothwell, Third Husband of Mary, Queen of Scots." The balance of this present work will be a "Summing up," founded on the author's personal examination of over two hundred works in English, French and German. The author's Trilogy, "Mary, Queen of Scots, a Study," "A Vindication of James Hepburn, &c.," and "James Hepburn, Earl of Bothwell," are intended to present the character of a "REAL MAN,"—traduced through over three centuries—in a true light and demonstrate how villainously he has been misrepresented, calumniated, and—pardon the expression, but it is the only one applicable in this case—consistently belied.

Sowing.

> " Through the large, stormy splendors of the night,
> When clouds made war, and spears of moonlight strove
> To penetrate their serried ranks and prove
> That stronger than the darkness was the light,
> Yet failed before the storm-clouds' gathered might,
> *I heard a voice cry: 'Strong indeed is* LOVE,
> *But stronger* FATE *and* DEATH, *who hold above*
> *Their pitiless high court in Love's despite.*' "
>   LOUISE CHANDLER MOULTON, in *"Lippincott's Magazine."*

> " But O, that day, when first I rose, a cripple from my lair—
> Threw wide the casement, breathed my fill of fresh and wholesome air—
> Drank in new life, and felt once more the pulse's stirring play—
> O, madly in my heart is writ the record of that day !
> I thought to hear the gorcock crow, or ouzel whistle shrill,
> When lo ! a gallant company came riding up the hill.
> No banner was displayed on high, no sign of war was seen,
> No armed band, with spear and brand, encompassed Scotland's *Queen*,
> She came, on gentle errand bound,—the bounteous and the free—
> *She came to cheer her wounded knight, she came to smile on me.*
> She waited not for guard or groom, but passed into the hall ;
> Around her were the four MARIES, herself the rose of all.
> I never thought that woman's voice could thrill my being so,
> As when she thanked me for my zeal in accents soft and low.
> I saw the tear within her eye, when, bending down to me,
> She placed her lily hand in mine, and bade me quit my knee.
> ' Dear lord,' she said, ' 'tis woman's right to comfort when she may :
> Then chafe not, if we take by storm your Border-keep to-day.
> We come not to invade your hall, or rudely mar your rest :
> Though well I know, at fitter time, I were a welcome guest.
> But could I quit the Border-side without my thanks to him
> Who paid his service far too well, at risk of life and limb ?
> Ah, BOTHWELL ! *you have bravely done*, and all my thanks are poor ;
> *Would God that more were bent like you to make my throne secure !*
> *True heart ! strong arm !* I cannot place a chaplet on your brow,
> For the old laws of chivalry are dead and vanished now ;
> *But, trust me, never was a Queen more debtor to a peer,*
> *Than I, brave Earl, am proud to own, before the presence here !* ' "
>   AYTOUN'S *"Bothwell,"* II., vii., viii.

HE story of MARY STUART, DARNLEY, BOTH-WELL, and the implacable enemy of all three, but particularly the last, MURRAY, has not as yet been clearly understood or its true particulars manifested. To comprehend it, it is necessary to disentangle manifold considerations of cause and effect. Each of these is entirely independent of the others in its, and their, progress of development, and yet so strangely are they inter-twisted as to seem at times inseparable. In the first place, the head and front of all the offending was the mischief-maker, Mary's bastard brother, James Stuart (Murray), who through the backing of Knox and the Reformed clergy and nobility hoped in some way to overcome the drawback of his illegitimacy and become King of Scotland. Still, as Petrick justly observes, the turbulent Scottish nobility did not want a king, a master, and above all an illegitimate one. They were unwilling to accept such a one, and unfit to have a good ruler. They were not even loyal to their "Sovereign by the grace of God." Not one of the Stuarts can be said to have died a natural death: two were assassinated, one fell in battle, one was killed by the bursting of a cannon, and two died of broken hearts through the treason of their chief and trusted magnates. Besides these crowned examples, one crowned prince was starved to death by his own uncle aiming at the crown.

According to Robert Birrel's Diary, "There hes beine in this Kingdome of Scotland one hundereth and fyve kings of quhilk ther wes slaine fyftic sex." ("*Fragments of Scottish History*, p. 3.")

Sudden and violent ends seemed to be the natural terminations of the reigns of Scottish monarchs. This was proved when Murray did accomplish his purposes and became Regent, June 24th, 1567. Like many another bad citizen, he was proving himself an able ruler, sufficiently so to win the title of the "Good Regent" when he was assassinated, 23d January, 1570. He had enjoyed the aim of his career thirty-one months. Lenox, another firebrand, next, the Second Regent, was shot 4th September, 1571, within twenty months. John Erskine, or Areskin as Rapin styles him, the Earl of Mar, the Third Regent, died with suspicion of poison, 28th October (15th November?), 1572, within fourteen months, and the hoary-headed villain, Morton, the Fourth Regent, after five years of rule, October, 1572—September, 1577, although he had resigned, nevertheless lost his head 1st June, 1581. All these wretches, as regarded Mary and Bothwell, saw the cup of realization dashed from their lips as they were drinking. Murray and Morton, the first and last, richly deserved their dooms, Lenox won it and Mar got it. By this time James VI., the legitimate king, was old enough to sit upon his throne as the complete representative of royalty, but his position was very uneasy. His reign was anything but peaceful. Conspiracies succeeded each other, rather against those who ruled in his name than against the ruler. Inheriting the Crown of England, he found himself monarch of a different race. There was no rebellion among his new people during his reign, but turbulence did not end in Scotland for over a century and a half subsequently. Cromwell was the only one who could keep England, Scotland and Ireland, all three so different and antagonistic, quiet. He was indeed in every sense a Protector. What Cromwell made himself in 1653, Murray was already striving after, in hope, a century previous. Cromwell died a *natural* death after a rule of nearly five years, Murray came to a *violent* end in less than two.

Mary but fulfilled the destiny of her race. Raumer justly styles the history of her dynasty "The Tragedy of the Stuarts," and observes, "As there are ill-fated persons, there are also ill-fated families." Mirabeau (French), pursuing a similar train of thought, endorses this view of the German historian and philosopher, "Though I am far from adopting the gloomy and irreligious mania of fanaticism, yet it is impossible not to believe that there are very estimable beings who, from a concurrence of disastrous circumstances accumulated on their heads, seem to be destined to a calamitous existence." Mary exemplified the truth of this individually and intensified its general application.

Every human being is a product, neither more nor less—the result of mingled material combinations and developments. Jonathan Edwards sets forth an analogous theory, an idea, if not in the exact words, in doctrine. He says the will or desire to do is free, but the will or desire is nevertheless dependent on a long series of antecedent causes, of which the origin is so remote as to defy recognition. What is this but another word for "inevitable decree," which is simply Fate.

>"But vainly doth a man contend with Fate."
>
>"Sir, and King, thy Fate
>That comes on all men born hath come on thee."

are the words of Laing in his "Helen of Troy." That but expresses the bed-rock belief of antiquity, that even the gods were subject to the "inevitable," whose laws were as binding on the Olympian immortals as upon the mortals who were their dependents and victims. Under different names, but endowed with the same irresistible powers, "Hathors in Egypt," "Μοιραι among the Greeks, or Fata in the Latin belief," all gods, men and things were subject to their decrees. It is difficult to distinguish between the laws of Necessity and those of Nature. "She" [Nature], says Auerbach, "goes her steady appointed course, from eternity to eternity." Coleridge thought that "Shakespeare wished to show how even such a character as Hamlet is at last obliged to be the sport of chance," or Fate. His case,

> "Like mortal schemes by fortune cros't."

> "Vainly did my magic sleight
> Send the lover [Bothwell] from her [Mary's] sight."

However forced asunder, they had to come together until all was accomplished—"No spot where human hearts are beating can escape the cruel entanglements of Fate." "The curtains of yesterday drop down, the curtains of to-morrow roll up; but *yesterday* and *to-morrow* both ARE." "To the divine knowledge, the *future* must be as much *present* as the present itself." Mary simply fulfilled in sorrow and suffering her destiny. It was necessary to England's future that she should fail and fall. Reform in Church and State hinged upon this, and the world to-day is reaping the benefits of her misery—the bitter consequences of her very criminal love for Bothwell—sown in folly and crime, and watered with her tears through twenty years.

> "No, no, fair heretic [to principle], it needs must be,"

as Sir John Suckling sang truthfully.

Bothwell was not *her* evil genius, she was *his*. She was not only, as Babington White styles her, "The false and frail accomplice of Bothwell," but the cause and negative instigator of "the only crime chargeable to him"—"a nobleman, who as it can be proved, had hitherto been guilty of nothing dishonorable" (p. 54 *supra*). "Man's destiny is woman; she it is who opens the thread of his life—dark or golden" (Hamerling's "*Aspasia*"), and

Paracelsus, wisest among the observers of nature, declares "Woman is under the sovereign influence of a single organ." (Michelet, X., 50-1.) Everything connected with Mary's career* has been distorted favorably by her own champions and advocates or for evil by the opposition. Impartiality discovers no truth, even in her portraiture. She was not the lovely woman she has been represented by pencil, brush or pen. Her pictures, generally accepted as correct, are mere ideals. She was fascinating, grace itself—a very Circe. Longfellow has some lines in

---

*Among the many curious publications on this never-aging subject, there is a Tragedy. "The ISLAND QUEENS, or *The Death of Mary, Queen of Scotland*." By J. Banks, 4to, 1684. This piece was prohibited the stage; for which reason the author thought proper to publish it, both in defence of himself and it. The story is founded on the *Scotch* and *English* histories, to which the author has closely and impartially adhered, and well preserved that power of affecting the passions, which runs through all his works and sometimes makes ample amends for the want of poetry and language. It is reprinted without date, with the title of "The ALBION QUEENS, or *The Death*, &c. [Bell's British Theatre, Vol. 22?]. To this edition are the names added of *Wilkes Booth, Oldfield, Porter*, &c., in *Dramatis Personæ*, from which it should seem that it was afterwards allowed the liberty of being performed."

"These remarks are from *The Companion to the Play House: or, an historical account of all the Dramatic Writers* (*and their Works*) that have appeared in Great Britain and Ireland, from the commencement of our Theatrical Exhibitions, down to the present year, 1764. Composed in the form of a dictionary, for the more readily turning to any particular author or performance. In two volumes. London: printed for T. Becket and P. A. Dehoudt, in the Strand; C. Henderson, at the Royal Exchange; and F. Davies, in Russel Street, Covent Garden, 1764."

"Hyperion" depicting another Mary, which probably presents the truth of Mary Stuart:

> —"She was not fair,
> Nor beautiful—those words express her not;
> But, O, her looks had something excellent,
> That wants a name:"—

These lines exactly epitomize the previous conclusions of the author in his "Study" on Mary, and "Vindication" of Bothwell. Or, as Lovelace rhymes:

> "The melody
> Of every grace
> And music of her face."

Mary embodied the Charms of "Nature's three daughters—Beauty [or what was accepted as such in her, a queen], Love [the passion], and [undoubtedly] Wit."

Or, again, to borrow the words of an unpublished tragedy:

> "Many a village maid, in face and form,
> The child of Nature, 's far more beautiful
> Than Mary, Queen, so peerless in men's eyes:—
> But she's a queen, therefore a deity,
> And, to defects, all blinded by her rank,
> See in her face the sea-born Aphrodite.
> She's not so lovely as report avers—
> Although most lovable as all admit—
> She is too tall, too vig'rous in her port;
> A full man's heart is beating in her bosom;
> And more than once she's pray'd to be a man
> With helm on head and girt with sword and dagg,
> Astride a gallant steed like Border-Chief:
> Yet in her eye there 's such demoniac light

  Can kindle passion in a breast of ice,
  And lure, as serpent fascinates a bird :
  We've seen her do it. Blazing into flame
  Her heat could melt a mass of iron ore :
  'Tis not her beauty won her Hepburn's love,
  But something kin to tropic heat at pole.
  Magnificently clad, her lusty form
  Captures the men as springtime 'livens flies :
  And though she plays, as cat plays with a mouse.
  With lovers bowing 'fore her sov'reign grace,
  By never yielding has Earl Bothwell won :
  As spell more potent overcomes the less :
  And binds the weaker with more potent sway :
  His magic's been an over-mast'ring will.
  Her mother's grandeur and her sire's finesse
  Make her omnipotent in swaying men :
  When young she rul'd them with her gentle lures :
  A full grown woman with her subtle wiles ;
  And thus, pre-eminent in female guile,
  She leads the wolves as Orpheus moved the trees :
  Carried away by Darnley's courtly airs,
  She soon discerned the caitiff 'neath the style,
  And then returning to her stifled love,
  She found herself compell'd, as 't were by Fate,
  Into embrace of stalwart Bothwell's arms,
  As hunted deer rush wildly in the net."

Partisans, of her creed, exhibit her as a victim and a martyr. "Nothing in [her] life became [her] like the leaving it." She has found knight-errants, even among those who do not believe as she did, if she believed—in the real sense of belief—anything; bewitched by her own sorceries, and magnetized by her sad story. Is her story true as it has usually been told by them ? No ! A thousand times,

No! Bothwell was the victim of her Circean lures, as she became the victim of his desires. Bothwell was a "real man," a man ahead of his time. "Men who dare to be the first in great movements are ever self-immolated victims." He belonged to no party; he swore by no other's formula or oath; he planned, strove, fought—yes, even loved for the good of Scotland. He was more upright and magnanimous than Murray, more virtuous than Morton and the whole of that "healthy crowd," who betrayed him and their country, and more honest and chivalric than Kircaldy, the tool and spy of the Elizabethan cabinet, but he was less astute than "The Chameleon" Lethington, and less brutal than Ruthven or Lindsay, who were nothing more than aristocratic ruffians and murderers.

"A noticeable man, with large grey eyes," he justified Churchhill's principle, that "The vices of a generous man are better than those of a cold-blooded hypocrite, ingrate and traitor," like Murray, *cum suis*—or even Knox!

The diabolical subtlety of the Scottish nobility was shown in nothing more clearly than in their refusal to allow their monarchs to enjoy the protection of a regular body-guard. The conspiracies at the same era against the monarchs of France were not more dangerous and embittered than those against Mary; but in the former case there were numerous and highly disciplined organizations which afforded trustworthy protection to the royal person and ministry. The rebellious Scottish nobility were well aware, that if Mary could organize a guard solely dependent on herself, even of a few hundred men, she would be at once beyond the immediate reach of their machinations. Had Mary and Bothwell been able to array five hundred regulars, in addition to the few hundred faithful Borderers who adhered with constancy and courage to Bothwell, with two such corps, supported by what artillery might be carried into the field, the royal pair would have bid defiance to all that the rebels could have brought together for a single decisive collision. This is all that was necessary, for it is well known that the last revolt could not have maintained itself for a week. Carberry Hill, 1567, was fatal to Bothwell, because the Confederate Lords could marshal a greater number of trustworthy troops, and Langside, 1568, to Mary, for the reason that Murray was able to array discipline against indiscipline, however devoted and reckless.

Bothwell stood alone, as inaccessible to English bribes; and, had he succeeded and shared a stable throne with Mary, the union of Scotland and England, under Mary's pedantic, "slobbering" son, "the wisest fool in Christendom," would have been an impossibility. The time, however, had arrived that the British islands should become united under one crown. Destiny works with strange, uncouth and often cruel instruments, and by tortuous ways, and its motives and motors and movements are inscrutable and almost invariably misrepresented and misunderstood.

All accepted history is in less or greater degree a fearful lie, "a splendid fiction," founded remotely in ignorance, unsusceptible of enlightenment at the time, and on wilful falsehood, which has worn a rut so deep that succeeding historians can hardly extricate themselves from it.

> "And oft repeating [the panegyrics of Mary and malisons on Bothwell], they [historians] believe them true."

It is only within this generation that the story of the Mælstrom has been shown to be without foundation, and only within a year or two that the "Upas Tree" and its "Death Valley" has been proved to be an utter falsehood. "I am gradually coming to disbelieve everything that has been asserted," was the despairing utterance of William Smith.* Undoubtedly "Religious history is partial in its verdicts." What is more and most to the point, "*The story of James I. having had the Castle Fotheringay razed, as the scene of his mother's death, is pretty, but false.*" "The site of Fotheringay now [1882] belongs to the most moneyed man in England—Lord Overstone, son of a London and Lancashire banker, who has a great estate there. The castle began to be dismantled in 1625. [This date proves James had nothing to do with its demolition,

---
* See "Milledulcia," 1857, "The impossibilities of History, Cranmer," 43–44, "The Fallacy of Traditions," 209–'10.

because he died 27th March of that year.] Sir Robert Colton bought the hall in which the Queen was executed, and removed it to Covington, now Mr. Heathcote's, in Huntingdonshire; some of the stone went to build a chapel at Finshade, not far distant; and the remainder of the material was used in works to render the Nene, which flows by it, navigable."

A sensational writer, like a ghoul, disinterred the remains of England's second greatest poet, to prey upon them, and to fill the world with the story of a foulness originating in a bitterness of which none but a jealous wife, who considers herself deeply aggrieved, is capable. "A further examination [of a recently discovered correspondence of Byron] confirms the opinion we expressed—(is the language of a sterling British periodical)—would be to prove the groundlessness of the horrible suggestions made public in 1869.   *   *   *   There is nothing in the documents [now ready for publication] that does not redound to the credit of Lord Byron or his sister." Just so the more that is revealed in regard to Bothwell places that cruelly maligned patriot in a better light; and so it will ever be if the investigation is conducted on honorable principles by parties who can divest themselves of bigotry, partiality, prejudice and wilful blindness.

>   "Though from our birth the faculty divine
>   Is chain'd and tortured—cabin'd, crib'd, confined,
>   And bred in darkness, lest the truth should shine

> Too brightly on the unprepared mind,
> *The beam pours in, for Time and* SKILL *will couch the Blind."*

The writer simply pities those who cannot see, and he will not indulge in the disgust their wilful stupidity that justice and intelligence might justly arouse. "Ephraim is a cake not turned," *i. e.*, only "one-half baked." "Ephraim is joined unto idols, let him alone." Mary Stuart is an idol to the partisan and bigot. "Ephraim is a silly dove," "a wild ass alone by himself: Ephraim hath hired lovers." It is perfectly ridiculous to attempt to judge the XVI. century by the present era.

Strange to say, it seems impossible in writing of Mary, Queen of Scots, not to make a psychological study of her, and absolutely feeling and taking as much interest in it as a doctor does in a dissection. Doubtless there have been worse women; but, as far as her impulses were concerned, she was about "as bad as they make them." Her powers of fascination were boundless, and she used them to their fullest extent wherever her interests seemed to indicate they might be of service to herself or conducive to her purposes. She was habituated to look upon murder with complacency, and immorality as not only pardonable, but commendable. Her passions, when aroused, appear to have been uncontrolled; and her love to have been simply material—for what was there in the hobble-de-hoy carpet-knight Darnley, or, to say the worst of him, in the border-chieftain, the indomitable moss-trooper, Bothwell, to arouse *her* instincts, except the lusty vigor of the one or the absolute manhood of the other. Bothwell has always hitherto been maligned. He *must* have been a "real man," but perhaps an extremely rough-hewn one, full of that, however, which pleases the majority of women, chief of all virtues, courage.

Renan, amid all his half-truths—neutrals—because a Frenchman as well as an Orientalist, seemed to be afraid to utter more than half-truths ; to throw the gauntlet fair and square in the teeth of Roman Catholicism, inasmuch as that was the recognized religion of France—did and does, nevertheless, utter once in a while grand, independent, pregnant sentences. In his Anti-Christ (Chapter XX., 543–4) he observed, "in spite of the many violent shocks given to Truth, such fearless firebrands, as Bar Gioras and John of Gischala, will never become great citizens ; but they will play their parts, and the future will discover, perhaps, that they, better than men of sense, saw farther into the secret designs of Destiny."

That observation applies forcibly to Mary, Queen of Scots. She was to the Union of England and of Scotland very much what Bar Gioras and John of Gischala were to the catastrophe at Jerusalem, agents for the dissolution of existences, which, dissolving like the seed in the ground, still bore within themselves the germ that, nourished by their own putrescence, produced plants to grow, to flower and to fruit in grander new developments. "The ruin of

Jerusalem and of the temple," continues Renan, "was for Christianity a fortune without limits. If the reasoning assigned by Tacitus to Titus is correctly reported, the victorious general believed that the destruction of the Temple would be the ruin of Christianity as well as of Judaism. Never did any human being deceive himself so completely."

Mary, Queen of Scots, was undeniably the rightful heir to the Crown of Scotland, and she was posessed, at the same time, of strong hereditary claims to that of England also; but she was a bigoted Papist. Her ultraism in belief and morality—or rather the want of the latter—smoothed the ascent for the march of the Reformation in Scotland to a plane elevated even with that in England.

Her execution made the throne of Elizabeth perfectly secure. Had Mary been otherwise than heartless while passionate, she would not have been driven from her ancestral realm and deprived of her royal rights. The axe that cut off her head severed at the same time every legal claim, which, in her, endangered the crown and existence of Elizabeth. The latter, dying without an heir, transmitted at once her own rights, to her godson, by selection, James, as well as those established by the death of his mother, Mary, and those which he inherited through his sonship. These brought about the union of two kingdoms, so long arrayed in hostility—and with conquered Ireland—completed the Empire of Great Britain.

"HANDWRITING ON THE WALL OF ENGLAND."

	1066 A.D.	William the Conqueror.
First Great Act of English History.	468 years. 46.8 47th Decade.	First Great Act. Popery or Egyptian Bondage.
Protestantism, or the Woman's Church.	1534	
Second Great Act.—First Hand	First Finger Second Finger Third Finger Fourth Finger Thumb . . .	HENRY VIII. Protestant Reformation. EDWARD VI. LADY JANE GREY. Sacrifice. MARY [Roman] Catholic ELIZABETH. Founder of the [Anglican] Church
	1603	MARY QUEEN OF SCOTS. [1587] Female Curtain
Third Great Act.—Second Hand	First Finger Second Finger Third Finger Fourth Finger Thumb . . .	JAMES I. CHARLES I. Prisoner, 1646. [Executed 1649.] Interregnum. CHARLES II. Sacrifice of King and People. JAMES II.[Rom.]Catholic WILLIAM. Founder of Protestant Constitution.
	1702	
	1714	ANNE. Female Curtain.
Fourth Great Act.—Third Hand . . .	First Finger Second Finger Third Finger Fourth Finger Thumb . . .	GEORGE I. GEORGE II. GEORGE III. Sacrifice of blood and money. GEORGE IV. WILLIAM. Parliamentary Reform.
	1837	
Dawn of the Fifth Act. This being an act of mercy, does not necessarily involve the removal of the Queen. Perhaps the contrary. But I do not pretend to prophesy, only to reason from analogy.		VICTORIA. Female Curtain.

"From this ['Handwriting on the Wall of England'] it is evident that the history of England is arranged dramatically by the all-wise and all-powerful Manager of the universal theatre, and that we are on the eve [1873] of commencing the fifth or last act. The history of the world from the beginning is arranged in the same order, and it all displays throughout, in a variety of modes, the same legitimate arrangement, for it is all written by the hand of the only Great Dramatist who can be imagined to live from eternity to eternity. The unities of time and place are strictly attended to, with the exception perhaps of a few perturbations like those exhibited in the planetary movements, which perturbations are merely the infinitesimal representatives of human liberty, which is only as a drop in the ocean compared to the DIVINE NECESSITY, by which all things that take place are in wisdom and irresistible power ordained.

"You will observe that in the Middle Finger there is always a sacrifice, for it represents the Mountain of Sacrifice when arranged in the order of time. The second great act is the Exodus of the Protestant Church—its coming out of Egypt, and fighting for an independent existence. It accomplishes its end in the fifth little or subordinate act, under Queen Elizabeth, but not without blood. Jane Grey, who was a half-crowned, or proclaimed queen, was in this dramatic five [the second grand act] the victim. She was the royal female martyr of the Protestant Church, which is represented by a woman. Mary, her sacrificer, was Catholic; and thus the fourth act represents, as it uniformly does, apostacy or rebellion, or departure from the principle which characterizes the era. After the fourth, the thumb appears in Elizabeth, and the Church is established, its Articles agreed upon in 1562, and confirmed in 1571 by Act of Parliament. Thus the Exodus closes. A woman, however, of another family was heir to the throne, namely, Mary, Queen of

Scots, and she was sacrificed. Her curtain, therefore, is black [in the tabulated exposition], as the succession passed through her dead body. Her death was inevitable upon the principles of dramatic propriety. * * * Jane Grey had already died for the Protestant Church. Mary must die for the [Roman] Catholic Church—for the Protestant Church is both Protestant and Catholic—and she is brought from Scotland on purpose, because Scotland, being a spiritual Church with Christ as its supreme head, represents the principle of spiritual Catholicity in Great Britain. England having a lay, or civil, head of the Church, its Catholicity is formal.

"The three great acts begin with the United Kingdoms of England and Scotland, each having contributed its royal, female victim. James I. distinguished his reign with a new translation of the Bible. And regarding himself and all crowned heads as God's vicegerents on earth, he inculcated the doctrine of the Divine right of Kings, and the passive obedience of subjects, both in Church and State. This reveals the character of the third great act. It is a fight for a Constitution as well as a Church, some intelligible principle upon which the rights of king and people may be reconciled with religious principle. The fight, of course, begins with the second act, although it is announced in the first. Charles I., therefore, in pure dramatic order, contends with the People, and as the stars in their courses are leading towards universal in opposition to particular interest, the people gain the victory; he is made prisoner in 1646. Then the Monarchy ceased, and Presbytery is established, and the Scotch Church reigns triumphant, and draws up the Westminster Confession of Faith in company with English divines. The Sacrificial era, which is the third, then begins. The King is sacrificed as the representative of Royalty—the State and the People sacrifice one another in the civil wars. When the sacrifice ceases, the Restoration takes place in Charles II., who is the third crowned head of the era, or act. After that, of course, a departure from principles takes place in the fourth act. King James II. becomes traitor to the ruling principle, attempts to restore [Roman] Catholicism, and is obliged to flee the kingdom. Then the thumb appears in William III., who settles the Protestant constitution upon *Low* Dutch principles—the material power taking the precedence, and the multitudinous Parliament gaining a legitimate and recognized ascendancy. Thus closes the great Levitical era of English history. The great era of sacrifice are the cloven mount of republicanism and monarchy.

"Then the female curtain drops again; for woman represents the negative principle in law, and she thus with strict propriety divides the eras. Here the Parliaments of Scotland and England are united. When the curtain of Queen Anne rises, a new act commences. It is the *High* Dutch era of the Brunswick family. It is the spirit of Germany in England. Germany represents the Universal Man. Its ideas are therefore large; but as the first is always material, and the forerunner type, or representative of a successor, the universalism of the Brunswick era is purely material. Therefore the Church is overborne at its commencement. The Convocation is entirely suppressed, and the nation devotes itself with unprecedented zeal and assiduity to the pursuit of its commercial or material interests. This being the fourth, is the great Numerical era of the history of England. Materialism is in the ascendant. It flourishes amongst the people, the clergy, and the nobility; and science and philosophy almost silence the voice of the Church in the private walks of society. The sacrifice of this era therefore is pecuniary, and it takes place as usual in the third act—the reign of George III., on the cloven mountain of the king and the regent. Here the severity is mitigated in respect to the king, and his mind only is affected—his person is saved; because the Numerical era requires the sacrifice of money chiefly, as representing material interests—blood-money. And blood-money it has had. The national debt is this blood-money, the great sacrifice of the numerical era. This being also a universal era—an Alleman or German era—the external empire is greatly enlarged in India, and the wars are Continental, conducted upon a great scale. George IV. constituting the fourth act of the drama, an apostacy of course is demanded in his reign by the law of the drama, and apostacy is mildly and delicately performed, for we are approaching mild and delicate times, in the repeal of the Test and Corporation Acts, and in the Act of Catholic Emancipation—Catholicity once more in the fourth act—apostacy from rigid Protestant principle. George means 'husbandman, or man of the earth'—admirably representing the materiality of the period. The first George was a rude, unpolished man; the last was a finished gentleman, but wholly material and sensual. William, the 'man of the sea,' closed the drama in the fifth act, by means of a new constitution—Parliamentary Reform. The sea is a Catholic representative. The four great rivers run into the sea from the earth. The Georges, or earthmen, terminate their reign in a sea-man. This is a still nearer approach to universalism, and as the sea represents purity, purifying the corruptible rivers that flow into it, so Parliamentary Reform attempts to cure corruption. But being only a type, and not the substance, it does not accomplish its end. The end is accomplished in the fifth great act, not in the minor fifth.

"The female curtain drops once more, and the name of Victoria is painted upon it. Her name is propitious; and as we are approaching a mild and gentle government of the world by the Great Dramatist, the Queen has no reason to fear for herself. But remarkable changes are on the eve of taking place; and her relationship with Church and State must submit to the law of Divine necessity, which forbids a woman to sit at the head of a doctrinal Church. Her proper position is the head of the ceremonial and dramatic Church, the Church of good-manners. The change about to take place may be imagined by examining the three female curtains. The first curtain of Queen Mary united the monarchies of Scotland and England; the second united the Parliament of Scotland and England. What should the third unite?" ("The Coming Man," II., 330-335.)

Wonderful to consider are the steps by which the Inevitable advances to its objective. Even the "wise-fool" James, son of Mary, and godson of Elizabeth, was a means to an end. An embryo in the womb of Mary, he felt the shock given to the mother by the murder, at her feet, of her favorite, her Ahitophel, Rizzio. The offspring of Darnley weak in will, and of Mary strong in will, his very inherited feebleness of will was requisite to the pacific unification of the Anglo-Scottish island. Entirely destitute of force of character, he presented no stumbling block to a perfect identification of adverse or conflicting interests. Had he been a strong personality, he would not have tamely acquiesced in the judicial murder of his mother. Had he been a thorough Scotchman, he would have been unfit to assume the rule over Englishmen. Circumstances transmuted his very vices into negative virtues. The little good that he inherited from Mary, added to the great power he inherited from Elizabeth, constituted him a timely make-shift. The tendency to arbitrary king-ship transmitted to him through blood by his real mother, Mary, and through election by his god-mother, Elizabeth, developed into Charles I., another necessity of the time. Without such a one as the latter, there had been no chance of a Cromwell, whose rise laid the bases of the Liberties of England. The Failure of the Commonwealth paved the way for the return of the Stuarts. Their vices and weaknesses, inherited from Mary, Queen of Scots, re-asserted themselves with opportunities, and made the advent of William III.—another necessity for progress—King of Great Britain. By blood through his wife, and by might through his sword, and by choice through the temper of men's minds, he came, "the right man at the right time," "to honor the crown of England"—as Hazlitt justly observed—"by the wearing of it." He raised the superstructure—the building of which would have been impossible but for two such reigns as those of Charles II. and James II. that were the *products* of a bigotry inherited from Mary, Queen of Scots, upon a foundation, laid strong and deep, by Cromwell and the Commonwealth. Those, again, could never have become realities but for the senseless attempts at arbitrary power exhibited in the reigns of James I. and Charles I., heirlooms, direct, through son and grandson of Mary, Queen of Scots; in whom the exhibition of like qualities was the cause of the loss of her crown, the flight from her realm, and the scaffold at Fotheringay Castle.

"No man," says Wisdom, "is a necessity to God;" but philosophy also reveals the fact that Providence often makes the very deficencies of a mortal the apparent necessities that constitute the stepping-stones of the Inexorable in its strides, leading, or dragging, on Human Progress as it were, by the hand.

The speech placed by Webster, in 1612, in his "eminently interesting" tragedy, "The White Devil," reads like an echo of the opinion of the majority of the English and Scotch people upon Mary Stuart, when, 1587, the axe fell upon her neck:

> "Miserable creature!
> If thou persist in this, 't is damnable.
> Do'st thou imagine thou can'st slide on blood,
> And not be tainted with a shameful fall?
> Or, like the black and melancholick yew-tree,
> Do'st think to root thyself in dead men's graves,
> And yet to prosper? Instruction to thee
> Comes like sweet showers to over-harden'd ground;
> They wet, but pierce not deep. And so I leave thee,
> With all the furies hanging 'bout thy neck."

Destiny judges not so. As in "Manfred," it declares the implacable "MUST BE" of Mary Stuart.

> "*Made* [her] *a thing, which I, who pity not,
> Yet pardon those who pity.*"

JAMES ERLE BOITHUILLE.
(AS HE HIMSELF WROTE IT.)

JAMES HEPBURNE, ERLE OF BOTHELL.
(AS THE SCOTCH PRONOUNCED IT.)

Monticello.—" It is a wonder to your noble friends,
That you, having, as 't were, enter'd the world
With a free sceptre in your able hand,
And to the use of nature well applied
High gifts of learning, should in your prime age
Neglect your [I?] awful throne for the soft down
Of an insatiate bed. O, my lord,
The drunkard, after all his lavish cups,
Is dry, and then is sober ! so at length,
When you awake from this lascivious dream,
Repentance then will follow, like the sting
Plac'd in the adder's tail. Wretched are the princes
When fortune blasteth but a petty flower
Of their unwieldy crowns, or ravisheth
But one pearl from their sceptres ; but, alas !
*When they to wilful shipwreck lose good fame,
All princely titles perish with their name.*"
    JOHN WEBSTER'S *Tragedy, "The White Devil, or Vittoria Corombona."*

Mosby.—" Silence speaks best for me. His death once known,
I must forswear the fact, and give these tools
To public justice—and not live in fear. (*Aside.*)
Thy heart is mine. I ask but for my own. (*To Alicia.*)
Truth, gratitude, and honor bind you to me
Or else you never lov'd."
    Alicia.—" Then why this struggle ?
Not loved ! "
    GEORGE LILLO'S *Tragedy, "Arden of Feversham."*

I N 1565—wrote Lamartine in 1859— "Bothwell was no longer in the flower of his youth; but although he had lost an eye by a wound, he was still *handsome*." *

"Blackwood cites Bothwell 'for his beauty,' which must have been natural, since even his enemy, Agnes Strickland, admits. 'Bothwell does not appear to have affected fine dress.'" "*His beauty was not effeminate,* like Darnley's, nor melancholy and pensive like Rizzio's, *but of that rude and manly order which gives to passion the energy of heroism.*" He was tall, athletic, "columnar;" wore a thick brown beard, with which his mustache mingled; presented a stately warrior figure; was a consummate rider and master of the weapons of the day, an excellent commander, possessing all the attributes of a leader and general. "The licentiousness of his manners, * * had made him well known at the Court of Holyrood. He had many attachments among the women of that Court. * * * One of those mistresses, Lady Reves, * celebrated by Brantome, * * was the confidante of the Queen. *She had retained for Bothwell an admiration which survived their intimacy.*

The Queen, who amused herself by interrogating her confidante regarding the exploits and amours of her old favorite, allowed herself to be gradually attracted towards him by a sentiment which, at first, assumed the appearance of a mere good-natured curiosity. The confidante divining, or believing she divined, the yet unexpressed desires of the Queen, introduced Bothwell one evening into the garden, and even to the apartment of her mistress. This secret meeting forever sealed the ascendancy of Bothwell over the Queen. Her passion, though hidden, was, for that reason, still more commanding, and became for the first time apparent to all some weeks after this interview, on the occasion of a wound Bothwell had received in a Border feud, on the Marches of which he had the command. On hearing of this, Mary * * rode, without resting by the way, to the Hermitage, where he had been carried, assured herself with her own eyes of the danger he had run, and returned the same day " [to Jedburgh]. "The Earl of Bothwell," writes at this time the French ambassador to Catharine of Medici, "*is out of danger, at which the Queen is well pleased. To have lost him would have been no small loss indeed to her.*"

She herself avows her anxiety in verses composed on the occasion:

> "When first my master he became,
> For him I shed full many a tear;
> But now this new and dire alarm
> Destroys in me both life and fear!"

"*After his cure Bothwell became master of the kingdom.*"

"The career of Earl Bothwell had been one tissue of inconsistencies." Nevertheless, he did not by any means deserve the abuse poured upon him, amounting to what Robert Hall aptly styled "distilled damnation."

"Revolting at the ecclesiastical executions which about the period of James V.'s death so greatly disgusted the Scottish people, [James, not] his father became a reformer at an early period in life." His father, "like all the leaders in that great movement which was fated to convulse the land, accepted a secret pension from the English court to maintain his wild extravagance; but when blows were struck and banners displayed, when the army of the Protestants took the field against Mary of Guise [Queen Dowager Regent], young Bothwell, in 1559, assumed the command of her French auxiliaries, and acted with vigor and valor in her cause.

"Afterwards he went on an embassy to Paris; where, by the gallantry of his air, the splendor of his retinue, and the versatility of his talents for flattery, diplomacy, and intrigue, together with his dutiful and graceful demeanor, he particularly recommended himself to Mary of Scotland, the young queen of France.

"Four years afterwards, when Mary was seated on her father's throne, he had returned to Scotland with her; but engaging in a desperate conspiracy for the destruction of his mortal foe, the Earl of Moray, then in the zenith of his power and royal favor, he had been indefinitely banished the court and kingdom. Filled with rage against Moray, who wielded the whole power at the court and council of his too facile sister, Bothwell, finding his star thus completely eclipsed by a rival to whom he was fully equal in bravery and ambition, though inferior in subtlety and guile, and that his strong and stately castles, his fertile provinces and rich domains, were gifted away to feudal and political foemen, sought the Danish court, where he had intrigued so far that at the period when our story opens (1560 or '5?) a conspiracy had been formed to place all the fortresses of Orkney and Shetland in the hands of Frederick II., who, in return, was to create Lord Bothwell Prince of the Northern Isles. This plot had gradually been developing; and the Earl, in furtherance of his daring and revengeful scheme, was now on his way back to Orkney, where he possessed various fiefs and adherents, especially one powerful baron of the house of Balfour of Monkquhanny.

"To a face and form that were singularly noble and prepossessing, the unfortunate Earl of Bothwell united a bearing alike gallant and courtly; while his known courage and suavity of manner, in the noonday of his fortune, made him the favorite equally of the great and the humble." "Beginning from his very youth, * * * immediately after the death of his father, who was one of the first Erles of the realm, and his house was the foremost in reputation by reason of the nobleness and antiquity of the same, and great offices that were hereditary in the family." (Mary Stuart.) "*He was the darling of the common people for his courage and liberality, and the envy of the court.*" "James Hepburne, a man generally esteemed and applauded." (Crawford, 42.) Bothwell was "One of the handsomest men of his time," as old Crawford tells us, and Gilbert Stuart clinches this by admitting that "When he won the favor of the Queen, he was in the prime of youth, and extremely handsome." Even Murray's panegyrist agrees with Mary's champion, Stuart. To sum up the matter, it would seem that if Bothwell must rank among the fallen angels, he was nevertheless invested with all the glorious external attractions of the grandest of the condemned celestial hierarchy; not a sleek, cunning, plausible, however brave, but not bold, Belial; but an audacious, fearless and impulsive Moloch. Perhaps Bothwell was in reality what Rodogune appears, in Nicholas Rowe's tragedy of the 'Royal Convert' (*circa* 1700), "a personage truly tragical, of high spirit and violent passions, great with tempestuous dignity, and wicked, *with a soul that would have been* HEROIC, *if it had been virtuous,"* according to Dr. Johnson's ideas.

"Without being yet a confirmed profligate, he had plunged deeply into all the excesses and gaieties of the age, especially when in France and Italy; for at home in Scotland, when under the Draconian laws and iron rule of the new [Reformed (Knox's)] *regime*, the arena of such follies, even to a powerful baron, was very circumscribed." "Though of a happy and thoughtless temperament," "he was "a reckless, and often (when crossed in his pride and purposes) of a ferocious disposition."

"His heart was naturally good, and his first impulses were ever those of warmth, generosity, and gratitude; and these principles, under proper direction, when united to his talent, courage, and ambition, might have made him an ornament to his country. His early rectitude of purpose had led him to trust others too indiscriminately; his warmth, to sudden attachments and dangerous quarrels; his generosity, to lavish extravagance.* Early in life he is said to have loved deeply and

---

* Buckingham, another partial advocate for Mary (I., 171), mentions "His extreme wealth,"—("The greatest landlord in this country" [Southern Scotland], *Paris apud* Goodall, I., 139) "his valor" and "preeminence in bravery and martial destruction;" "glorious as had been his career," (B. I., 184);—"of our own subjects there was none, either for the reputation of his house, or for the worthiness of himself, as well in wisdom, valor and all other good qualities, to be preferred or yet compared to him." (Mary Stuart, herself, 1567.) "Nor shall we omit his service done a little time before in the wars against England, wherein he gave great proof of his valiantness, courage and good conduct, that notwithstanding he was then of very young age, yet he was chosen out as most fit of all our nobility to be our Lieutenant General upon the Borders, having the whole charge as well to defend us as to assail. At

unhappily, but with all the ardor of which first passion is capable of firing a brave and generous heart. Who the object of his

which time [1535], he made many noble enterprises not unknown to both the realms, by which he acquired a singular reputation in both." (Mary Stuart, 1565.) "He was unanimously chosen General to the Army when very young, merely upon the score of his bravery." (Crawford, 53.) "Among the noblemen whose names constantly meet our eye" [1560-1565], was one" * * * "whose after career justifies us in selecting him, and indulging him with a more special notice. James Hepburn, Earl of Bothwell, the descendant of a long line of illustrious ancestry, succeeded, in 1556, to the estates and honors of his father, Patrick, and although a member of the Reformed Church, attached himself finally to the party of the Regent, in opposition to the rebellious Murray, being appointed by her lieutenant general of her forces and honored with special marks of her favor and approbation; *but his* LOYALTY *at length compelled his retreat into France.* There he entered into the service of Mary, was constituted Captain of the [Royal French] Scottish Guard, and obtained several marks of distinction for his enterprise and valor, and on his return to Scotland, 1560 [with the Queen] was noted by Throckmorton as a 'glorious, rash and hazardous young man,' whose motions were to be watched, and whose actions were to be feared by his foes. Although a firm and consistent Protestant, refusing even to sacrifice in form to the religious notions of his queen, yet his loyalty and consistency,—the more remarkable when contrasted with the duplicity and villainy of many of those around him—procured him the favor of his queen. But Murray was his enemy, and summoned him to a public trial, on a charge of having conspired against his life, and as Murray came to the place appointed for the trial with a body of five thousand men, Bothwell thought it most prudent to avoid the impending danger by departure from the country. When, however, a short lapse of time had exposed to Mary the baseness of her brother, and when, unmindful of the favor and advancement which he owed to her, he had taken up arms to oppose her marriage, she began to perceive how little weight was to be accorded to the assertions of such an accuser; and, recalling Bothwell from his exile, she placed him at the head of the royal troops;— * * * raised to the honor and

love had been was then unknown; one report averred her to be a French princess, and the Magister Absalom Beyer shrewdly dignity which his past service and loyalty well deserved, while his accuser, Murray, was suffering in exile the merited punishment of his treason. To attempt to sketch the character of Bothwell, is to tread on ground so insecure and so disputed, that prudence would induce an abstinence from so dangerous a theme, *but justice has high claims to be regarded; and, even at the risk of offending the deeply-rooted prejudice of many*, I shall venture upon the attempt. Setting aside, for the moment, the truth of his assumed participation in the murder of Darnley, [Scoto-Brittanicus alludes to "his supposed share:" in that evil deed,] * * * we shall, I think, see nothing in his general character which will merit the extreme obloquy which has been cast upon it ever since the age in which he lived. *Bravery, beyond the reach of doubt; loyalty which could never be shaken by the highest temptations which were offered for its desertion; and fidelity to all the trusts which were reposed in him*, are elements of character which certainly deserve some portion of our respect. But it would be useless and uncandid to deny that these high qualities were clouded by many faults, even if they were not obscured by weighty crimes. An ambition which was jealous of the slightest obstacle to its advance; a degree of political recklessness which was, unfortunately, very characteristic of the Scottish aristocracy in that age, and which was augmented, if not caused, by the license which they permitted to themselves in [their] depredations upon the church, and which led them to look with some degree of contempt upon religion itself; and a want of scruple with regard to the means which he employed for the attainment of the objects he desired, are very dark traits in his disposition, and were, unhappily, not peculiar to himself. But to Mary none of these less favorable characteristics were likely to become known. The mutual position in which they were placed exhibited to her only his loyalty, his courage and his fidelity; and she liberally rewarded these: while she would have shrunk from the contemplation of the other elements of his disposition." Buckingham's "Mary Stuart" (1., 91-95). Bothwell must have been a very lovable man, since women once in love with him never ceased to feel the warmest interest in his fortunes, and continued to be not only his friends, but his agents for the furtherance of his interests."

guesses, that this means no other than the Dauphiness, Mary Stuart—but of this more anon.

"There was now a dash of the cynic in his nature, and he was fast schooling himself to consider women merely what he was in his gayer moments, habitually averring them to be, the mere instruments of pleasure, and tools of ambition.

"The unhappy influence of that ill-placed or unrequited love, had thrown a long shadow on the career of Bothwell; and as the sun of his fortune set, that shadow grew darker and deeper. But there were times, when his cooler reflection had tamed his wild impulses, that a sudden act of generosity and chivalry would evince the greatness of that heart, which an unhappy combination of circumstances, a prospect the most alluring that ever opened to man, and the influence of evil counsel spurring on a restless ambition, hurried into those dark and terrible schemes of power and greatness that blighted his name and fame for ever!" Buckingham adds (1, 215), "Bothwell was a man whose early career should have led us to hope for a brighter close, and whose character is one of the darkest mysteries which history presents to our contemplation. His unconquerable fidelity to his sovereign, amid all temptations which surrounded him, had procured so large a share of her favor, that it was not very wonderful that he should have dared to aspire even to the highest honor, and look to her hand as the reward of his long and loyal service."

It is all well enough for modernized manhood in swallow tails and white chokers, who scarcely enjoy a real movement of the soul throughout their money-seeking or money-wasting existences, or mawkish sentimental womanhood cramped within their Worth-stayed dresses, to sit in judgment upon Bothwell. But where is the man who, to attain the woman he loves—for love covers all—would not sweep a rival from his path as quickly as an insect, if he dared. The trouble with Bothwell was, he made a blunder.* As was said of the "Massacre of St. Bartholomew" and the "Revocation of the Edict of Nantes," and the "Military Execution of Glencoe," and the "Assassination of the Duke d'Enghien," they were worse than crimes, they were stupid blunders. Had Bothwell been a refined Italian or Frenchman, he would have accomplished the same result without noise and without display. Darnley would suddenly and simply have ceased to be. Unfortunately, they did not know how to do those things properly in Scotland. They were bunglers, hacking an enemy, or rival, or oppressor to pieces, as they did Archbishop Sharpe even as late as 1679. Morton was the only one who seems to have profited by Continental examples. Mar dined with him one day, and after his meal felt uncomfortable and died, vacating the Regency in favor of his host. The Earl of Atholl supped with Morton 24th April, 1578, and, curious coincidence, likewise died of indigestion next day. Perhaps the copper casseroles were not cleansed of verdigris, or a toadstool got among the

* Until within two days before the murder, Bothwell wished to do it decently, with cold steel, and openly, "à la Cæsar Borgia," the boldest of executives when any one stood in the way; but his associates induced him to change his intention, (A. S. M. S., I., 391). Why? That the explosion of the powder might blurt out the truth and burthen Bothwell, not them, with an universal obloquy undeserved, as can be proved—which has lasted until this very day.

mushrooms. Bothwell was ruder in his ministrations, but the object and end were the same. Why overwhelm him with obloquy and let Bothwellhaugh, Kircaldy, Crawford, Morton and an hundred others go free. The fact is he blundered, and Nemesis did not mitigate a pang to the mortal or his memory. He is the Œdipus of modern tragedy in his suffering and the Œgisthus of evil repute. Visconti does not receive the thousandth part of the execration heaped upon, him and yet the Italian was as fiendishly cruel to women as to men. Bothwell intended to blow up one, and Visconti tortured hundreds to death and had them torn with his bloodhounds or crushed in his iron telescoping prisons. The Milanese is scarcely alluded to, and the Scotchman is damned in prose, poetry, romance and history. He is a perfect victim of the bitterest " Irony of Fate."

"Happy is the man," exclaims Virgil, "who is skilled in tracing effects up to their causes." Equally happy should be the author who honestly endeavors to do so, and is enabled to embody, agreeably, the results of his labors. This is strictly apposite to the consideration of Bothwell. The cause of the obloquy heaped upon the "fair," "the great," "Erle" was, in the first instance, his original success against the finally triumphant party, especially in winning the hand of Mary, and in the second his failure to maintain himself in the possession of what he had so boldly won. As Kant remarks, "Success is justly considered the test of merit, even where it is attributable to an unworthy origin," literally "To have the conclusion right is the chief point (requisite), even if it may be done (reached) from false premises." Victor Hugo is more generous and honest, but less worldly-wise. He declares that "History is the mere dupe of Success."

While so many regard Mary Stuart as resembling "The White Devil," of Webster's Tragedy of "Vittoria Corombona," first printed in 1612, others, as numerous, seem to contemplate Bothwell, as displayed in the character of "Schedoni, the Monk," in Miss Radcliffe's novel, "The Italian," published in 1797.

"The White Devil of Venice," in the opinion of Charles Lamb, "sets off a bad cause so speciously, and pleads with such an innocent boldness, that we seem to see that matchless beauty of her face which inspires such gay confidence into her, and are ready to expect when she had done her pleadings, that her very judges, her accusers, the grave ambassadors who sit as spectators, and all the court, will rise and make proffer to defend her in spite of the utmost conviction of her guilt."

On the other hand, the Monk is "as strongly drawn a character as ever stalked through the regions of romance, equally detestable for the crimes he has formerly perpetrated and those which he is willing to commit; formidable from his talents and energy; at once a hypocrite and a profligate, unfeeling, unrelenting, and implacable. The romance in which he dominated abounds—according to Sir Walter Scott—with "the new and powerful machinery afforded by the Popish religion, when established in its paramount superiority and thereby [the author] had at her disposal monks, spies, dungeons, the mute obedience of the bigot and the dark and domineering spirit of the crafty priest." Any such implication on Bothwell is cruel!

These references to works of fiction are the more justifiable as there are many facts elicited in them that escape historians or are neglected as unimportant; whereas they are the solvents of much that is otherwise either sealed or misunderstood.* The great Prussian general, von Moltke,

*There are two tragedies of the time of Elizabeth, "Arden of Feversham," 1592, and "The Warning to Fair Women," 1599, which seem to have been founded on the results of the connection between MARY and BOTHWELL—pronounced in the Scottish dialect, "BOTHEL." The former is sometimes attributed to Shakespeare. It was translated into German by Tieck. A tragedy on the same subject was composed by George Lillo, 1693–1739. Arden was a gentleman of Feversham, who was murdered by his wife, Alicia, and her paramour, Mosby. In "The Warning to Fair Women," a London merchant is murdered in like manner as Arden and Darnley, by his wife and her lover. Bothwell's temptation is exemplified in the lines of Shakespeare's poem, "A Lover's Complaint,"

"O father, what a hell of witchcraft lies
In the small orb of one particular tear."—

one of the many tears shed by Mary over the conduct of the ill-conditioned and ungrateful Darnley, the more fearful in their effects on Bothwell since the latter were augmented by the belief that he had been supplanted in his suit and hopes by the successful rival who caused them to be shed. Again, in "The Maid's Tragedy," 1619, Beaumont and Fletcher may have derived their inspiration from a perusal of the famous "Casket Letters," from Mary to Bothwell, in portraying the character of *Evadne*, "Her naked, unblushing impudence," says Hazlitt, "her utter insensibility to any motive but her own pride and inclination—her *heroic superiority* to any signs of shame or scruples of conscience are well described."

declares that poets alone confer abiding fame, and it is very likely that a more truthful record of Bothwell will survive in verse and romance than in works styled history which, as a rule, are mere exhibitions of party spirit and prejudice. Swinburne, in his "Chastelard" and "Bothwell," is just towards the latter and affords a fair idea of his love, rise and fall; and White Melville, in his novel, "The Queen's Maries," exhibits more evidences of close search for facts in connection with the Earl than the majority of historians. The same remark holds better in respect to James Grant's "Bothwell," and he refers to incidents in James Hepburn's early manhood which have been neglected by almost every authority, and yet they colored his whole after-life. That Bothwell, sent out to France in 1558 by the Queen Regent, fell in love with Mary Stuart before she married the Dauphin, is alluded to in chronicles of the day, and also that he was not the desperate man he afterwards became until Darnley made his appearance and crushed for the nonce his hopes.

It is very remarkable that Catherine de Medicis, while rejecting the divine truths of revelation, caused seas of blood to be shed in the religious struggles she fomented and was a firm believer in astrology. The royal sorceress one day consulted her favorite seer as to the fate of Mary Stuart. Nostradamus answered, "I perceive blood," and predicted that the young Queen would be a victim to the fatal heritage of her race. When Mary was about sixteen years old, and when as yet she was scarcely betrothed in form to the Dauphin, Bothwell, in the course of one of his numerous voyages between Scotland and the Continent, saw "*la Reinette d'Ecosse*" and fell in love with her. He was then about twenty-two years of age, and although any suit at that time was hopeless for him, he was always true to this love at first sight. After the death of her husband, Francis, the two noblemen who afterwards successively became her husbands, visited her in France. Darnley was scarcely more than a boy, but Bothwell, already, in 1560 exhibiting rare ability, had become a man of mark. He remained in attendance upon Mary for upwards of four months, and she consulted him continually on matters of the highest importance and placed implicit reliance in his judgment. Agnes Strickland, with whom the Earl is no favorite, admits that he undoubtedly possessed literary talent and sufficient political importance to merit the closest supervision of the English ambassador in France, who notified his government that he exhibited qualities of the highest order, on which account it behooved his adversaries to keep a sharp eye upon him [III., 159–60]. He had already lost the sight of one eye (the left), but neither in a dishonorable manner nor in the course of a piratical cruise, as is almost invariably charged. The wound which destroyed its vision was received in a personal encounter [v. 228. 2] with Cockburn of Ormiston, when, in November, 1559, he tore the English subsidy from that agent of the

Rebel or Confederate Lords. Although the sight was gone, the organ was apparently uninjured, and the scar which remained, so far from being unsightly, was becoming to the martial visage of a born soldier. Miss Strickland, besides acknowledging his cultivation and capacity, is likewise forced to concede that Bothwell, in his hatred to Romanism, was a staunch Reformer, and so determined in his principles that, in spite of his ardent love for Mary, the Queen, could never induce him to concede the slightest conformity to the observances of the creed of which she—except when under his influence—was so devoted and zealous a member.

One of the charges brought against Bothwell, after he accompanied Mary back to Scotland, was that he intended to slay Murray and carry off Mary and wed her. It is a great pity he did not execute this plan, if he in reality entertained it (see 35–36, and note *supra*). Was there anything surprising in Bothwell's hatred of Murray, who had been and was his life-long bitterest enemy and a cold-blooded villain, neither more nor less, in every way, towards man and woman, where it served his purposes. If no other proof existed of this charge, his treatment of Christian, the Countess and unfortunate heiress of Buchan, would establish the fact. Having first sought the young lady's hand, he stripped her of her large possessions, and when he had impoverished her and enriched himself, he forced her to marry his uterine step-brother, far beneath her in rank. In this connection it is curious to learn that Murray's brother, another bastard of James V., John, Prior of Coldingham, married Bothwell's sister, and Bothwell himself, after Darnley's public marriage, married Jane Gordon, daughter of the Roman Catholic Earl of Huntly, whom he, as a Protestant, assisted Murray to ruin when the latter was the Prime Minister of Mary. The political vagaries of this period are utterly incomprehensible. Diabolical is almost too polite a term to apply to them. They present no redeeming aspect.

Whatever apparent or real temporary animosity Mary at any period displayed towards Bothwell was entirely due to the influence of Murray, which was succeeded by the inexplicable ascendancy of Rizzio; that was especially due to the fact that he was a secret agent of the Jesuits and the Pope. He it was engineered the courtship of the papist, Darnley, who made his appearance at a time when Bothwell was under a cloud, through the machinations of Murray and his own tendency to frolic. Those prejudiced against Bothwell conceal that Murray wanted to poison him.

Napoleon remarked, on the way to Marengo, that if he was killed at that time, his career, brilliant as it had been, would not fill ten pages of history. The whole story of the gradual conquest and dominion of the Saxons in England is confined in ordinary histories to about as many pages as it occupied centuries. The same remarks apply to the narrative of a great many historical phases, but not to the case of Mary Stuart. The most important portion of her career fills only a little over two years; yet it has been the subject of hundreds of volumes, and has enlisted the pens of some of the ablest writers in every language. Why? Not for the reason that most people suppose; but because she was an agency to throw down the past, control the present and assist in erecting the future. She was the socket-joint on which turned the fate of the Reformation in the British Isles. Yes, and thus in many respects, upon her and Bothwell, pivoted the impulse, if not all the future of Anglo-Saxondom—which completes the whole of—humanity.

The fact that portentous events did hinge upon her involves inevitably the close consideration of Bothwell.

If Mary was the first, Bothwell was the second great quantity in the equation of the times, and their intimate connection lasted, clearly visible, but a little over a year; recognizably but little over two years, although perceptibly to close observation for a much longer period. As the crisis of the fortunes of Mary and of Scotland occurred within the two years of the intimate relations of Mary with Bothwell, this it is makes him so important a factor in the effects developing therefrom, which were gradually felt in ever-increasing circumference, until it may be said that, like the circle in the water, cited as a parallel by Shakspeare, the ripple set in motion by the loves of Mary and Bothwell have broken and to-day break, according to times, places, and circumstances—upon the horizon, nearer or farther, of human development.

Raumer—as quoted—justly observed that there are fated individuals—using the word fated in an unhappy sense—and fated families. This remark might be extended to embrace fated nations and fated races. Mary Stuart's life was one tissue of mistakes. These errors were neither her fault nor her crime. *Every human being is a product,* and the elements which entered into her creation produced effects such as must inevitably result from an amalgamation like to theirs in any power, so to speak, exerting the influence of a sovereign, as pertinently observed by the author of "The Modern Hagar" on the death of a child immediately after its birth, "A chain of evil that might have warped souls for a century—unto the third and fourth generation—was broken in the welding."

Bothwell was a much nobler product than Mary. His antecedents were better. The Hepburns were greater men in their sphere than the Stuarts in theirs, although the latter occupied a higher one, a throne. Mary's race or components were bad on both sides and in every direction. This was clearly demonstrated in the author's "Study," "Mary, Queen of Scots." Bothwell's father was a wild slip, "a gay Lothario," but not worse than his compeers. His grandfather was a grand character. The record of his mother, Agnes Sinclair, "a virtuous lady of the highest rank" (A. S.—V. 229, 1) is unstained. She was divorced by a self-seeking husband, planning for a higher, but not a better mate, the Queen-Dowager-Regent, Mary of Lorraine.

Agnes lived a good wife ever, an affectionate mother, careful of the interests of her only son, and died, leaving all she possessed to his illegitimate son (Schiern, 4-53.). His legitimate daughter by Queen Mary disappeared, of her all certain traces—as has been shown—have been lost.

Agnes Strickland (Q. of S.—V. 316) commenting on this birth uses very unsatisfactory language, "*There is no* SUBSTANTIAL reason to believe, * * * that Mary ever gave birth to any other child" than James VI. "Substantial!" What does she mean by this? She cannot disprove it, and equally credible witnesses affirm it. Throckmorton mentions her pregnancy as admitted by herself. Miss Strickland (IV. 53) mentions her "painful and dangerous illness" at Lochleven, "exactly nine months from the period," Bothwell is charged to have forced her in Dunbar Castle, and the good and virtuous Castlenau and Le Laboureur, Counsellor and Almoner to the King of France, attest the existence, fate and demise of a daughter. All the evidence against the birth of this unhappy child is *negative*; all the proof in favor of it is *positive*. In a court of justice which of these pleadings would prevail? Throckmorton had no interest in misrepresenting Mary's admission of her pregnancy. Miss Strickland, a panegyrist and partial advocate, concedes the painful illness at the natural epoch, and also eulogises Castlenau as honest, who, the latter, furnishes us with the evidence of the birth. Where bigotry and prejudice and interest combine to deny a fact which disinterested records confirm, whoever doubts the latter ranks himself with the former, who belong to the class who "neither will they be persuaded, though one rose from the dead."

God bless the good mothers: like Bothwell's, Agnes Sinclair, whoever is blessed with such is blessed indeed!

In many respects Bothwell was an eminent man. He was a brave soldier and a capable leader. The French ambassador, du Croc, a veteran, admired his dispositions for the last battle he set in array. He was a statesman, indeed, for his times, and as a politician he would have ranked with the highest if he had been *less* honest. He was a patriot in the best sense of the word, devoid of hypocrisy and a believer in the religion, or rather creed, he had chosen without affectation or cant. As a subordinate he was an extraordinary example of fidelity amid almost universal faithlessness. His was a lovable nature, and powerful in inspiring a corresponding passion.

"I held the Queen in no captivity [at Dunbar], *but I loved and honored her with such humility as she deserved,*" are the words of Bothwell, when with years and captivity he had time for reflection and had no reason to misrepresent the slightest fact.

It is curious how much can be proved through the self-contradicting testimony of his traducers. Their evidence demonstrates the falsehood of Buchanan's inconsistent untruths and Brantome's prejudiced Gallic misrepresentation.

When, in 1563, Bothwell, like Harold, the great son of Godwin, was driven to an inimical shore by a tempest—in the same manner as the grand Saxon had been—he was unjustly seized and unrighteously imprisoned by the mean Elizabeth. Just like Bothwell, the subsequent victor of Stamford Bridge and the victim of Sanguelac was dishonorably trepanned by William the Conqueror. Mary Stuart exercised efficient influence for the man she loved; Edward the Confessor had not or did not exert any in favor of the Thegn, in whom he trusted implicitly, even while he did not feel for him any affection. At this time the English agent, Randal, or Randolph, who especially had occasioned Bothwell's detention, writes to Cecil, dated Edinburgh, 3d June, 1563 "I beseech your grace, send him where you will, only not to Dover Castle, not so much for fear of my aged mother, but my sister is young and has many daughters." Now does it stand to reason that a man, stigmatized by Buchanan as resembling "an ape in fine clothes," and by Brantome as "the ugliest and awkwardest man ever seen," could have been dangerous among women of rank? A second Englishman—another of the accredited meddlers in Scottish affairs, who was particularly hostile to Bothwell—Sir William Drury, writing to Cecil, charges the Earl with "inordinateness toward women." When illicit connections occur between cultivated men and women in the higher ranks of society, as a rule, the man is not the seducer, but the seduced. To this rule there are exceptions; but in this case, as in all others, the exceptions prove the rule. Respectable people, so styled, condemn the man because it is the fashion to do so and suits the purposes of moralists. Again, mannerism is very frequently mistaken for immorality, and the refinement of courtesy—sometimes styled gallantry—for absolute vice. The judgment of this world is almost always fallacious. The proverb, "there is no smoke without fire," is about as true in its general application as many of the comprehensive adages which will not bear critical investigation. There may be a huge column of smoke with a very little fire, and a fearful conflagration with hardly any visible smoke. Kindle a small fire, and heap damp combustibles upon it without preventing the circulation of air, and it will send up a veritable pillar of smoke which can be seen for miles. Haul together hundreds of loads of dry brush, apply the torch to windward, and in a few minutes a conflagration will ensue which will snap out tongues of flame laterally that make it perilous to stand in the vicinity, and shoot up a pillar of fire that often rivals in altitude the ordinary evolutions of smoke. The author has burned huge piles of damp leaves and vegetable matter, and also thousands of loads of brush, green and dry, in clearing up extensive woodlands throughout a period of forty years, and knows these parallels to be correct and these facts to be true. Identical deductions hold good with regard to the passions of individuals. The same decision in the Court of Love will not apply with justice to scarcely any two cases brought before it.

> "The mind hath a thousand eyes,
> The heart but one ;
> Yet the life of a whole life dies
> When love is done."

But, to cease from moralizing at large, and to return to the immediate consideration of Bothwell. Let us see what unprejudiced gentlemen wrote about him at the age of twenty-eight to thirty.

At the same time while Randolph was persecuting Bothwell so bitterly, one of the young Earl's keepers in England, Sir Henry Percy, recommended him to Cecil, with the testimony that "he is very wise, and not the man he was reported to be." "His behavior has been courteous and honorable, keeping his promise." ("Calendar of State Papers, Foreign Series," 1563, p. 129; 1564–5, p. 83. Sir John Forster also writes at that time to Cecil, that Bothwell, "all time of his abode here, behaved himself as to him appertained." ("Calendar of State Papers, Foreign Series," 1564–5, p. 75.)

It is a strong point in his favor—however the over-virtuous may desire to reject the evidence—his mistresses, even after the more intimate tie had been severed, continued to the last most faithful and active instruments for the advancement of his fortunes.

It is, indeed, very interesting to discover how women,

once in love with Bothwell, never lost their interest in him, and absolutely, contrary to the rule in such cases, became his most faithful agents in furthering his plans. For instance, if there is any truth in the private records of the times, Lady Reres, one of his intimates, was his most effectual ally in bringing him and Queen Mary together. She was the daughter of the Earl of Angus, and cousin of the Earl of Morton. Her sister, Margaret Douglas, known as Lady Buccleuch, wife of Sir Walter Scott, of Buccleuch (according to Froude, IX., 7 (2), see Scheirn, 53 (3 and 4). 54 (2), 55 (1)), was another of the many *chere amies* of the Earl, and also influential between the Queen and him, so much so, indeed, that she was accused of accomplishing her purposes by witchcraft, a charge which, by-the-bye, was likewise brought against the Earl, and urged vindictively against him by Buchanan, the Scotch ambassador to Frederick II. of Denmark, when Bothwell's extradition was the subject of so much negotiation and pressure by the Regency of Scotland and the Government of England.

It is still more curious to observe how every writer, even those the most abandoned to their Scottish Mariolatry, when conscience and circumstances compel them to admit the merits of Bothwell, fall back on the scurrilous Buchanan, "the prince of literary prostitutes," to neutralize their unwilling praise with his calumnies, or else refer to an inimical witness, Brantome, who it is not certain (Burton, IV., 174, and others), ever saw Bothwell with his own eyes.

"James Hepburne, Earl of Bothwell, though some of the leading features of his character had hardly shown themselves at the period of which we speak [1561, when Mary returned to Scotland], merits, nevertheless, from the part he subsequently acted, especial notice at present. He had succeeded his father in his titles and estates in the year 1556, when he was five or six and twenty years of age. [This is a gross error; he was only nineteen or twenty. He was born in 1536 or 1537, and only nineteen or twenty at the time referred to, and but fifty when he died.] He enjoyed not only large estates, but the hereditary offices of Lord High Admiral of Scotland, Sheriff of Berwick, Haddington and Edinburgh, and Baillie of Lauderdale. With the exception of the Duke of Chatelherault, he was the most powerful nobleman in the Southern districts of Scotland. Soon after coming to his titles he began to take an active share in public business. In addition to his other offices, he was appointed the Queen's Lieutenant on the Borders, and Keeper of Hermitage Castle, by the Queen Regent, *to whom he always remained faithful*, in opposition to the Lord James [Murray], and what was then termed the English faction. He went over to France on the death of Francis II., to pay his duty to Mary, and on his return to Scotland was by her intrusted with the discharge of an *important commission* regarding the government. Though all former differences were now supposed to have been forgotten, there was not, nor did there ever exist, a very cordial agreement between the Earls of Murray and Bothwell. They were both about the same age, but their dispositions were very different. Murray was self-possessed, full of foresight, prudent and wary. Bothwell was bold, reckless and extravagant. His youth had been devoted to every species of dissipation; and even in manhood he seemed more intent on pleasure than on business. This was a sort of life which Murray despised, and perhaps he calculated that Bothwell would never aim at any other. But, though guided by no steady principles, and devoted to licentiousness, Bothwell was, nevertheless, not the mere man of pleasure. *He was all his life celebrated for daring and lawless exploits*, and vanity or passion were motives whose force he was never able to resist. Unlike Murray, who, when he had an end in view, made his advances toward it as cautiously as an Indian hunter, Bothwell dashed right through, as careless of the means by which he was to accomplish his object as of the consequences that were to ensue. *His manner was of that frank, open, and uncalculating kind, which frequently catches a superficial observer.* They who did not study him more closely were apt to imagine that he was merely a blustering, good-natured, violent, headstrong man, whose manners must inevitably have degenerated into vulgarity, had he not been nobly born and accustomed to the society of his peers. But much more serious conclusions might have been drawn [as in regard to Julius Cæsar] by those who had penetration enough to see under the dark cloak of dissoluteness in which he wrapped himself and his designs."

Bell, perhaps, sought to do Bothwell justice, but his desire to clear his heroine, Mary, would not permit him to do so. To tell the truth, Bothwell stands erect and prominent in his better qualities among his contemporaries. He resembles a grand, polished and ornamented shaft, which has retained its perpendicular amid similar erections, its fellows of even date, which, shaken by a moral and political earthquake, if not thrown down, lean in one direction or another, or lie prostrate in the mire of their meaner characteristics, or half hidden *amid* the rank and dank growth of their vices and their crimes. He was certainly more honest and more bold than his only real rival in power and influence, the sly, self-seeking Murray, the pet of the clergy. Besides this Stuart, there is no other Scottish nobleman who deserves to be named in the same breath with Bothwell.

Agnes Strickland, who is positively wicked at times in her vituperation and misrepresentation of Bothwell, is, nevertheless, compelled to make admissions in his favor, which neutralize volumes of abuse. She says (I., 139–140), "Covetousness was not his besetting sin," and that he "had refused to enrich himself with English bribes when deprived of all his living in Scotland." Of what other Scottish noble but he could the same be said? What does this mean? He was unalterably true in good or evil estate to his sovereign, his government and his country. "However deserving of censure, he had resisted every temptation either to act as the secret service man of England or to trouble Mary's government by raising a revolt against her in [his own territories] Liddesdale, during his imprisonment at Berwick, which he might well have done; his forbearance was deservedly appreciated by his sovereign." (*Ibid* 229.) "As LONG AS HE [Bothwell] REMAINED FAITHFUL TO HIS DUTY, SHE [Mary] WAS SAFE." (1566, *Ibid* 351.) To impugn his complete intrepidity is to descend to the meanest vilification, of the lowest. If he had not been consummately brave and expert in the management of arms, why was he always ready to venture his person in the field? and if he was simply a braggart, why did the men he challenged always shirk or refuse, or slink out of the encounter, as did the miserable Morton, at Carberry Hill? The atrocious abuse of Bothwell does not hang together. It would contradict, or stultify itself if prejudice had not petrified itself into something insoluble to proof and reason.

In 1565, amid her 18,000 men, "*of Loyal friends, the Queen could really count on none but* BOTHWELL, *young Athol, and perhaps Huntly, the rest were as like to turn against her as to stand by her.*" (Froude, VIII., 213-14). This makes Mary's conduct at Carberry Hill utterly beyond the grasp of common sense. In allowing herself to be separated from Bothwell she abandoned everything trustworthy. It was sheer insanity.

Blooming.

Ernesto.—   "'T is true
He thither came a private Gentleman,
But young and brave, and of a Family
Ancient and Noble as the Empire holds.
The Honours he has gained are justly his:
He purchas'd them in War; thrice has he led
An Army 'gainst the Rebels, and as often
Return'd with Victory; the world has not
A truer Soldier, or a better Subject."
OTWAY's *Tragedy,* "*The Orphan.*"

—" Ha! not love her!
Witness, ye heav'ns, if e'er was love like mine!
Witness, ye hours, that saw my joys and pains!
My joys and pains that were for her alone.
When I stood wond'ring at her awful beauties,
Gaz'd on her eyes, or languish'd on her lips,
Did she e'er joy, but I was all in raptures,
Or ever grieve, but I was all in tears?"
RICHARD BARFORD's *Tragedy,* "*Virgin Queen.*" 1729.

"Love, like a wren upon the eagle's wing,
Shall perch superior on Ambition's plume,
And mock the lordly passion in its flight."
JAMES DARCY's *Tragedy,* "*Love and Ambition.*" 1732.

HE difficulties of presenting a concise and, withal, a clear statement of facts, were admitted by the celebrated Pascal, master of his language, as he remarks at the end of Letter XVI. of his famous " Provincials." "I have made this dissertation longer *because I did not have time nor leisure to make it shorter.*" In any event could he have made it more concise without obscuring its clearness.

Terence, 1900 years before, said, "There may be too much, even of a good thing." The human brain is very much like the human stomach. Good writing and good health depend very much on the digestive and assimilative powers of these organs. To receive facts or food and so digest either that the one will turn what it has taken in into *excellent* writing, or the other into *perfectly healthy* blood, is what few mortal brains or stomachs are capable of doing. These remarks are particularly pertinent to the consideration of the case of Bothwell and his times; and the results of a careful analysis will prove most conclusively the truth of Shakespeare's idea, that "pleasant vices become scourges." James the Fifth, the "King of the Commons," was very common or indiscriminate in his loves. Among his illegitimate children, the best known is James, the Prior of St. Andrews, better known as the Earl of Moray, or Murray. As a physiognomist remarks, after studying his portrait, "His face gives him away," *i. e.*, reveals his character.

It abounds with traits that deceive the multitude of ordinary observers, and disgusts the few who possess the gifts of insight and reflection. In spite of his seniority of birth, his bar-sinister precluded any right to the throne of his father. Notwithstanding, that was the *objective* of his life, and to its attainment he was willing to sacrifice everything which honest men esteem. Gratitude and rectitude were qualities of which he knew not the signification.

Mary Stuart, his father's legal heiress and his sister, who should have been the object of his sleepless care and tenderest solicitude, was the victim of his unceasing machinations and criminal attempts.

From the first, Bothwell's loyalty of service and affection aroused Murray's utterly selfish enmity. After getting rid of this fearless obstacle to his plans for a time—as he hoped for all time—the soul-less Murray transferred his hatred to Darnley, when the latter became betrothed to Mary. The papist creed of the royal pair made Murray and Knox coadjutors in every attempt to weaken or overthrow their authority. Knox, however worthy of respect as the prime moral agent in securing the triumph of the Reformation in Scotland, was full of defects as an individual. To him "the end justified the means;" and, while wide awake and eloquent as to the vices of Mary, he was often blind to the iniquities of his associates. He even winked at murder if it advanced his cause, as in the case of Rizzio. And yet, to his credit be it said, that Knox, in his own "work" [writings], Bothwell is "never mentioned without a certain unmistakeable sympathy" (Schiern 183). Murray was always a traitor at heart. After Mary's marriage with Darnley was an accomplished fact, Murray's treason in *purpose* became so in *deed*. The only Scottish nobleman who was capable of checkmating Murray was Bothwell. He had been driven from the country at the instigation of Murray. Nothing but Bothwell's loyalty, ability and courage were equal to save the Queen from "the Bastard." Bothwell was summoned home, and with James Hepburn, at the head of her forces, Mary was soon and easily able to chase out Murray and his brother rebels. The brief campaign by which she triumphed under Bothwell's leadership is known in Scottish history as the "Runabout-raid," because, as soon as Murray and his associates settled down in any position which they deemed defensible, Bothwell ran them out of it, and finally out of the country.

Mary's weakness in continually condoning treason, her folly in forgiving unrepentant enemies, was only equaled by her strength of will for the gratification of her passionate nature, as was manifested by her sudden self-abandonment to Darnley's superficial attractions and almost as sudden a revulsion of feeling in favor of Bothwell.

With an obtuseness to her best interests, she pardoned where she should have executed, and the recipients of her highest bounty proceeded to inaugurate another League or Bond, ostensibly to get rid of Rizzio, who was the power behind the throne, but in reality to sweep away from the path of Murray and his faction, not only the favorite, and the husband, Darnley, but the Queen and the child in her bosom. Their removal would have left the throne vacant for Murray. Darnley, silly fool, dupe and tool, lent himself to the designs of his deadly enemy. Rizzio was murdered 9th March, 1566 ; how is well known. But the

Queen, who, as Froude (IX., 158) remarks, "had happily a tough, healthy nature," survived a scene and shock which would have destroyed most women in her condition. Bothwell was to have been included in the massacre. He escaped to frustrate the success of the plan. Darnley, a traitor to his consort and his sovereign, in order to rehabilitate himself with her, betrayed in turn his associates, of whom he had been the instrument, and of whom he was to be the victim. Mary's want of common sense throughout all this is as remarkable as her self-will.

She had sacrificed friends and supporters to enrich Murray and his supporters by confiscations and grants of crown lands. By the latter she had impoverished the Throne. By the law of Scotland these acts of folly could be remedied, provided they were revoked before she had attained her twenty-fifth year, a term near at hand in 1567. Darnley, aware of this, could find his revenge by influencing the Queen to such a course against Murray, Morton, and their "Bonded" associates. It was well known that Bothwell was desperately in love with the Queen, and that her passion for him was equally violent. With a fiendish astuteness these nominal reformers in religion and politics entered into another bond, under the leadership of Murray, to get rid of Darnley, ostensibly for the benefit of Bothwell, and in reality solely for the advantage of themselves.

Bothwell, carried away by his "overpowering love" for

the woman, although a patriot and an honest man in every other respect, yielded to the temptation, and in intent, but not in deed, became a partner in an iniquity by which Darnley perished, just eleven months after Darnley, in conjunction with his own after-murderers, had assassinated his best friend, Rizzio. Darnley did not lose his life through anything that Bothwell did, but by the hands of the strangler, the Scottish Thug, Sir Archibald Douglas, the cousin of Morton, the *Alter Ego* in sin of the arch sinner Murray. The last felt that he was now on the threshold of success. By inflaming the public mind with the idea that Mary and her paramour were associates in the murder of her husband, he assured himself, if a marriage between the lovers could be accomplished, both might be crushed under the load of obloquy which would be aroused against them. Murray led off in the devilish design. He was the first to sign the Ainslie Supper Bond, which urged the Queen to marry Bothwell, and pledged the fortunes and fidelity of those who signed the Bond to defend and support the Queen and her third husband, James Hepburn. The ink was scarcely dry on the Bond before the human devils who subscribed it secretly entered into another to sacrifice Bothwell and the Queen. Fate was their friend, and Mary, with a folly as incomprehensible as inconsistent, threw away the game, allowed Bothwell to be driven from her side, gave herself up to her enemies, and became first a prisoner, and then a fugitive.

Murray had triumphed. Mary's son, heir to the throne, being an infant, Murray became Regent—was virtually King. For two short years he enjoyed the fruits of his life-long treachery. Then *Ate* stepped in, and through an agent as vile in his ingratitude to Murray as the latter had been to Mary, slew Murray; and one by one, within a very few years, each one of his associates in crime perished by the bullet, by poison, by the axe, by the halter, or by some other sudden violence, artificial or natural. Then, out of the revolting putrescence of folly, passion, sin and crime, grew up, flowered, and fruited the success of Reform, and the Union of Three Crowns, the sovereignty of the British Islands, in the son of Mary.

It seems to be the endeavor of every one who has written respecting the closer relations of Mary and Bothwell, to prove that their season of love—even if they admit their love was mutual—was of very brief duration; with strange phases, at most comprised within two years. How long Mary took a warm interest in him is not so susceptible of proof; but that Bothwell was in love with her as early as 1558, when he went to France in connection with her betrothal to the Dauphin, is admitted by more than one writer, either as a fact or as a surmise. Whether he saw her again until he encountered her at Joinville, in 1560, is not so certain. In that year he was sent over by her mother, the Queen-Dowager-Regent, on an important political mission, and remained four months in close communion with Mary, enjoying her fullest confidence and consulted daily by her on many questions of vital consequence connected with her present and future. That she acted on his advice, and that his counsels were most wise, is undeniable. She learned to appreciate the literary and political capacity of which she had ample proof, and the trust that she acquired in his mental superiority was afterwards fortified by the experience she had reason to regard with gratitude in consequence of his invariable trustworthiness in arms and in council, his loyalty and his heroism.

When Bothwell first enjoyed her society he was only eighteen years of age, although already showing the ability of riper age, and in 1560 he was not over twenty-four, in the full possession of acknowledged virile beauty and manly courage. In truth, as soon as his father died, in 1556, he evinced "The spirit of a youth that means to be of note."

It is also certain that Bothwell returned to Scotland with her, but whether or not in the same vessel is nowhere stated. He may have been in the ship with the Earl of Eglintoun, which was stopped by the English vessels-of-war. If he was afterwards or at any time under a cloud for a shorter or longer period in his own country or in exile, the disfavor was not due to himself, but to the malice of the wicked Murray, who was implacable in regard to every one whom he deemed an obstacle to his greed and to his ambition. Doubtless Bothwell's habits may have offended Mary from time to time; not his vices, for to such she had been accustomed during her sojourn in France, but to the manner in which he gave way to his indulgence.

Mary's relations with Bothwell must have been more or less intimate, because her favorite brother, Lord John Stuart, Prior of Coldingham, married Bothwell's only sister, Jane Hepburn, 11th January, 1561-2. The nuptials "were celebrated with great splendor at Crichton Castle. The fetes were prolonged for three days, during which time Mary, matronized by his widowed mother, was Bothwell's guest. The family connection established between them by that marriage placed them on more familiar terms than might otherwise have been the case. What more natural, if Bothwell had been a man likely to please the Queen, then a widow, than that courtship should have been commenced between them on an occasion so auspicious for love-making as a festive Scottish wedding in a lonely castle at Yule-tide, when all was mirth and social joy, and regal cares forgotten for a season? What objection could have been urged against her contracting matrimony with him at that time? Bothwell was one of the great territorialists, Hereditary Lord Admiral, Lord Lieutenant of the Borders, a valiant soldier, and a Protestant. John Knox himself would have been willing to pronounce the bridal benediction of his feudal chief and the blooming Queen, in the hope that she would accompany her anti-Popish bridegroom to the preaching, learn from his stern lessons the monstrousness of female domination, and submit the sceptre and the sword of empire to a king-matrimonial of the Reformed faith."*

The only issue of this marriage of John Stuart and Jane Hepburn was a son, Francis, who stood in an equal degree of relationship to Mary and to Bothwell, being the nephew of both, thus forming an additional strong connecting link between them. Lord John died in 1563, three years before Mary and Bothwell were drawn most closely together, and Mary always cherished a great affection for the little boy to whom she had given the name of her first husband, Francis. This son was a real Hepburn, and turned out a wild slip, and by his wayward boldness showed that his Uncle James lived over again in his sister's child, who was devoid of fear and full of wild enterprise.†

Whatever may have been the feelings of Mary toward Bothwell, their course was turned aside by the appearance

---

* Here let it be observed that it is very questionable if Mary would have conceded full royal rights to any one, or, if she did so, submit to a co-equal exercise of sovereignty by a consort. Perhaps the key to much of her enigmatical conduct is the fact that, as soon as she felt her neck within a bow of the matrimonial yoke, her whole powers were exerted to relieve herself of the constriction and control. Moreover, this may explain her strange conduct at times, particularly after her marriage with Bothwell, arising from a mere struggle for mastery. As long as the relative positions of lover and sweetheart were maintained, it was a sliding scale, dependent solely on feeling. Marriage brought in a new quantity, and instead of two positive poles, mutually attractive, there were now a positive and a negative, repellant.

† "John Stuart had already died at Inverness about the close of 1563. His widow entered, in the year 1566, into a second marriage with John

of Darnley. This "beardless Adonis" captured her fancy, and Bothwell for a short time was "out in the cold."

Sinclair, of Caithness, and after the death of the latter, in 1573, into a third, with Archibald Douglas, a relative of the Earl of Morton. Bothwell's sister, during her first brief union to John Stuart, bore a son, Francis Stuart, to whom Mary became godmother, and of whom his maternal uncle [James, Earl of Bothwell] at a late period assumed the office of guardian. Named, as it would seem, after Mary's first husband, and by his father's early death specially commended to her care, Francis Stuart received even in his childhood, while the Queen was still at the head of the Government of Scotland, many proofs of her kindness, and was afterwards, in a testament made at Sheffield during her imprisonment, recommended, as her brother's son and her own godson, to the favorable regard of James VI., particularly in order that he might succeed to the Bothwell estates [those of her third husband]. James VI. consequently considered Francis Stuart as his cousin, and, although belonging to an illegitimate branch of the family, created him, in 1581, Earl of Bothwell and Lord High Admiral of Scotland, having at the same time made over to him all the rest of his uncle's long-forfeited possessions and offices. His character was, notwithstanding, too much like that of his uncle [James], and his political life was also as stormy as his. However ungrateful the new Earl of Bothwell afterwards showed himself towards James VI., he never in the least forgot the kindness with which Mary had followed him from his cradle. *He told James VI to his face that if he submitted to Elizabeth's prosecution against his imprisoned mother, he deserved to be hanged ; and when the tidings of her execution reached Scotland, he exclaimed that a coat of mail was now the only mourning he should wear, and put forth all his efforts to set on foot a hostile attack upon England.* Seven years afterwards he was obliged to seek refuge in the wild highlands of the North, and subsequently to betake himself to the Orkneys, whence he at length continued his flight over the Shetland Isles to France. In 1600, the French Government compelled him to withdraw into Spain, whence he betook himself to Naples, and there, after he had gone over to Romanism, he ended his life in the year 1612, having, it is alleged, died of grief at the death, by accident, of the eldest son of James VI., Prince Henry Frederick." "Schiern's Bothwell," appendix (Note B. to P. 57), 407-'8.

Handfasted to Darnley early in April, she was married to him 29th July of the same year, 1565. Before the public ceremony she gave tokens of regret at her precipitate choice of a yoke-fellow.

The consideration now reaches a point which has given rise to a great deal of discussion. After the marriage with Darnley, Bothwell had been recalled, as the only man who could support the Queen against the bastard Murray. Why did Mary promote his marriage with Jane Gordon if she hated Darnley so desperately and loved Bothwell so dearly? The English minister wrote home, 18th February, 1566, "I know now for certain that this Queen repenteth her marriage [with Darnley],* and she hateth him and all his kin." Burton (IV., 139) answers every objection in two short sentences:

"The interest taken by Queen Mary in this marriage has been pitted against the many presumptions that her heart then belonged to Bothwell. But experience in poor human nature teaches us that people, terrified by the pressure of temptation, do sometimes set up barriers against it, which they afterward make frantic efforts to get over."

---

*Feuillet, in his *Histoire d'une Parisienne,*" has some pertinent observations on a similar antagonism between man and wife. "This man [Darnley], constituted solely of physical energy, had held his own against the anxieties by which he had been secretly tortured for weeks. His moral force had weakened under the astonishment, under the prolonged impression of that sombre hatred, that premeditated, astute, implacable vengeance

Whatever barrier Mary was thus erecting against herself, and however impassable she considered it to be, Bothwell had already planned the way to break it or sweep it away. His project was the reëstablishment of a Roman Catholic Court, invested with the power to pronounce divorces, especially where such were sought on a plea of which he felt that he was to be the victim. Habituated to treating women as children and playthings, he was stupefied and even terrified at having encountered, all at once, in one of these frail and despised beings, a profundity of perception and a force of will against which all his personal forces, physical vigor, fortune, social position, conjugal authority, were impotent and of no account whatever."

"The conclusion of the matter is this: in the moral order of things monsters are not produced. God does not create them, and [Mary] the angel, by her husband's brutality, was transformed into a monster." As a bystander observed, "I see something in the pupil of her eye which would not greatly please me were I her husband."

"Her (Mary's) education was essentially that of the French Court, and it affords a general solution of some of the moral difficulties connected with her career to collect from the sad history of the times the principles she must have then imbibed." "Appleton's Picturesque Cylopædia of Biography."

"The first Stuart on the English throne [James VI. of Scotland and I. of England] *was a true son of the* (mean and cowardly Darnley and of the intellectual but) *vicious beauty*, the mother, Mary, Queen of Scots. He (James) was a hard, cruel, weak, degraded creature." "*A perished kernel.*"—Ewall's "Stories from State Papers," 11-71.

which the Papists never failed to adjudge sufficient to untie the marriage knot. Upon the advice of Bothwell, Mary reconstituted this Court, and, when the time came that a divorce was desirable, Mary did all in her power to bring the matter before this tribunal and hasten the proceedings which set Bothwell free to marry her. All parties interested then concurred in using every means to remove all obstacles to the union of Mary and Bothwell, and the Protestant and Papist authorities ran a race, neck and neck, to legalize the divorce, without which Mary could not have married Bothwell, 15 May, 1567. It is utterly ridiculous to attempt to explain away the patent fact that, without Mary was willing, and all parties agreeable, the marriage between the Queen and the Earl could not have been accomplished. Mary's champions and defenders may shout themselves hoarse without weakening in the slightest degree Hume's consummate argument, that until her friends can show that Mary did not marry Bothwell, they had brought forward nothing to exonerate her. As to the question, how early Mary entered into those intimate relations with Bothwell—which not even her passionate affection for him can excuse, in a strictly moral light—is not so clear, nor is this so important if the fact can be shown that they did exist for some time before the death of Darnley. That they did as early as the summer of 1556 is attested by her own hand, in one of the famous Sonnets addressed to Bothwell by her after he had such a narrow escape from death on the 6th of October, 1556. After this Mary seemed determined to aid him to the fullest extent of her ability in hastening the crisis. Then and thence resulted the death of Darnley, the divorce of Bothwell from his wife, Mary's marriage with him, and her complete surrender of herself to him, as it were, in the very presence of her husband's corpse.*

Mary's conduct at Borthwick Castle demonstrates that, so far as she was concerned, she was determined to cast in her lot with him; but her conduct, as well as his own, at Carberry Hill, is one of those "weakenings" which puzzle the clearest head and most philosophical mind. That she should have consented to let Bothwell leave her without striking a blow, and have insisted upon surrendering herself helplessly to his and her mortal enemies, is one of those mysteries which neither experience nor philosophy can solve.* History, it is true, abounds with mysteries, but pre-

---

* "Amid the confusion and general stupor, Jeanne, suddenly sobered, kept her feet, cold, impassable, resting one hand on her chair; her lovely face—once so pure and noble—seemingly concealed beneath the mask of Tisiphone, it manifested that mingling of horror and savage joy (satisfaction) which might have been discovered in the expression of Mary Stuart when she heard the explosion which avenged her upon the murderer of Rizzio."—Feuillet's "*Histoire d'une Parisienne.*"

* What an awful fatality must that have been which led Mary Stuart * * * ; but the hand of Nemesis is upon *the false and frail accomplice* of Bothwell. She rejects all advice." * * * [Babington White's "Circe."] The author is speaking of the equal feasibility of Mary's escape to France after Langside as to England. His view is just, for the French galleys took her on board at Dumbar-

sents none greater than the abandonment of Mary and the fruiting of his ambition and ("supposed") crime, by Bothwell. After striving for years to obtain, his relinquishment of his success without a struggle is among the most incomprehensible faintings in manhood on record. Some explanation may be discovered in the supposition that he had formerly found his strength and influence renewed and increased in exile; but even then the chance was so desperate and dubious, his desertion of his own cause, without a shot being fired or a blow struck, ranks with the inexplicable. It is one of the instances of the self-betrayal of a brave man which taxes the ingenuity of his biographer to excuse it: that is, if the historical writer has had any knowledge of manhood in adversity. Mary was doubtless at fault more than Bothwell; but since he had triumphed over her in his marriage and in accomplishing all his previous purposes, his will should have risen, with opposition and the occasion, to a greater triumph. What conversation passed between them in their parting exchange of thoughts, hopes and affection is a mystery as great as the result. Impartiality can only suggest that all powers, even the boldest, have their moments of weakness, and this was one of Bothwell's. The decision of the Queen and of her consort on this occasion must be assigned to the same class

---

ton when she was a child, and transported her to France, which was a onger and a more dangerous transit. The same remark, however, is equally applicable to her action at Carberry Hill.

of inexplicable events as Hooker's throwing away all his advantages on the 1st of May, 1863, at Chancellorsville, after he had out-generaled Lee by such magnificent strategy as to evoke the highest praises of the best judges of war. It was a self-surrender similar to that which called forth the cruel criticism of Field Marshal the Duke of Berwick upon the parallel action of Louis XIV., 7th June, 1693. Berwick, courtier as he was, could not keep silent, and in bitterness of spirit he declared that the King's treason to himself was incomprehensible; that there could have been no good reason for it; that he could never learn anything to justify it; and that the only conclusion he could come to was that it was God's will it should be so. The Elector of Bavaria expressed about the same idea after the battle of Ramillies, 23d May, 1706; and, since it is admitted that the physical courage of both Mary and Bothwell was indisputable, all that can be said to throw the slightest glimmer of light upon such suicidal madness on their part is to refer the whole matter to the immediate influence of Providence, and remember the story of Jehosaphat and Ahab at Ramoth-Gilead, where God allowed "a lying spirit to go out" and "entice" Ahab, and "prevail" in leading him to his destruction. In the case of Mary and Bothwell, "the lying spirit" was Kirkaldy of Grange, and he prevailed.* *"Fiat voluntas tua"* was one of the

---

* It has even been surmised that Mary was struck with Kircaldy, and that he was fascinated by Mary (Burton, V., 129), on this occasion

mottoes of the Templars. "Thy will be done." "And it was so!"

Among the many letters written and received on the subject of "Mary, Queen of Scots, a Study," two contain observations which cannot be omitted. It is said of Marshal Clark, Napoleon's Minister of War, that, after the campaign of "One hundred days," in the summer of 1815, and while he continued to enjoy the favor of the restored Louis XVIII., "Those whose base extortions he had repressed in other times now joined their clamors against him, and the Royalists [Queen's party] cared not to say a word in his defence." Compare Dr. Petrick's conclusions—exactly Bothwell's case.

Again, "I believe I told you that I became curiously interested in the story of Mary and Bothwell. I know a living woman who is exactly such a creature as the Queen was, and I know a living man who is as exactly such a being as the Earl, only I believe the *living Earl*—if he had been there three hundred and fifteen years ago—would have fought it out to the bitter end at Carberry Hill. In

---

and he eventually became another of her victims. There is no doubt that some unrecognized influence began soon after to work upon him, and converted him into one of her champions. Having hunted out Bothwell in 1567, he espoused her cause in 1569, took up arms in her behalf and perished like Bothwell through Murray's "foul accomplice,' Morton, and the latter's English allies. Kirkaldy betrayed Mary at Carberry Hill in 1567, and he was betrayed by his own troops in Edinburgh Castle in 1573, six years afterward captured and ignominiously hung by Morton.

fact I know he would, because he belongs to a race who have held high commands in battle, and have either conquered, fought it out to the last, or died sword in hand on the field. I also think the living woman would have "caved," just as the Queen of Scots did; not from want of physical courage, but from what the Yankees term "inward cussedness," or that moral cowardice which arises from utter selfishness.

"Causes of good or evil seem to accumulate, when a very slight thing is the beginning of a succession of blessings or curses. All things conspire, till the recipients of blessings are smothered, or the victims of curses are crushed. Till the cup is full, overflowing, till the burden is unbearable, merciless, till good becomes satiety, or evil cruelty—all the world seems to delight in contributing or robbing, deifying or anathematizing."

> "Never stoops the soaring vulture
> On his quarry in the desert,
> On the sick or wounded bison,
> But another vulture watching
> From his high aerial lookout,
> Sees the downward plunge and follows;
> And a third pursues the second,
> Coming from the invisible ether,
> First a speck and then a vulture,
> Till the air is dark with pinions.
> So disasters come not singly;
> But as if they watched and waited,
> Scanning one another's motions,
> When the first descends, the others
> Follow, follow, gathering flock-wise
> Round their victim, sick and wounded
> First a shadow, then a sorrow,
> Till the air is dark with anguish."
>   RUSSELL's *Library Notes,* "*Types.*"

Fruiting.

"*But though its greatness* [like Bothwell's] *has departed, its beauty remains.* Unlike its once proud masters, Decay, though it has destroyed, has not corrupted it; nay, has entranced its majesty, if not its beauty. The few grey hairs that palsy stirs upon the head of Eld, and which in man we pitifully call his "glory;" the trembling limbs that hardly serve to bear him to the wished for grave have here no parallel. The lichen and grey moss efface the ravages that Time has wrought upon the crumbling pile, the ivy binds its broken ruins together, and hides its scars, or crowns them with eternal green, and in every cleft and crevice through the summer long, the wild rose and the wall flower *swing their incense over this shrine of Time, and fill the air with sweetness.*"

JAMES PAYNE, "*Kit; a Memory.*"

—" All men must die:
BODIES ARE ONLY SHADOWS."
"*Mandingo Song,*" "*Savage Africa.*"

"Go to the battle. It is not lead [the bullet] that kills. It is FATE which strikes us and which makes us die." "*Wollof War Song,*" WILLIAM'S "*Negro Race in America.*"

"It is not in my power [to turn back], an irresistible impulse forces me onward to the overthrow of Rome." ALARIC.

"What course shall I steer?" asked the pilot; "Where God pleases to send me; Against that [nation] which God wills to punish." GENSERIC.

"To every thing there is a season, and a time to every purpose under'the heaven: A time to love, and a time to hate; a time of war, and a time of peace."

"*Ecclesiastes,*" III., 1 and 8.

N the foregoing presentation and absolute refutation of the false charges preferred by so many writers against Bothwell, sufficient proofs have been adduced to demonstrate that Bothwell's first criminal intent was suggested by that prime agent of evil, the astute Lethington, or, as he is better known, Maitland, in obedience to the odious craft of Murray and

the insidious destitution of principle of the latter's "old accomplice," the foul Morton. No felonious conception can be imputed to James Hepburn until he became reconciled to Murray and to that illegitimate Stuart's *Adlatus* and father of lies, Morton. To judge of either of these two it is only necessary to recall the proverbs, "A man is known by his friends and associates," or "Tell me a man's companions and I will tell you the man." Justly, indeed, the Hon. John St. John, in his Tragedy, "Mary, Queen of Scots," makes the Queen declare:

> "O, I was destined in my native land
> To heavier ills; *to Darnley's cruelty ;*
> MURRAY'S AMBITION : MORTON'S TREACHERY :
> My subjects mean desertion of their Queen ;
> Their base revolt, and baser calumnie."

BANKS, *in his "Albion's Queens,"* (see Note, p. 76, *supra*), endorses this:

> "Thou [MORTON] 'st done
> No ill to me, but as thy nature :
> *A wolf can do but as a wolf*—thou hast it
> Tho' Heaven thy horrid crimes may ne'er forget ;
> But let my son revenge [he did] his father's murder,
> Which thou too surely did'st, and laid'st the stain on me."

It would be an attempt false to the purpose of this Trilogy—Mary, James Hepburn, and Bothwell—to endeavor to disprove or gloss over the fact that Bothwell's illicit love for Mary, and her return of such a passion for him, constituted the corner-stone of his subsequent co-operation in the "taking off" of Darnley. He realized the ideal of James Thomson, in his tragedy of "Agamemnon," 1733:

> " Love, to the future blind, each sober thought,
> Each consequence despising, scorning all,
> But what its own enchanting dreams suggest."

Mary's surroundings in her girlhood and youth were incompatible with any sound comprehension of virtue. Her principal attendant, even when she left Scotland in 1548, was Lady Fleming, her aunt, an illegitimate daughter of James V. Chalmers more than once styles the Bastard Murray "her *minion*." What can he mean by this term? Or, again, of Henry Brookes, in his better known tragedy of "*Gustavus Vasa*," 1739:

> " Love is a passion whose effects are various :
> It ever brings some charge upon the soul,
> Some virtue, or some vice, till then unknown,
> Degrades the hero, and makes cowards valiant.
> ——When it pours upon a youthful temper,
> Open and apt to take the torrent in,
> It owns no limits, no restraint it knows,
> But sweeps down all, tho' Heav'n and Hell oppose :
> Ev'n Virtue rears in vain her sacred mound,
> Raz'd in its rage, or in its swellings drown'd."

Still it must be borne in mind that Bothwell was enamored of Mary from the first time that he saw her, and also that she simultaneously experienced a confiding and intimate appreciation of his worth. From that time forward *she leaned upon him, and was thrust more and more into his arms ;* and had it not been for the insidious Murray, it is likely that James Hepburn, and NOT Henry Stuart (Darnley), would have been her second—not her third—consort. As justly observed (page 54, *supra*), Bothwell "was a nobleman, who had hitherto been guilty of nothing dishonorable;" that being a man—as Lamartine admits—"gifted with superhuman daring," he was the only one who felt no fear in undertaking the doing of a deed which the other nobles suggested and devised, incited "thereto" by Murray, "looking through his fingers." That in this Bond he was the Douglas, who had the audacity to "Bell-the-Cat," "and, which none other dared to attempt—according to the morals of the times when it occurred—it [the removal of Darnley] is certainly not dishonoring for Bothwell." Finally, startling as the statement may seem, "Bothwell's [actual] participation in the murder of Darnley has not been strictly proved." Chalmers (1, 141) uses explicit language. "Murray and Maitland condemned him [Darnley] to the *bowstring*," and Archibald Douglas, Morton's cousin, played the part of a Turkish mute, and applied what answered to a *bowstring* in its effects.

Another of the false charges against Bothwell is that he was guilty of ingratitude to Mary, by dragging her down to ruin through his own selfishness, after she had loaded him with benefits and rewards. This is utterly ridiculous.

He had served her mother, the Queen-Dowager-Regent,

with unexampled fidelity against the "Lords of the Congregation," the rebellious nobility; and, after her death, Mary, herself, with equal loyalty. He had shown himself from the beginning the latter's wisest counsellor; preserved her from Murray, Morton and their party; led her armies; pacified the Borders; restored order throughout the realm: and it was not until he had rescued her from the assassins of Rizzio, in the spring of 1566, that he received his first reward (page 48–9, *supra*). Bothwell owed nothing to Mary up to this time. His dignities, his position, his possessions, his influence, were all inherited and inherent. He was born, 1536 or 1537, Lord High Admiral of Scotland, and as such his cradle was his first cabin. While a boy he had fought to suppress, not to abet, piracy. In his nineteenth or twentieth year he already took an active part in public affairs, and was a member of Parliament. When only twenty-one he represented his country at the solemn betrothal of Mary to Francis, when and where he first saw his subsequent sweetheart and wife. The same year he was in the field as a military commander, and in 1558, at most aged twenty-two, he was appointed Lieutenant General of the Scottish Southerly Frontier (Marches or Borders) and Constable of the Headquarters of the turbulent territory, Hermitage Castle. In regard to this appointment, Mary thus expressed herself at a later date: "Notwithstanding he wes yan of verie younge aige, yit wes he chosin out as maist fit of the haill nobilitie to be oure Lieutenent-Generall upoun the bordouris, having the haill charge alsweill to defend as to assayle." (Labanoff, "*Lettres, Instructions et Memoires de Marie Stuart.*" Vol. II., p. 34.)

As Lieutenant, or Warden, Bothwell invaded England, made a destructive raid, and defeated one of the famous perilous-to-encounter Percys, in a noted and notable cavalry engagement. Of this invasion he himself remarks: "I inflicted irreparable damage on the frontiers, and especially upon the [turbulent and inimical] population." In 1559, the "hitherto successful Bothwell" was sent, with a combined force of French and Scotch soldiers, to preserve the "famous fortress" or Castle of Stirling; in 1560 he was sent over to the French Court, over which presided Mary and Francis, to seek military co-operation: likewise into Denmark and Germany for the same purpose. In the spring of 1561 he rejoined Mary, now a widow, and remained at her Court in France until he left that country, and with her, on the same fleet if not in the same ship, returned to Scotland, and became a member of the Royal Privy Council. It may be said that this Council was due to his advice and selection of its members.

In 1560 he was made "*Gentilhomme de la Chambre*" (Chamberlain) to the King of France, with a handsome donation, and, in 1564, when the false Murray drove him forth into exile, the new King of France, Charles IX., made him, on Mary's recommendation, Captain of his

Scottish Body-Guard. In 1563-4, Elizabeth, contrary to right and honor, threw him, when thrown on her coasts by a storm, into captivity, and held him in duress as a dangerous enemy to English intrigue until Mary herself effected or compelled his release. Bothwell was the only man in Scotland that Murray feared. It was at this time, Randolf indicates "the first traces" "of the Queen's partiality for Bothwell." (Burton, IV., 110.) In 1565, all his former dignities, offices and influence were completely restored. In 1566 he was the Queen's Lieutenant General, or military *Alter Ego*, and commanded the Royal army which dispersed the insurgent forces and drove forth Elizabeth's fawning, thoroughly disciplined spaniel, Murray, and the other rebel lords, into the arms of their abettor, the false Machiavellian English Queen. The blows which slew Rizzio were aimed as well at Mary, at Bothwell and the rest of those faithful to her. When Bothwell brought her back within nine days in triumph, she made him Provost of Edinburgh Castle and Custodian or Constable of Dunbar. These were the first acknowledgments of his invaluable services, accompanied with emoluments, that Bothwell had as yet received at the hands of Mary. They did not in reality elevate him a single step, and it was not until he was about to marry her that the Queen made him Duke of the Orkneys—an empty title, as it turned out—a delusion and a snare. In the previous works, "Mary, Queen of Scots," a "Study," and "James Hepburn, a

Vindication," it has been shown that Mary's partiality for Bothwell dates back much farther—perhaps to the earliest months of her first widowhood— than writers are willing to allow. That they did not develop into the absorbing passion that afterwards possessed her is undoubtedly attributable to the malign and adverse influence of her illegitimate half-brother, "the Bastard" Murray. He was jealous of Bothwell as a soldier, as a statesman, and as a suitor, and he poisoned the Queen's mind against the only "REAL MAN" who approached her. Murray persecuted Bothwell to the extent of the power derived from his relationship, both through blood and "Bonds," or political partisanship, from the time of Mary's return home down to the minute that the bullet of Bothwellhaugh avenged James, Earl of Bothwell. It is likely that Bothwell's mode of life had something to do with diverting Mary's feelings from him to Darnley; but, like the pendulum driven to the left by the application of concealed machinery is brought back as soon as it has reached the limits of its sweep, and swings as far to the right, so Mary's sudden "access," which threw her into the arms of Darnley, as soon as she discovered her mistake, brought her back with equal velocity into the embrace of Bothwell. How soon? That it is impossible to prove. There is no direct testimony. Everything is circumstantial. Nevertheless the chain of evidence is very strong that, before Mary was publicly married to Darnley, she was already, from passion as well as politics, attracted more and more to Bothwell. Solomon, whose "Song of Songs" "breathes such impassioned love," truly declares: "Love is strong as death; jealousy is cruel as the grave." Many waters cannot quench love, neither can the floods drown it; if a man would give his whole substance for love, it would utterly be contemned." Bothwell won; Mary gave!

Yes, the more carefully that the critic—if he be unbiassed—prosecutes his scrutiny, the more he will be convinced of this. It is easy to deny; it is difficult to disprove. It is more facile to assert, and it is not as hard to demonstrate, that she was from time to time deeply, nay, desperately, in love with Bothwell.

> "Who journeys far in knowledge grows,
> If wise, to wisdom more attains;
> The more the outer world he knows
> The more the inner vision gains—
> The knowledge of the world within;
> He clearer sees with deeper ken
> That human souls are all akin,
> Though diverse are the lives of men."

The proverb reads, "The course of true love never did run smooth." It held good in this case. As St. Augustine says in his "Confessions," "I loved not yet, yet I loved to love. * * * I sought what I might love, in love with loving;" or, as Dante puts it in his "Divine Comedy:"

"Love, that exempts no one beloved from loving,
Seized me [Mary] with pleasure of this man [Bothwell] so strongly,"
That, as thou seest, it doth not yet desert me ;
[Even in, and after, her captivity at Lochleven.]
Love has conducted us unto one death ;
Caina [lowest Hell] waiteth him [Murray] who quenched our life !
[Whither Bothwellhaugh's bullets sent the treacherous Bastard.]

Campbell goes so far as to state that Mary was "blinded by resentment" against Elizabeth's opposition to her marriage with Darnley, "as well as by love" for him, and, from these mingled motives, was impelled by indignation as well as by passion into consummating the union, which soon cost him his life and later hers.

Dargaud—sneer at his correctness who may—develops the rapid action of the tragic drama with trustworthy distinctness. The relations of Mary and of Bothwell had arrived at such a fever heat about the time that the Earl was wounded by John Elliot, of the Park, that a cataclysm was inevitable. It was simply cause and effect.*

---

* "To the man on whose career and character the correspondence of the day affords us these casual lights let us now return, at that critical point where all eyes were bent on him, and on the *Queen along with him, as in some shape to be sharers in a common destiny.* It was becoming evident that there was something in her sentiments towards him of a warmer nature than those who closely observed it could rationally attribute either to a just sense of his public merits or to simple gratitude for his services to herself. That she should fix her love on him has always been deemed something approaching the unnatural : but, when the circumstances are considered, the conclusion ceases to become so absolutely startling. *Mary was evidently one of those to whom at times—and to her the times were apt to come in quick succession*—a

Looking up into a clear blue sky, considering the condition of the atmosphere, and observing other circumstances inappreciable to those without experience in such matters, enables the careful observer to pronounce this serenity "a weather-breeder." The night closes in without particular change to attract the attention of admiring ignorance. Still there are indications perceptible to the seer, and the morning breaks in gloom and tempest. Knox, in a measure, was right, that "literary prostitute" Buchanan also, Murray, the whole tribe in some degree; but, like birds of prey, they saw nothing in this storm but the promise of gratification for their coarse but natural appetites. Mary returned from her trying gallop to the Hermitage to visit her wounded lover, and, in spite of the inevitable fatigue, instead of seeking repose, spent a large portion of the night in writing to him. This developed the fierce fever which nearly burned out her life. She rose from that

great affair of the heart is a necessity of life; the necessity now increased in intensity by her utter disappointment in her last attachment, and *the loathing she entertained towards its object*. Who, then, were near her to be the first refuge for her fugitive affections? None but her own nobles, for she was not in a position to treat with a foreign prince; and, in looking around among the most eminent of these, including Huntly, the brother of a former suitor, Argyle, Athole and Arran, *there were none who, on the ground of rank and position, had claims much higher than Bothwell's,* unless it might be Arran, by reason of his royal blood, and he was already a rejected suitor." (Burton, IV., 172.) Burton (IV., 95) speaks of her *policy* in 1563, "when she was not under the influence of the *violent* attachments to which she afterwards yielded."

sick-bed another woman. Bothwell left his couch—to which the wound received in her service had consigned him—and, only half recovered, hastened to her side; Darnley also came. How was each one received? There is no doubt as to the difference. From this time forward Bothwell rose privately and publicly in her esteem; and, as Bothwell rose, Darnley fell, stumbled, plunged into the pit his follies, cowardice and debaucheries had dug for him, and lost his life. Was Bothwell to blame that he delivered the nation and its queen from such a compound of ambition and imbecility! Since the beginning of the world history teems with similar instances. Is left-handed Ehud blamed for slaying the tyrant Eglon? Was not Jehu exalted for the destruction of Ahaziah and Jezebel? Are not Harmodius and Aristogiton honored for killing one of the Pisistratidæ, oppressors of Athens? Is not Brutus hailed as "the Last of the Romans," although he struck down his benefactor, Julius Cæsar! The Roman Catholics glorified with blasphemous honors the monk Clement, who emulated Ehud in killing Henry III.; and is not Charlotte Corday almost sanctified by the best of people for stabbing Marat? Did Bothwell intend to do more than either one of these, and was he not incited to do whatever he did by the preachings of Knox, the founder of the Scottish Church, and his coadjutors in the work of reformation? It is now positively known that Darnley did not lose his life either through the means employed by Bothwell or at his hands. Darnley was slain by Archibald Douglas, cousin to Darnley, and relative and confidant of Murray and Morton. Out upon such injustice! It was to the interest of Murray's party to throw the guilt upon Bothwell, to ruin him, to persecute him to his life's end, to defame his memory, and to hand him down as the vilest criminal in Scotland, *whereas he was the only* REAL MAN *of his generation*. As was said of the great Hohenstaufen emperor, "Frederick II., with many of the noblest qualities which could captivate the admiration of his own age, in some respects might appear misplaced, and by many centuries prematurely born." Or, again, "In all ages there have been false [undeserved] reputations, founded on some individual judgment, whose authority has prevailed without examination, until, at last, criticism discusses, the truth penetrates, and the phantom of prejudice vanishes. Such has been the reputation of" James Hepburn. "But the eye of Providence, which sees everything from eternity, perceives all this; and that same Providence disposes everything she has predestinated, in the order it deserves. As Homer says of the sun, it sees everything and hears everything."

Bothwell, as a politician, was too honest for his time, or any time. He served through loyalty, true to his motto, "Kiip Trest" ("Be Faithful"), through sheer loyalty to the Queen-Dowager and purest loyalty, fondest love (in many ways the terms are synonymous) to Mary,

Queen and woman. The scales of his magnanimity, adjusted to weigh most precious objects, were incompetent to weigh the sordid, soul-less creatures with whom he had to work, whose religion, patriotism and honor were founded on greed. With all his experience and education he did not appreciate that all revolutions were founded on personal interests, *pecunia*, money and lands. If he had lived to this day he would have seen this truth confirmed. The Netherlanders, who stood fiery death and fiercer torture because it reached individuals, or only a portion of the population, not the whole, would not stand the "tenth penny," Alva's *alcobala*, because it affected every one—every one felt and no one could avoid the extortion. The people of the Thirteen Colonies rebelled because the Mother Country justly sought to impose upon them a small portion of the burden of the expense of their defence against the French and savages. The South took up arms to carry their "peculiar institution," Slavery, on to Free Soil, and protect their property and traffic in human chattels.

So it has been and so it ever will be. The Scotch nobility wanted to retain what they had gripped, and acquire more of the confiscated Church lands, and Bothwell sought to curb their growing power, to maintain the royal authority, and to administer justice without regard to creed or greed. It is susceptible of proof that he did this almost without reward, and even at last with no adequate compensation from this source. All that he held he inherited from his great-grandfather, the first Earl Patrick, except his government of Edinburgh Castle and the Castlery of Dunbar, which were the recompense of his mighty fidelity; he

"Who never sold the truth to serve the hour,
  Nor palter'd with Eternal God for power;"—

he, who never placed his neck in the yoke of a Knox—who, lording so long over the consciences of Scotland, thought enough of his own appetites and interests to share at sixty the matrimonial yoke with a rich and noble maiden of fifteen;—he, who planted himself as a barrier to the aggressions of the "Lords of the Congregation;" who had he but filled the maws of this hungry pack with plunder, or reduced them to beggary, and given their possessions to a new tribe of "wild (Nepaul) dogs" and jackals, and had he been contented with the woman, Mary, he might have continued to live on and to love. He fell and lost all because he was a patriot without groveling objects. Had he left the administration and its advantages to the vile aristocracy whose mouths watered for the latter alone, as hungry wolves contemplate a flock of fat sheep, he would not have been branded as a "pirate," and died in exile and captivity. He sought at once to love the Queen as a "real man," and to govern the country as a real ruler. In Scotland two such *roles*, in his day, were incompatible. Love brims earth's cup. Let mortals be content with that. If the goblet of life be filled with that draught, pure and complete, none other will be conceded. The law of compensation will yield no more because, with means to live, Fortune can bestow no more. Wreathe the cup with the most exquisite wild flowers grown amid the thorns along the path of life, and Fate may smile and bless the gift. Encrust the chalice with gems, and at once it becomes the coveted prize of the envious, the sensual and the violent, or the prey of the stealthy or the rapacious robber.

> "Pains of love be sweeter far
> Than all other pleasures are."

Harvesting

> "This is Love's house, and this is Love's hour of bliss;
>   Through the dark grove her windows shine like stars;
> List to those flute-players, mark well the bars
> Of that sweet prelude, each note like a kiss
> That longer grows and tenderer, till you miss
>   The music in the passion. Nothing jars
>   On soul or sense: no fateful boding mars
> Joy's perfectness; what end shall be of this?
>
> Love hath her day, but Love's day vanisheth;
>   Vacant her chambers now, below, above;
> Her flutes no longer breathe melodious breath;
>   Dark are her windows now as is the grove;
> And echoes of the falling feet of Death
>   Reverberate through the empty house of Love."
>   *"Love's Day."—The Academy.*

IT is impossible, without entering into the most minute details and at length, to furnish to readers any adequate idea of the utter villainy of the principal Scotch nobility in the time of Mary. They had scarcely signed the Bond at the celebrated Ainslie [Annesley] Supper, 19th April, 1567,* urging the Queen to marry Bothwell, and sol-

---

* But what was the purport of this celebrated Bond? The writers—after rehearsing the facts which we have already detailed, that the Earl of Bothwell, having been openly calumniated as guilty of the death

emnly pledging "their lives, their fortunes and their sacred honors," their complete support to her and to him, if the marriage did follow, than—even before the nuptial

---

of the late King, as well by placards over the city as by the letters of the Earl of Lennox, had been tried and found innocent by the noblemen, his peers, appointed to conduct the inquest—declare that *the nobleness of his lineage, the magnitude of his services, and their own friendship towards him in all times past, together with that common bond of interest which unites all noblemen together,* as equally subject to the calumnies of their enemies, and the vain bruits of the common people, induce them *to come forward and avouch his perfect innocence, and to promise upon their faith and honor, and truth in their bodies as they are noblemen,* and as they shall answer to God, to defend him in all time to come against all, whosoever they may be, who shall utter slander against his name; and, moreover, considering that the Queen was without a husband, and that *none could be found so fitting for that dignity as himself,* they promise to sustain him in his endeavors to perfect such a marriage, and to render him all assistance against any who shall endeavor to oppose or to prevent it. [If there were no evident tokens of Mary's fondness and partiality for Bothwell, why should he have been selected for so high a dignity and reward?] And should they violate their solemn promise, they call down upon their own heads the vengeance of posterity, and beseech that they may "never have Reputatioun or Credite in na Tyme heiraftir, but be accounted unworthie and faithles Traytors." The annals of history are filled with many sad and melancholy instances of human treachery and human crime, and our own [English] nation has not been free from such blots upon its brilliant escutcheon; but when we see the same men who have thus, under the most solemn obligations which can bind the mind of man, *dedicate their lives, their fortunes and their honor to the support and defence of a single man,* and the furtherance of his marriage with their Queen, declaring a few short months afterwards that he was undoubtedly guilty of the perpetration of the crime, from the imputation of which they there declared him free, and averring that their sovereign, "by hir unknot was tied—they were making arrangements for another "Bond" to pull down the Earl and ruin the Queen. (See Letter of the British spy and tool, Kircaldy of Grange, to the English Earl of Bedford, dated the next day, 20th of April, 1567.) Burton (IV., 235) states that they were concerting their plans for this infernal treachery before the marriage, 15th May, 1567. That is to say they had handicapped the Ainslie-Tavern-Bond by another, calculated to annul their pledges, which had been freely and unreservedly given a few weeks previously. Among the excuses they alleged to whitewash themselves for rising against Bothwell and the Queen, was the charge that the former intended to get possession of the young prince (afterwards James VI.) and make way with him, to assure to himself and to his issue the Crown and the Succession in Scotland. That such issue there would be, Mary herself deemed probable. (Froude, IX., 65.) This lame attempt at exon-

godlie and dishonorable proceeding in a priveit mariage with him soddenlie and unprovisitlie," was proved beyond a doubt to have participated in that crime, the whole dark array of human guilt seems brightened by the contrast, and the vile act of perfidy stands forth the blackest in the annals of our race. Bright, indeed, was the spirit of prophecy which illuminated their minds when they penned those last words of their sacred Bond, when they declared that, if they violated that pledge, they should " nevir have Reputatioun or Credite in na Tyme heiraftir, but be accounted *unworthie and faithles Traytors.*" Their own lips have pronounced the verdict on their fame, and posterity shall confirm the awful sentence for the profit and edification of an admiring world." ("Memoirs of Mary Stuart, Queen of Scotland," by L. Stanhope F. Buckingham. London, 1844, pp. 177-80.

cration falls to the ground, since it is known that their threefold treason was determined at least a week before either the Queen or Bothwell had manifested the faintest design—or, according to any evidence, entertained the slightest idea—of asking or seeking the guardianship of the Royal child. They had no reason for their suspicions except the suggestion of their own guilty minds, sufficiently capable of engendering such a criminal plot. Whatever course he followed, Bothwell's objective had always been, and was, a grand one. Primarily it was the good of his country, and the hope of bringing order out of chaos. Secondly, it was the possession of Mary Stuart, the object of "the overpowering force of love [which] had already swept away his long tried fidelity." (Buckingham, I., 182.) It is a pity Bothwell had not eaten freely of "Ant's Eggs," which, according to popular superstition, "are an Antidote to Love." Even in this, however, his design was invested with a certain nobility of purpose. From her hand he hoped to receive the sceptre, and from his marriage with her derive the legitimization of an authority which would enable him to bless Scotland with something like a stable and efficient government. That he loved Mary as no other man ever loved her, and that she loved him—as much as her Stuart-Guisan nature—spasmodically and sporadically—would allow, and as she loved no other man, is susceptible of the clearest proof, except to those who resemble the Papists and Southern Rebels, and are positively unable to see the truth through the atmosphere of their interests and their ignorance, their prejudices and their passions.

Mary Stuart's life—to repeat—was one tissue of mistakes. She started out with the grand error of making Elizabeth her enemy by a public claim to the Crown of England. She endeavored to excuse this on the ground that the act was not her own, but that of her father-in-law, Henry II., King of France. This would be a plausible explanation if she had not adhered to the assumption throughout life, and when she was entirely independent of all control. This obstinacy brought her to the scaffold. Moreover, her indiscretions—beginning as soon as her first husband, Francis, died—were unintermittent. (Burton, IV., 172-3.) She was a perfect "Medusa among Beauties." Every one of her lovers in succession came to a terrible end; with one exception, the noble d'Amville. He alone, in time, had the strength of soul to break the spell. From Chastelard to Babington, to love Mary Stuart, or to be favored by her, was equivalent to a sentence of death. Just consider the list after her return to Scotland; for uncertainty—like one of the dense fogs of the land of her nativity—invests the period of her widowhood in France. She must have in reality possessed the fabulous "Capon's stone," capable of ensuring love. Even the vile Murray expiated his brief intervals of favor by assassination. Chastelard, by the hands of the executioner, heads the death-roll; Sir John Gordon, avowedly the handsomest man in Scotland, **was decapitated in her presence**; Rizzio was basely and barbarously murdered at her knees, her second husband abetting and assisting; Darnley was strangled, NOT *killed by an explosion, and* NOT *by Bothwell;* Bothwell, after fearful vicissitudes, perished in confinement; the Earl of Arundel died in the Tower and the Duke of Norfolk on the block there; the Earl of Northumberland lost his head by the axe at York; and the Earl of Westmoreland died in poverty and exile. As for minor victims to her fascination, the rack, the noose, the axe and the gibbet were their inevitable fate.

Mary Stuart's mother, Mary of Guise, Queen-Dowager-Regent, trusted implicitly in Bothwell. Mary herself accorded to him her fullest confidence in emergencies, from the first time they met at Joinville. Had she remained faithful to these first impressions, all would have gone well. Knox would have sanctioned and blessed the union of the Queen and his hereditary chief, to whom he ever, with more or less fondness, inclined, and the Reformers, as a body, in spite of the rascality of their lords, would have followed the anointed of the great Scottish Reformer and the most consistent Protestant of the whole nobility. But, unfortunately, she allowed herself to be beguiled by the arch-hypocrite Murray, and he led her astray and plunged her deeper and deeper into the fatal slough of his arts, or lured her into the meshes of his boundless ambition.

Although a bigoted Roman Catholic, among her first acts, after her return to Scotland, was to assist her intriguing relative to ruin the House of Huntley, the principal prop of her creed. What for? To build up the fortunes of her false brother, who was her most truculent enemy, and thus, by the spoliation of her staunchest friends, to found and fence the fortunes of her bitterest enemies. Unless she had so greatly enriched Murray, he could not have compassed her downfall. Had she married Bothwell when she returned to Scotland, all would have gone well. He was a Protestant who, while unshakable in his convictions, was wholly destitute of bigotry. He would have rallied the Calvinistic pack to her support —the hungry and remorseless pack, which, allowed to follow Murray's lead, hunted Mary to her doom. She passed over devoted fidelity when it might have proved her salvation, and was captured—"captured" is the only word applicable—by the "mere external graces and accomplishments" of a courtly but "silly young fool," and soul-less, "well-made, long lad"—an immature man, just as fit to be a king-consort as the astute Murray was to be a subject. The "deep-seeing ecclesiastic," Mary's uncle, the Cardinal de Lorraine, sent two confidential messengers to his niece, and implored her, through Roullart, to give up Darnley "if she valued her future happiness," styling him, with astonishing perspicacity, "*un gentil hutaudeau*" (an obsolete epithet of contempt equivalent to a "high-born, quarrelsome coxcomb") "unmeet in any respect to be her consort." Unfortunately things had gone too far. Darnley already possessed her person. Handfasted to him in the beginning of April, 1565, she learned too late the truth of her relative's judgment. She was already surfeited with him when the mistress, in fact,—by a sort of brutal usage or custom in Scotland—became the fully legalized wife, on the 29th of July following. For this outrage on manners and morals, her church—the Roman Catholic, a church which is never false to its Jesuit creed, expediency, that the end justifies the means—and the Papal agent, Rizzio, are alone responsible. All this time her heart of hearts belonged to Bothwell. This cannot be proved by direct, however demonstrable by indirect, evidence. At the public marriage with Darnley (Froude, VIII., 190)—

"For some strange reason," the Queen appeared "at the altar in a mourning dress of black velvet, such as she wore the doleful day of the burial of her husband [Francis]. Whether it was an accident—whether the doom of the house of Stuart haunted her at this hour with its fatal foreshadowings—or *whether simply for a great political purpose*, she was *doing an* ACT WHICH IN ITSELF SHE LOATHED, it is impossible to tell; *but that black drapery struck the spectators with a cold, uneasy awe.*"

The public marriage with Darnley evoked from its originator and manipulator, Rizzio, the secret agent of the Papacy, "the exultant exclamation, '*Te Deum laudamus*' —it is done, and cannot be broken." Blind fool! He praised God for what? For bringing about his own downfall and death! He did not foresee that, within eight months, Darnley would compass his murder. Nor did he foresee that a week after Bothwell would be summoned home, destined to avenge him on Darnley, and overturn all for which the exultant Piedmontese had labored and was to suffer.

In "Mary, Queen of Scots, a Study," and in "James Hepburn, Earl of Bothwell, a (the first) Vindication," sufficient has been said in detail of the removal of Darnley. All that seems needful in this immediate connection is to repeat that "Mary was thrust more and more into the arms of Bothwell" (page 49, *supra*) from the moment he returned home to her support. By handfasting she became the legalized or morganatic mistress of Darnley early in April, 1565; by choice she was the *chere-amie* of Bothwell (Dargaud), before Darnley was a year older, perhaps much sooner.

That Sir Walter Scott, with all his chivalric admiration of Mary Stuart, did not believe in her innocence is admitted by the Queen's warmest advocates. That she lured Darnley—once, and for a short period, the object of a frenzied passion—to his doom is undoubted. The more the facts are studied, the more conclusive must be the judgment of the impartial against her. Amid the direct and circumstantial evidence, her letters (known generally as the "Casket Letters") to Bothwell are the most important proof.

In spite of all the volumes published and testimony that has accumulated, in almost every language of Europe, to prove that the "Casket Letters" and Sonnets and Documents found in the Silver Box, belonging to Bothwell, and delivered over to his enemies by the double traitor, Balfour—are forgeries, the writer reiterates, after more careful consideration, that *their authenticity is undoubted*. After over two years' study of all the testimony, pro and con, his verdict—that of no incompetent critic—must be that *they carry within themselves inherent proof that they are not inventions*, except in the primary sense of the word— i. e., they were accidentally discovered. To emphasize, *the Casket Letters are not* FORGERIES. Those documents are not anomalies. Many women in different classes of life, in more or less polished language, have addressed letters to their lovers as full of passion as those of Mary, demonstrating as complete surrenders of heart and soul to the object of their love, to whom they had abandoned themselves and devoted themselves whether for good or for evil. They are exactly such communications as would be sent to a Bothwell. now idolized by a Mary Stuart hating a Darnley, a detested and detestable husband, than whom a meaner creature never lived ; and, *as she did write them*, they clear up every difficulty which appears to invest the otherwise enigmatical tie that bound the Queen and the Earl to each other with mysterious intensity. They prove, moreover, that in whatever degree Bothwell was criminal in blasting away the obstacle, Darnley, between Mary and himself, she, in an equal if not a greater degree, was guilty as instigator, perhaps; as accomplice, assuredly; as spy and lure, certainly; as a receiver of whatever was acquired by the crime, a partner from first to last, at every step, in every degree, in every phase, and in every particular action. Among other arguments urged that Mary did not compose or write these letters, &c., is their orthography, calligraphy, language, style, and sentiment. No one wrote more unevenly in every respect than she did at different times. In a little French work entitled, "The Art of Judging the Characters of Men and Their Handwriting," is shown a letter of Mary Stuart, "who at times wrote elegantly, though usually in uneven lines; when *in haste* and distress of mind; in several letters during her imprisonment which I have read *much the contrary;*" *i. e.*, not elegantly or as ordinarily. This is another strong proof of the authenticity of Mary's letters to Bothwell, which were indited both "*in haste* and distress of mind," or perturbation of mind (D'Israeli's "Curiosities of Literature," IV., 47). As further proof against her see the curious inedited holograph letter recently discovered, among others of Mary, in the Charter Room of the Earl of Moray, Donibristle House, to the Commendator of St. Colmes Inch, in a mixed dialect of English, Scotch and French. Although a perfectly original document from the hand of the Queen, it is admitted by Agnes Strickland, her *too partial* biographer, to be "almost as unintelligible as if written in Welsh." It was indited during Mary's captivity at Bolton Castle, in England, and is dated 23d July, 1568. Such spelling as this epistle exhibits is incomprehensible in a woman of the Queen's capabilities, education, and opportunities. The best proof against Mary is feminine nature in general, and her own in particular, and there is nothing in any of the papers, charged to be hers, in prose or poetry, that is not strictly consistent with both.

It seems almost impossible for a student of this period to tear himself away from discussing the validity of the Casket Letters and Documents. To a person of experience, a man of the world, they carry within themselves every proof of their authenticity. This internal evidence, again, is corroborated by external circumstances. Whoever denies that Mary's infatuation or passion for Bothwell is not demonstrated by them, as well as by her open conduct, is either too prejudiced to judge fairly, or too ignorant of women and the world to be competent to judge at all. Here, apparently out of place in this connection, it seems pertinent to anticipate in regard to the charge of Bothwell's unkindness to Mary, after their public marriage, a similar rule of investigation must be applied. If Bothwell and Mary's connection dated back for the long period alleged, and as good as proven—although a Scotch jury might let them off with the dubious verdict of "guilty, but not proven"—a comparison of testimonies will demonstrate that their *honeymoon* was only *nominal*, and that, since the edge of possession had long since been turned, it was no honeymoon—in the real sense of the word—at all. Bothwell knew Mary and her failings or proclivities, and since it is admitted that strong love and fierce jealousy are inseparable, this conjunction of excitations, together with the difficulties of his situation, may have made the Earl-Consort less gentle than a "spoiled beauty" was willing to submit to without grievous complaint. The conditions of courting and of marriage, differ vastly in the great majority of cases. Marriage, according to the proverb, "is the Grave of Love." Moreover, Mary was easily discomposed. When crossed, and when in that condition of mind, and in her condition of body—all proved by her faintings and other unmistakable signs—she doubtless used strong phrases not meant in earnest, however forcibly expressed. People undertake to apply to her case rules of judgment which are altogether inapplicable in the nature of things and to women, from queen to quean: since all women in love are alike, whether crowned or in rags. Moral laws and conventional restraints are all very well in the abstract, but whoever has been behind the scenes and seen the litter-strewn corners of life is well **aware** that a writer must have been very much of a Bohemian, who undertakes to write on subjects that lie entirely beyond the area of the dignity of parlor manners and the proprieties of full-dress-parade or fashionable receptions.

Burton (IV., 228-'9) assures us that:

"The beginning of their wedded life [publicly accepted as such] resembled that of any innocent young couple, affluent in the sources of magnificence and luxury.* They were a *good*

---

* " Some business had to be done, however, and, among other things, came up the proper diplomatic communication of the events to foreign Courts. A long document of extreme interest contains her instructions to William Chisholm, Bishop of Dunblane, sent as a special envoy to France to convey the intelligence and make suitable explanations. This document is curiously wavering and inconsistent. It begins with a eulogistic biography of her husband—what the French would call an *eloge*. His great services and merits are set forth at length; and since it has to be admitted that he was sometimes under the cloud of the royal displeasure, this is attributed to the envyings that ever dog high merit, and are successful for a time in obscuring it. In this portion of the document it is made clear that Bothwell amply deserved his preferment.

"Having shown what she had done was exactly what in justice and duty she should have done, she next tells how the surrounding conditions coerced her, so that, as a political necessity, she could not do otherwise. She found that his eminent services to the state and to her own person had not been achieved without exciting ambitious thoughts. She saw the somewhat audacious tenor of these, and tried to administer a judicious check to them. She failed. There was another element besides ambition which made him rash and headstrong in his acts—a devouring love for her. These combined motives conduced to rash acts, which brought her into his power. Then, when she considered her position, it was not merely that she was at the mercy of a man exulting in the consciousness of unparalled heroism and statesmanship, and frantically in love with herself, but her whole nature was with him. She referred to the Bond signed at the notable [Ainslie] supper as a great demonstration of the chiefs of the state, such as a sovereign cannot without danger resist. The current in Bothwell's favor was so strong that not one man in Scotland appeared to stand up for her. Then she bethought herself if she was right in her obstinate resistance. She be-

deal seen in public, and frequently rode together in much bravery. Stories were told how when he, still preserving the etiquette of sovereign and subject, would attend her cap in hand, she would playfully snatch it and place it on his head. It may, indeed, be counted one of the most remarkable phenomena of the whole situation that one of the subtlest and acutest women ever born should, in her fool's paradise, have been totally unconscious of the volcano she was treading on."

Any man of the world who has seen much of life, and been behind the scenes, must know that just such letters as are attributed to Mary Stuart have been written under similar cir-

---

gan to yield to the wishes of her people, and at the same time her heart relented to the *merits and the deep affection* of her lover. Further, wearied out by the turbulence of the country she was to rule over, she feels how great a relief it will be to herself, how great a gain to law and order, that she shall have for her husband *a man who has command in his nature*, and can be trusted to rule her fierce subjects. These, indeed, would never 'digest a foreign husband;' and of her own subjects 'there was none, either for the reputation of his house or for the worthiness of himself, as well in wisdom, valiantness, as in all other good qualities, to be preferred or yet compared to him whom we have taken.' Again the document takes a twist. There must be something said to palliate the extraordinary haste in this royal marriage. Such alliances were generally affairs on which a sort of congress of friendly royalties deliberated. It was but common decorum that she should have consulted the King of France, the Queen Mother, her uncle, the Cardinal, and some others. Here, again, she throws the blame on the importunity of her lover and the impatient pressure of the ruling powers of the country. Then, as if the writer felt alarm that what she said in her own vindication must react against the other, she pleads vehemently that all her friends must be the friends of him who is inseparably joined to her. The past is past. If he has been to blame, it was because *his devotion overcame his discretion*." (Burton's "History of Scotland." Vol. IV., pages 229-230.)

cumstances by passionate women to the objects of inordinate and illicit affection again, and again, in every age. Human nature never changes. The mode of expression, perhaps, may vary with the times, but the ideas are always identical. Froude has been charged with bigoted prejudice against Mary. Even that does not invalidate his facts. Before those can be disregarded they must be disproved. All the advocates and champions who have come forward to exonerate Mary are no more than knight errants fighting windmills, unless they can demonstrate that he falsified the records. Examine his chapter xvi., vol. ix. The English Lords who considered these letters were convinced that Mary wrote them. Burton, (iv., xlvii., 278,) draws a conclusion, which is the only explanation of Mary's "giving in" and signing her abdication at Loch Leven. He says that it was her knowledge of the existence of these letters that cowed her, and not the brutal conduct of the Rebel Lords that induced her to set her seal to her own unthroning. Mary's friends admit that Burton is fair, and, yet, Burton is more severe in his measured language than Froude in his asperity, and the former's arguments that the Casket Letters are genuine are not only unanswerable, but convincing. There is no question but that Bothwell was the master spirit. Still Mary was the temptress. A careless study of her character finds traits which at first seem incompatible with the spirit of the letters; but a closer analysis proves that her true character is revealed in them. The want of refinement on which her friends found their denial is due to the time and not to her, and, being consistent with the time, do not invalidate the fact that a Queen wrote them. Another foundation on which her defenders build high is that she was a poet of ability. She was not; and it is very doubtful if the prettiest verses attributed to her were not written at a later date by a bright Frenchman, in the same way that the noted wit,

Rougemont, manufactured bon-mots for the Count d' Artois, and that Cambronne uttered a filthy word which Victor Hugo transmuted into a deathless, despairing outburst of heroism. Whether Mary did or did not write the few lines of her "Adieu to France," or other poetry attributed to her, had she not been a Queen, her versification would be deemed by an accomplished editor worthy of the waste basket. The "Casket Letters" are those of a passionate woman, loathing her husband and loving another man. They are as true to nature as a howl to a wolf or a roar to a lion. Whether or not Bothwell deserved such self-abandonment is something that cannot be brought into the question. Love is blind; Love is lunacy; and to discover why any woman loves any man *a l'outrance*, is a question as impossible to solve as to comprehend hieroglyphics without a key to them. Mary Stuart, of a "tough, healthy nature," which could accommodate itself to the brutality of her captivity at Loch Leven—" a lusty princess "—a full blooded woman, disgusted with an effeminate, debauched, " beardless Adonis," who caught her truant fancy, and yielded to the heroic roughness of the REAL MAN, Bothwell, in herself furnishes the clearest elucidation and the completest proof that the Casket Letters and Sonnets are genuine.*

"Amour! Amour quand tu nous tiens,
On peut bein dire : Adieu prudence!"

In this connection, the remark of the author of the "Heir of Redcliffe" is pertinent: "Hearts can find

---

* CASKET LETTERS.—Arnold Gædeke, Professor of History in the University of Heidelberg, in his "Maria Stuart," published in 1879, in his text proper, Appendixes I., II., III., has gone into a thorough analysis and examination of the Casket Letters, and his conclusions fully endorse the views expressed by the author.

more ways than you dream of" [to communicate their sentiments], "we had only to meet for the magnetism of mind to be felt." Exactly so! It was this magnetism of mind first drew Bothwell and Mary together, and it breathes or influences or manifests itself throughout the "Casket Letters and Sonnets." Mary appears in them as vividly present in spirit as if she spoke them in person.

People talk about the impassioned tone of the Casket Letters. Men and women felt and wrote four hundred years ago just as they feel and write to-day. Read Perkin Warbeck's love epistle to his ladye love, the " White Rose of Scotland," in 1492 [see author's "Bothwell, a Vindication," page 11] and Otway's love-letter to his mistress—composed under similar circumstances to those of Bothwell and Mary—two hundred years ago, of which the following is a transcript. Do Mary Stuart's Casket Letters breathe more fervent, absolute passion or affection, term it what you will?

To Madam: My Tyrant:—I endure too much Torment to be silent, and have endur'd it too long not to make the severest complaint. I love you, I dote on you; Desire makes me mad, when I am near you; and Despair, when I am from you. Sure, of all Miseries, Love is to me the most intolerable: It haunts me in my Sleep, perplexes me when waking; every melancholy Thought makes my Fears more powerful; and every delightful one makes my Wishes more unruly. In all other uneasy Chances of a man's Life, there is an immediate Recourse to some kind of Succour or another: In Wants we apply ourselves to our Friends; in Sickness to Physicians: But Love, the Sum, the Total of all Misfortunes, must be endur'd with Silence; no Friend so dear to trust with such a Secret, nor Remedy in Art so powerful as to remove its Anguish. Since the first day I saw you, I have hardly enjoyed one Hour of perfect Quiet. I lov'd you early; and no sooner had I beheld that soft bewitching Face of yours, but I felt in my Heart the very Foundation of all my Peace give way: But when you became another's, I must confess that I did then rebel, had foolish Pride enough to promise myself I would in Time recover my Liberty: In spight of my enslav'd Nature, I swore against myself, I would not love you: I affected a Resentment, stifled my Spirit, and would not let it bend so much as once to upbraid you, each Day it was my chance to see or to be near you: With stubborn Sufferance, I resolved to bear, and brave your Power: Nay, did it often too, successfully. Generally with Wine, or Conversation I diverted or appeas'd the Demon that possessed me; but when at Night, returning to my unhappy self, to give my Heart an Account why I had done it so unnatural a Violence, it was then I always paid a treble Interest for the short moments of Ease, which I had borrow'd; then every treacherous Thought rose up and took your part, nor left me 'till they had thrown me on my Bed, and open'd those Sluices of Tears, that were to run till Morning. This has been for some years my best Condition: Nay, Time itself, that decays all things else, has but increas'd and added to my Longings. I tell it you, and charge you to believe it, as you are generous (which sure you must be, for every thing, except your Neglect of me, persuades me that you are so) even at this time, tho' other Arms have held you, and so long trespass'd on those dear Joys that only were my Due. I love you with that Tenderness of Spirit, that Purity of Truth, and that Sincerity of Heart, that I could sacrifice the nearest Friends, or Interests I have on Earth, barely but to please you: If I had all the World, it should be yours; for with it I could be but miserable, if you were not mine. I appeal to yourself for Justice, if through the whole Actions of my Life, I have done any one thing that might not let you see how absolute your authority was over me. Your Commands have been always sacred to me; your Smiles have always transported me, and your Frowns aw'd me. In short, you will quickly become to me the greatest Blessing, or the greatest Curse, that ever Man was doomed to. I cannot so much as look on you without Confusion; Wishes and Fears rise up in War within me, and work a cursed Distraction thro' my Soul, that must, I am sure, in time have wretched Consequences: You only can, with that beadling Cordial, Love, assuage and calm my Torments; pity the Man then that would be proud to die for you and cannot live without you, and allow him thus far to boast too, that (take out Fortune from the Balance) you never were belov'd or courted by a Creature that had a nobler or juster Pretence to your Heart, than the Unfortunate (and even at this time) weeping OTWAY.

Blight.

> "I woke
> With his last word,
> And cried through tears and with uplifted hands:
> 'Come back, beloved; why to distant lands
> Row thy lone way? Oh! come and breathe again
> Thy perfumed words, spoke this time not in vain.
>   Come back!' but the wide vales
>   Return my yearning cry;
>   'Come back!' but far he sails;
>   He heeds not my sad cry.
> 'Oh! come again, great stranger; why depart?
> Come back to heal my pierced, anguished heart.'
>   I saw his airy skiff
>   Sail up beyond the sea,
>   Far o'er a cloudy cliff
>   That overhung the sea.
> And never may return the rapture of my dream?
> And never may I hear or know of him?
>   'Come, oh! come to me,—
>   Oh! hush, envenomed sea.'
>   'Farewell, [Marie], to thee.'
>   Would God I had awoke
>   Before my heart was broke."
>   —*All the Year Round*.

> "But now the hand of Fate is on the curtain,
> And gives the Scene to light."
>   DRYDEN.

NOTE.—If repetitions present themselves in these successive chapters they are not the result of inadvertence, but intention; endeavors to impress certain proofs and arguments the more forcibly, in order to make more appreciable the evidence in Bothwell's favor, and render more secure his acquittal or exoneration.

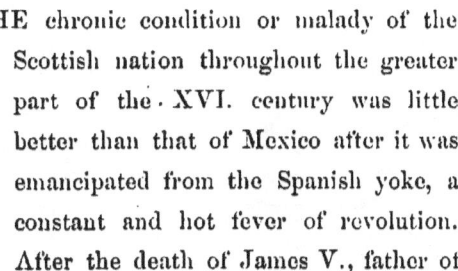HE chronic condition or malady of the Scottish nation throughout the greater part of the XVI. century was little better than that of Mexico after it was emancipated from the Spanish yoke, a constant and hot fever of revolution. After the death of James V., father of Mary, the Reformation, which had been kept down more particularly by Cardinal Beatoun, began to acquire a relative strength, such as it actually possessed in no other country. It grew stronger and stronger with every succeeding year, until it might have wrested the power from the Queen-Dowager, Mary of Guise, had it not been for the military intervention of the French. To the assistance of the Reform party Queen Elizabeth sent a fleet, under one of the ablest seamen and soundest commanders of the day, Admiral Winter, and an army under an excellent soldier and wise leader, Lord Grey. Between them the French were expelled. To this war, as regards the French fleet, as to previous and subsequent ones with the same nation and others, especially with Spain, would apply the motto of the medal struck to commemorate the overthrow of the Invincible Armada:*

---

* DIVINE ORDER.—" How often might a man, after he hath jumbled a set of letters in a bag, fling them out upon the ground before they would fall into an exact poem, yea, or so much as make a good discourse in prose? And may not a little book be as easily made by chance, as this great volume of the world? How long might a man be sprinkling colors upon a canvas with a careless hand before they could happen to make the exact picture of a man? And is a man easier made by chance than his picture? How long might twenty thousand

"*Afflavit Deus et dissipantur.*
(God the Almighty blew,
And the Armada went to every wind.)"

Well might the poet sing:

" Thank him who isled us [English] here, and roughly set
His Saxon in blown seas and storming showers."

Just preceding their expulsion of the French the Queen-Dowager died, displaying at her end a policy which, if it had been exhibited at an earlier date, might have made the royal cushion of her daughter much easier for its occupant. It was exactly the policy of Alexander Jannæus, King of Judea, in regard to the Pharisees, his life-long enemies and victims. His death-bed astuteness (B. C. 78) left his family in the possession of an authority which otherwise certainly would have been disputed.

The enforced withdrawal of the French from Scotland, under the impulsion of England, very much resembled that of the forces of Louis Napoleon, three hundred years afterwards, from Mexico. In 1560 the English said "Go!" and the French went. In 1865 the re-united United States notified the French " Either go, or—!" that is, more imperatively "Go!" and without the necessity of the application of force, they went. As in 1560 in Scotland, so in 1865 in Mexico, the departure of the French left the popular party in

---

blind men which should be sent out from the several remote parts of England, wander up and down before they would all meet upon Salisbury Plains, and fall into rank and file in the exact order of an army? And yet this is much more easy to be managed than how the innumerable blind parts of matter should rendezvous themselves into a world."
ARCHBISHOP JOHN TILLOTSON.

the ascendant. When Mary returned, in 1561, the "Lords of the Congregation" exercised the controlling power. Her acceptance of Murray, their leader, enabled her to tide over the first four years of her administration in a sort of sullen peace. Her sex and her graces, and her very impotence, had a great deal to do with the meanwhile acquiescence in her authority. As long as there was no king, and Murray controlled events, there was no actual outbreak. No doubt the courage, ability and fidelity of Bothwell acted as a balance-wheel, even in a so-shackly-piece of machinery. To use a very strong, but vulgar expression, Mary, undoubtedly, felt a "sneaking kindness" for the Earl from the first time that they were thrown together after the death of her husband, Francis II., at the time (1560) when he was sent out by her mother, Mary of Guise, to France on a political mission. Bothwell had experienced the same love at first sight for her, when they met before the betrothal in 1557–'8. This affection was growing stronger and stronger, and might have resulted in a union which would have consolidated the monarchy, when Darnley made his appearance, and with his airs and graces "captured" the Queen. Mary was a "lusty princess," to use the expression of Froude (VIII. 25), and her passionate nature took fire from the appetizing "long lad." Through the intermediation of Rizzio, who, by the elevation of Darnley, expected to fortify his own influence, and that of his church, Mary became in fact, although not in law,

Darnley's bed-fellow. Although this surrender of her person was not generally known, there were surmises of the true condition of affairs, and the mutterings of a storm were soon heard ominously. By the time that Mary was ready to marry Darnley, officially and publicly, she was not only tired of him, but evinced it.* (See 163, *Supra*, &c.)

The Reform party now rose in arms, but the enthusiasm of the nation for their charming Queen, engineered by Bothwell, who she herself selected as her military representative, her soldierly *Alter Ego*, conjured the menacing tempest, and those who had evoked it, after what was styled the "Run-about-raid,"—sometimes styled, also, the "Round-about-raid"—were forced to take refuge in England. Had they not possessed the support of Elizabeth, manipulated with dexterity by her astute Ministry—than whom abler political pilots never conned and steered a ship of state—Mary might now have enjoyed some years of

---

* "The sage and moderate statesman, Castelnau de Mauvissiere, was sent to Scotland to keep matters quiet, and a better messenger for such a purpose could not be found. Grave, conscientious, friendly and peaceful, he was beyond his age, and was peculiarly free of the impulsive, warlike and ostentatious propensities which have characterized his countrymen in all ages.

"It is significant that in the same memoir in which he describes the beginning of her headlong career (1565), *he mentions Bothwell as her right-hand man*, and likely to be made lieutenant-general of the kingdom—so ostensibly began this man's disastrous influence." (Burton, IV., 127-'8.)

tranquillity—that is, if she had a bold sagacious Bothwell by her side, instead of a cowardly imbecile, Darnley. Through the latters brutish stupidity and insane jealousy of Rizzio, who had engineered his elevation, a new conspiracy or "Bond" was formed against the Italian, which was aimed as well at Mary. It is pretty evident that if Mary, seven months gone with child, had perished at the same time with her Italian favorite, it would not have pained or disappointed the conspirators. If she *had* perished there and thus, Darnley would have been a feeble obstacle to the ulterior plans of the Murray party. Mary was a hardy creature and she survived the shock, to which ordinary women would have succumbed. Between her cajolery of Darnley, and the promptings of Bothwell, she again triumphed in the spring of 1566, as she had in the summer of the previous year. Darnley's betrayal of his associates, through the subtle influence of Mary, made the conspirators, who had thus become the victims of his treason to them—though not by any means through his loyalty to his wife—his implacable enemies. Mary, who had long given her implicit confidence, as well as her affection, to Bothwell, now threw herself completely into his stalwart arms (see 49, *supra*). This was a result, of which to avert the possibility, for political reasons, Mary had brought about the marriage between the Earl and Jane Gordon, sister of the Earl of Huntley, and daughter of the great

Earl Huntley, whom she had wickedly sacrificed, in 1563, to the fox-wolf-cunning-and-voracity of Murray.

It would have been far better for Mary Stuart if her surrender of herself to the REAL MAN, Bothwell, had occurred before she threw herself at the head of the imitation of manhood, the immature Darnley. In the former case her passions would have been gratified without breach of law, and the law would have given her a support in the columnar Bothwell, which she could not have found in any other mate. The fierce blaze of the mutual craving of Mary and Bothwell, fanned by her increasing aversion to her husband, which seems to have gradually inspired her with a disgust at times amounting to loathing, re-awakened in Bothwell all his original passion and wildest hopes. These hopes developed into the only real crime which is chargeable to him throughout life, the getting rid of Darnley, in order that he might occupy his every place. When Bothwell had been nearly killed in the performance of his duty as Warden of the Borders or Marches, and Mary flew as a dispairing sweetheart to the bedside of a severely wounded lover, the curtain rose on the first scene of a tragedy which closed with the ruin of both. From this time forward momentous events succeeded each other with a rapidity almost unparalleled. To get rid of Darnley, and insure himself the sole possession of Mary, and to become king-consort, and through this ownership and elevation to acquire influence and authority to restore peace and prosperity to his country—certainly a most laudable motive—Bothwell joined hand for the nonce with the Murray faction, and Mary herself became a co-conspirator with her most dangerous enemies to free herself for good and all of the hated and hateful creature who stood between her and her love. The relations between herself and Bothwell are clearly set forth in the papers found in the "Silver Casket," already considered at length. (See pages *supra*.)

Mary's deportment towards Darnley rendered him contemptible, and his own attitude made him detestable and dispicable in the eyes of all. How he strayed off to Glasgow and fell sick, according to some surmises from an insufficient dose of poison—such as, in 1582, sufficed for the removal of the third Regent, the "good (?) Earl of Mar;"—or was stricken down by a foul disease—said to have been brought back from America by the Spaniards; or Italy, by the French, 1492-'7—or by the small-pox: whatever was the cause, he was dangerously ill. There is little doubt that Darnley had a reasonable presentiment that, if he remained in Scotland, he was sure of but a very short lease of life. He had threatened to fly the country and take refuge in France. Such a step would have traversed the hopes of Mary, the desire of Bothwell, and the plans of the conspirators. Mary's objective was a union with Bothwell; Bothwell's the possession of Mary, and, with her, kingly power, and, with both, the restoration of Scottish affairs, and their establishment upon a sound basis. Mary's views were simply those of a woman in love; those of Bothwell of a man in love, but also of a statesman, a general, a governor, and a patriot. The other conspirators looked farther ahead than either to their own aggrandisement at the expense of both. Could they manage it so that Bothwell, with Mary as his decoy and accomplice, should, with their help, succeed in murdering Darnley; then these confederated rebel lords, acting with the support of public opinion and the clergy, calculated to bring about a cataclysm which would sweep away both Mary and Bothwell, if the Queen took advantage of the death of Darnley to marry the generally accepted murderer. In this manner only could the great Earl be hurled from his pride of place.

This was the project of the rebels, and it was based on their idea that, in getting rid of him, they demolished the greatest obstacle to their immediate and eventual success, seeing that he was the ablest and most powerful personality in Scotland. Feeling certain that Mary must be involved in his ruin, Murray and his peers, or rather assistants and "seids," could thereupon seize the reins of government, exercise an authority akin to royal and divide the spoils. They realized the words of the Psalmist, "Surely the wrath of man shall praise thee." They succeeded, but Nemesis avenged all. "While their meat was yet in their mouths, the wrath of God came upon them and slew the fattest of them, and smote down the chosen men of Israel." [Scotland]. Mary got her man; Bothwell grasped for one month the Royal power; Murray, Lenox, Mar, Morton, in succession, became Regents and perished; meaner agents mounted higher steps of the ladder of preferment and gain; and yet, by poetical as well as prosaic justice to each, became applicable the words of St. Luke in regard to the exulting Herod, "The Lord smote him, * * * and he gave up the ghost."

It is curious how differently the judgment apparently opposite or applicable to different individuals will be warped to condemn the one, to absolve another, to mitigate the penalty of a third, or, with a recommendation to mercy, excuse a fourth. If ever a human being lived who deliberately toled a confiding fellow-creature within reach of the deadly blow of a paramour—for after making every excuse and pleading every justification for him, Bothwell was a paramour in the present meaning of the word—Mary Stuart was the guilty one. He was her paramour in the remote sense of the word, which did not imply originally all that it does now, and he was the same in a bad sense.* Time, place, and circumstance,

---

* The following conversation from Dr. John Moore's "Zeluco" (1789), shows the same contradictory judgments upon Mary, one hundred years ago, as had already ruled, *pro* and *con*, for two hundred years and still rule throughout the world:

"'In what did he [Buchanan, the Historian] ever shew any want of honesty?' said Buchanan. 'In calumniating and endeavoring to blacken the reputation of his rightful sovereign, Mary, Queen of Scots,'

noble thoughts, great plans, patriotic objects, besides undoubted affection, were his justification. He was a man of one absorbing idea. It was gratified. He ought to have been satisfied. His honeymoon was a realization of the magnificent story, "One of the Nights of Cleopatra," that wild conception of Theophile Gautier. Bothwell was the hero of Scottish history, Meiamoun of Egyptian romance. The latter a noble, fearless, Egyptian gentleman—became reckless in his infatuated love for Cleopatra. Fortune vouchsafed the successful revelation of his passion; and the Queen rewarded his audacity with a night's possession of herself, with the proviso that, with the ensuing dawn, her audacious admirer should drink a deadly poison. Meiamoun willingly consents. He enjoyed and he perished. Bothwell was more favored. Instead

replied Targe, 'the most beautiful and accomplished princess that ever sat on a throne.' * * * * * *

"'I fear you are too nearly related to the false slanderer whose name you bear!' said Targe. 'I glory in the name; and should think myself greatly obliged to any man who could prove my relation to the great George Buchanan!' cried the other. 'He is nothing but a disloyal calumniator,' cried Targe, 'who attempted to support falsehoods by forgeries, which I thank heaven, are now fully detected!' 'You are thankful for a very small mercy!' resumed Buchanan, 'but since you provoke me to it, I will tell you in plain English that your bonnie Queen Mary was the strumpet of Bothwell, and the murderer of her husband!'"

Moore, in his "Fables," remarks of Mary very much as Shakespeare of Cressida:

"Her very shoe has power to wound."

of a night, Fate generously conceded a month. He likewise enjoyed, and to him the result was worse than the fatal draught provided by the daughter of Ptolemy.

Mary lured Darnley into the death-trap. Goodhall declared, one hundred years ago, that Bothwell did not murder Darnley, but that the same men-devils, who deliberately slew Rizzio, avenged the Italian by slaying the arch-plotter and tool, Darnley; he, who was as criminal in his Judas' kiss, which signalled the death of the arrogant musician-minister-of-state on the night of the 9th–10th March, 1566, as Mary was guilty with a like Judas' kiss on the night of 9th—10th February, 1567. It might be said her kiss served as the signal, as it were, for her revenge and her emancipation. The fiction generally accepted as absolute truth by the whole reading public, with the exception of a few critics, sets forth that Darnley perished by the explosion of a comparatively small amount of powder, *emptied* loosely into the room sometimes occupied by the Queen, and underneath the one in which Darnley slept. Undoubtedly Bothwell intended the accomplishment of the death of Darnley by blowing up the house, but erred in his calculations, because at that day, and especially so in Scotland, the explosive properties of gunpowder seem to have been very little understood. Loose powder, even in a very large quantity, would not have blown a stone building so solidly built as houses were then constructed— especially such an one as the Kirk of Field is described to have been—all to pieces. It would have simply wrecked the interior, lifted off the roof, blown out doors and windows, and shattered everything except the floors and arches. *In such a case, had Darnley's death resulted from the powder deposited loosely by Bothwell's agents, his corpse must have been blackened, charred and mutilated. This was not the case, but exactly the contrary. His body was found, without a sign of violence, two hundred and forty feet from the building, which was blown all to pieces.* How is this to be accounted for? *Thus!* Before Bothwell's servants had brought thither, into the "Kirk-o-Field," a single grain of powder, mines had been laid under the house, their chambers heavily charged; and everything thoroughly looked to. Bothwell's co-conspirators determined that there should be no failure, while they arranged matters so cleverly that the whole odium of the crime would fall upon the Earl, who was to profit immediately by it, they themselves indirectly. In any event, Darnley was to die. They would see to that. How then was it that the victim's body was found not singed, nor blurred, nor mutilated, so far from the house. Darnley, with a presentiment of evil, did not go to bed that night as promptly as usual, but sat up reading the Bible with his body-page, Taylor, who was found, near him, dead also. *Alarmed* at strange or unusual noises, which fell with startling and ominous force upon his sensitive hearing, attentive and suspicious, *he fled* from the house with Taylor, *before the explosion.* His hopes of escape, however, were all in vain, since the house was entirely surrounded by the conspirators. This has been demonstrated at length in the author's "Vindication" of the Earl, published, at length, in the *United Service*, for September and October, 1882. Darnley and his page were caught by Sir Archibald Douglas, his kinsman, and others, assisting, and, after a violent struggle, strangled. The victim plead for mercy in piteous language, which was overheard and recorded, and struggled for his life with all the strength of a young and desperate man. The clothes of Douglas were all grimy with mire in consequence. Why, then, should Bothwell dream that his preparations had slain Darnley? He could not have seen what occurred, because high walls rose between him and the crime. He did not. He was completely justified in always protesting his innocence. Why has so much abuse been poured out on Bothwell for his "supposed" murder of Darnley and so many excuses found for the public assassination of Cardinal Beatoun, by the Calvinists, 28th May, 1546, the sainted (*sic*) Kirkaldy participating and all the Reformers approving, and of Archbishop Sharpe by the Covenanters, 1st May, 1679. "The law and the testimony" must apply equally in all three cases. He intended that Darnley should be killed, and Mary approved of it, but neither were aware that their co-conspirators had previously mined the house scientifically, and had surrounded the premises with a cordon of vigilant and determined would-be murderers. These did the deed. Why? Because these men-devils were resolved that not only one but three were to be sacrificed. Darnley on the spot, and afterwards Bothwell, and then Mary, through the effects of the murder done by them upon the first named. After Darnley was dead and Bothwell and Mary driven into exile, or thrown into prison, or cast into the grave, then would come the seizure of the government and the division of the spoils. Darnley was the dupe in all and of all; Mary was the lure; Bothwell was the instrument and the dupe of Murray and his faction; and all three were victims in turn, and those who victimized perished, one by one, each in his turn, all without warning and without mercy.

"Life's a bondage to the 'tickers' stern, immutable decrees."*

Darnley was dead. Between Bothwell and Mary the only barrier remaining was extremely slight, and very easily removed. As heretofore shown, Bothwell in the previous year had induced Mary to revive the ancient jurisdiction of the Roman Catholic Consistorial Courts, which had been charged with trying the pleas of consanguinity acknowledged by that creed as valid reasons for divorce. This Roman Catholic Court was re-created or revived 23d December, 1556. As Bothwell was married to Jane (Irving,

---

* "My personal despair extended itself to all creation, and the *law of fatality arose before me in such appalling aspect that my reason was shaken by it.*" GEORGE SAND.

in his "Eminent Scotsmen," 227, styles her Elizabeth) Gordon, on the 24th February, 1566, any one not wilfully blind must acknowledge that, even at the time of the nuptials, or very soon after, Bothwell was looking forward to find means to bring about a union with Mary. He seemed to be convinced that in espousing Jane Gordon he was tying a knot which would be readily unloosed through her complaisant disposition "for a consideration." Castelnau, the French Ambassador, perceiving already, in September, 1565, that Mary had resolved upon following the dictates of her own passion, while he describes the beginning of her headlong career, he mentions "Bothwell as her right hand man, and likely to be made Lieutenant-General of the kingdom—so, ostensibly, began this man's disastrous influence." (Burton, IV., 128-9.) In the author's two former works on Mary and Bothwell, sufficient attention has been paid to the details of occurrences between the death of Darnley, 9th February, 1567, and Mary's third marriage with Bothwell on 15th May following. The latter was acquitted on his trial before the Privy Council and a Jury of his Peers, 12th April, 1567, and their verdict was ratified by the Scottish Parliament on the 14th of the same month. On the 19th, Bothwell gave a grand supper at the famous Annesley (Ainslie, Anslee) Tavern to the highest nobility and the first men of the country. Before the guests separated, the famous Bond was subscribed—Murray's signature assuredly heading the list (Buckingham I., 172–4), although, with his usual duplicity, he was not present at the entertainment—declaring Bothwell's innocence and urging his marriage with the Queen. On the 21st April, with her own connivance and approbation, Mary was met and escorted by Bothwell to Dunbar. There altogether willingly or unwillingly, as her foes or her friends allege, the same intimate relations at once existed, or were entered into, between Mary and Bothwell as, two years previously, between Mary and Darnley, after she had "handfasted" herself to the latter nearly four months before the public celebration of their union. Two strong points in favor of Bothwell's action, as consistent with Mary's wishes and careful collusion, are always ignored by her friends in treating of what they elect to style her "ravishing"—which was simply conducting her with the honor of a great lord and the humility of a grand lover to one of the chief military strongholds and royal residences of the kingdom. First, Agnes Strickland, and all her associates, in whitewashing Mary, dwell on the fact that the Queen was slightly attended when Bothwell met her at the appointed place, as agreed upon between them, and consequently could not resist him, and that there was no escort of 300 horsemen, as alluded to in the Casket Letter, styled "Supposititious." These champions ignore *she did have an escort of* 300 *the previous day*, but managed to dismiss, or get rid, of them, that there might not be the slightest obstacle to traverse Bothwell's nominal seizure, or to justify her in making even a seeming opposition. Mary has been defended with all the subtlety of criminal lawyers' exhausting casuistry to save a criminal, whereas Bothwell has scarcely found an advocate who would dare to enter a plea in his favor. Second, Schiern (242-6), who is no enemy of Mary, here steps in most opportunely with an argument which, supported as it is by documentary and circumstantial evidence, seems to be unanswerable.

"This impression was, however, soon forced to give way before the opinion which subsequently prevailed in Scotland, according to which no doubt could be entertained, even from the beginning, that what Bothwell had undertaken was done in consequence of an agreement with Mary. His conduct was more precisely accounted for at the time in three ways. It was, in Scotland, an old practice that papers were drawn up, by which any one obtained pardon for crimes, this was done so that only the chief crime was expressly mentioned, while merely a clause was added, describing in general terms what offences the person concerned had besides committed. Buchanan accordingly holds that as the murderers of the King, and especially Bothwell, were afraid that there might come a time when it would be seriously resolved to punish them for the deed, they had found out that by the help of such a clause they would be able to get the crime pardoned, the express mention of which in a document might appear as dangerous to the perpetrators as it would be unseemly for the pardoner. The murder of the Queen's husband could not be mentioned, but another crime of high treason, which was less odious, must be found out, under screen of which the murder of the King, as by a piece of sophistry, could be concealed and forgiven. An attack upon the Queen's exalted person was such an aggravated crime, and therefore nothing more fitting for the purpose could be contrived than that *feigned abduction*. Others explained the strange transaction by alleging that its design was to stop the mouths of those who had long thought that the Queen stood in a too intimate relation to the Earl. More natural than both far-fetched explanations is that which, while still seeing in the abduction merely a preconcerted piece of acting, interpreted it as a direct result of an immoderate love for Bothwell, which made her impatiently long to be able to call him her own. As they who favor this mode of explaining the hurried marriage proceed upon the supposition that *the passion had long before led Mary to give herself up to the Earl*, so one of her later defenders believes that he is able to expose the foolishness of any such explanation by asking the question: "Where was the necessity for a precipitate marriage at all? Was Mary so eager to become Bothwell's wife, with whom she indeed had long been indulging in an illicit intercourse, that she could not wait the time demanded by common decency to wear her widow's garb for Darnley? Was she really so entirely lost to every sense of female delicacy and public shame—so utterly dead to her own interests and reputation—or so very scrupulous about a little longer continuing her unlicensed amours, that, rather than suffer the delay of a few months, she would thus run the risk of involving herself in eternal infamy?" These questions are not without force for those against whom they are directed; *but, if the relation be apprehended somewhat differently, it would be possible to meet them. There is with regard to the abduction, and the subsequent sudden marriage, a circumstance which is not ordinarily taken into consideration in this connection*, but to which we might refer as an answer. *Immediately after Mary's third marriage her opponents declared that she had again become pregnant,* and, when the Queen was confined a prisoner at Lochleven, Sir Nicholas Throckmorton, who had been sent by Elizabeth to Scotland to negotiate her release, wrote in a letter from Edinburgh, of 18th July, 1567, to his mistress: 'I have also persuaded her to conform herself to renounce Bothwell for her husband, and to be content to suffer a divorce to pass betwixt them; she hath sent me word that she will in no ways consent unto that, but rather die, grounding herself upon this reason, taking herself to be seven weeks gone with child; by renouncing Bothwell, she should acknowledge herself to be with child of a bastard, and to have forfeited her honor, which she will not do to die for it.' *Might not Mary,* under the supposition of which she makes mention, have at this time or earlier believed her pregnancy to be of older date? And, if the Queen had such fear after Darnley's death, might not Bothwell then have found the final encouragement to venture on abduction, and the Queen afterwards an incentive for not at this time rejecting his hand? Even if the abduction to Dunbar had not taken place with the Queen's will, yet the opposition which she there exhibited to Bothwell was, at all events, so small in comparison with her former brave behavior during the catastrophe which put an end to Rizzio's life, that this weakness becomes the weightiest—and properly the only incontrovertible—reason for assuming *an earlier and more intimate understanding between her and the Earl* than she has plainly admitted. When some one mentioned to David Hume that a new treatise had been published, the author of which was believed to have successfully vindicated Mary, the historian only asked: 'Has he also proved that the Queen did not marry Bothwell?' and, when no affirmative answer could be given, he signified that the attempt had failed." (Schiern's "Bothwell," 242-'6.)

To confirm Professor Schiern's view, turn to Raumer ("Queen Elizabeth and Queen Mary," Letter xxviii., 1569. Edition of 1836, p. 161). "*Mary never spoke decidedly respecting* the murder of Darnley and *her connection with Bothwell, or produced any fact in support of her innocence.* When Sir Francis Knollys at length plainly put the question to her, she answered, as usual, in some general expressions, and began to weep; on this he broke off the subject." For whatever reasons, she changed her views, if she did do so, Lady Lennox, Darnley's mother, in 1570, believed Mary "indisputably guilty," and Mary's ambassador, the Bishop of Ross, when the terrors of death were upon him, "and while making a clean breast of it, he admitted to Dr. Wilson her [Mary's] share of the murder of Darnley." This admission is pass-key to all the rest.

On the 27th April, the Roman Catholic Consistorial Tribunal was authorized to entertain an action of divorce by Bothwell against his wife. The proceedings began 5th May, and judgment was given in his favor on the 7th. Whoever presumes to question Mary's complicity in the whole matter is simply ignorant that, to accomplish this "Mary had to come personally forward and issue a special authority to that end" (Burton, IV., 221). In the meanwhile Bothwell's wife sued for a divorce against her husband, before the Protestant Civil Court, on the ground of adultery, which was almost simultaneously granted on the 3d May. On the 5th April—mark this!—Sir James Macintosh says that the suit of the Countess of Bothwell against her husband "commenced almost *on the day which the Queen specified as that on which she alleged she had been violated by Bothwell.*" (Buckingham I., 197.) Mary and Bothwell were married according to both the Protestant and Roman Catholic rites. Bothwell's biographer, Schiern, who examined all the evidence on this disputed point, says the *double* marriage presents perfectly clear proof (p. 258 and note 1) that it was so celebrated according to the Reformed and Romanist manners. Buckingham (I., 200–'2) is equally explicit, and endeavors to explain it on the plea of compulsion. Other historians concur. How any doubt could have arisen or a mistake have occurred can be easily explained. Bothwell had always refused to allow the Roman Catholic clergy to interfere in his affairs, and, therefore, his Protestant rites were public, although, perhaps, to satisfy the prejudices of his bride, he consented to permit a more private marriage according to the Roman Catholic form. Can anything be more sly than Romanism? and Buckingham clears it up by stating "they were married according to the forms of BOTH churches, by Adam Bothwell, Bishop of Orkney, and a Catholic priest whose name has not been recorded."

Bothwell's attitude, as soon as he became lord of the land, was noble. His announcement of the accomplished fact to Charles IX. of France was dignified and worthy of his new position. What he wrote to Elizabeth of England was almost haughty and defiant. His letter to her like

"His tread rings iron, as to battleward."

The Murray faction had now attained their object. According *to their representations*, Bothwell had long been Mary's paramour: he and he alone had murdered her husband Darnley; Mary was his accomplice; immediately after the murder she had hastened to bring about a divorce—before a court constituted or revived by her Royal authority, and especially called upon by herself to act in this case—between Bothwell and his wife; and she, **an adulteress and the accomplice of the murderer, had profited by his deed to marry within ten days after the divorce, an adulterer, an assassin, and a regicide.** What is more, these noble conspirators accused her and her husband of not only being desirous of getting possession of her son by Darnley, the royal infant afterwards James VI., but even of attempting to poison him. This crime, of "burking" little James VI., was the very one Doctor Story confessed to in 1570. "It was nothing else than making way with the little King of Scots, in the belief that with his life would be removed the principal obstacle to his mother's [Mary's] marriage with some Catholic prince." (Froude, X., 94.) All of Bothwell and Mary's accusers were themselves the originators, abettors, executives of the crimes they charged upon the Queen and her consort, who only acted in accordance with their desires, their suggestions and in furtherance of their ends. Such treachery, hypocrisy, betraying and sacrificing is scarcely recorded elsewhere in history. Grant that Mary and Bothwell were guilty, what were their accusers? Bothwell's crime, if he was as culpable as charged against him, was the single one that can be brought against himself throughout, for his era, an unusually loyal and honorable career. Murray, Knox's sainted Murray, had been the contriver and instigator of crime after crime for the past seven years. He had kept his fingers out of the fire, but he had looked through his fingers at the execution of every guilty deed which he had instigated. As an example of an honest man and a faithful subject, as a brother and a minister of state, he was a consummate fraud. His co-adjutors, co-conspirators, accomplices, instruments, associates, were, according to poor Hamlet's expression, "as foul as Vulcan's stithy." In comparison to Murray's particular friend, Morton,* the concrete of corruption, Bothwell was a miracle of virtue, and, indeed, among the black flock of ravens which joined in hoarse congratulation over the corpse of Rizzio and rejoiced over the stark body of Darnley, Bothwell, amid such a repulsive brood, was exactly what Petrick styled him, that "*rara avis*, a

---

* The best evidence of the popular opinion in England as to the especial guilt of Morton is to be found in the many plays of the actual and succeeding periods, in which Mary Stuart is introduced. Several instances have already been adduced: the following is even more pertinent. It is from J. Bank's "*Albion Queens.*"

NORFOLK (*speaks*). "Now, only now's the time; *the traitor Morton*,
    The false, usurping Regent, is returned,
    With all the magazine of hell about him.
    The Queen, my lovely Albion Queen's in danger;
    And if thou wilt not straight advise thy friend,
    Mary's undone, and Norfolk is no more."

WHITE CROW." Mary had scarcely been united to the consort selected and urged upon her by her chief nobility—a consort whom they had solemnly pledged themselves to sustain against all enemies—than the very magnates who signed the Ainslie "Bond" in favor of the man of her choice and of her marriage with him, entered into a new "Bond" to destroy both. The falsity of their excuses for this was as vile in itself as consistent with their hypocrisy and villainy. Among other charges they alleged that they bonded to protect their infant king, and only rose against him because Bothwell had demanded the custody of the baby prince, whereas the whole of their action was inimical to him before Bothwell had even intimated anything which could be construed into a desire that the royal child should be delivered to his care.

Hitherto, as a rule, with a few honorable exceptions, writers who have treated of the principal events in the life of Bothwell constitute a chorus of different voices or tones, which in its union of effect is damnatory. This is the more surprising as every one of the singers has to depend on the same score or authorities in producing his music. And, yet, although the general result is adverse, the testimony emanating from the majority of composers unfavorable or partially favorable to him is anything but depreciative. In no event of his life is he made to appear so badly as at Carberry Hill; and, yet, even then, the French Ambassador, Du Croc, who disliked Bothwell, is compelled to admit, in his record of this Sunday spectacle, that Bothwell had not only profited by his military studies and experience, but by his early training in the "humanities."

"*I cannot but say that I saw a* GREAT CAPTAIN *present himself with the utmost confidence, and one who led his troops with bravery and prudence.*" How certain Bothwell still was of the issue of the day at the departure of Du Croc, he also showed, when, on seeing his foes cross the stream, he advised this mediator "to imitate him who wished to establish peace and friendship between the armies of Scipio and Hannibal when these two armies were about to come to blows, just as the two before them were going to do, but who, when he could do nothing and was unwilling to take part with either side, chose for himself a place as a spectator, and thus became witness of the grandest sight which he had ever seen; if Du Croc would now do the same he would never live to witness a greater entertainment, for he should see them fight bravely."

Despite this acknowledged capacity for leadership of Bothwell, it would have been impossible for a Frederic the Great to fight against a superior force, even as to numbers, of comparatively trained soldiers, variously estimated at from two to four thousand—under commanders of considerable experience—with a kernel of two hundred Arquebusiers constituting the Queen's body-guard, and another small troop of his own personal followers, backed by a rabble not more numerous than the array of old soldiers opposed to them.

The majority of historians, poets and romancers combine to accuse Bothwell of want of courage in abandoning Mary at Carberry Hill. Aytoun, who, in his poem, "Bothwell," is cruel enough to write (Part vi., xl.,)

> "Was it a dream ? Or did I hear
> A yell of scorn assail my ear,
> As frantic from the host I rode?
> The very charger I bestrode
> Rebelled in wrath against the rein,
> And strove to bear me back again !
> Lost, lost ! I cared not where I went—
> Lost, lost ! and none were there,
> Save those who sought in banishment
> A refuge from despair."—

in his note to this stanza, the same author is compelled to admit, contradicting himself (258), " I must do Bothwell the justice to say :   *   *   *   "*His challenges were not mere bravado, but he was almost insanely anxious to meet Morton in single combat. Bothwell was a man of great physical courage, which is more than can be said of the adversary* [Morton, the Ahitophel of the period] *whom he selected.*" *

* "I have endeavored, as nearly as poetical requirements would allow, to follow history accurately. I interpret the events thus. Bothwell, by carrying Mary off to Dunbar, at once consummated his own ruin. His fellow-conspirators might easily have rescued her from his hands ; but *their object was to have her married to him*, so they delayed. After the marriage had taken place, they lost no time, but strengthened themselves by calling in the aid of such of the Border barons as regarded with jealousy the increasing power of the House of Hepburn. They could also depend upon the assistance of the craftsmen of Edinburgh, a body trained to the use of arms, and not degenerate from

The real facts of the case are these. Bothwell and Mary advanced to Carberry Hill with a force of about 2500 their fathers, who had fought valiantly at Flodden. Bothwell, on the other hand, had none beyond his own troopers in whom he could place perfect reliance. The royal summons had brought to Dunbar many of the East-Lothian barons, headed by Lords Seton, Yester and Borthwick; but they were not partisans of Bothwell, and came simply on account of the Queen. Bothwell was perfectly aware of this, and of the Queen's desire to escape, if possible, from his hands; and that knowledge accounts for his behavior. I shall quote one more from Melville:

"'Both armies lay not far from Carberry: the Earl of Bothwell's men camped upon the hill, in a strength very advantageous; the Lords encamped at the foot of the hill. And albeit her Majesty there, I cannot call it her army, for many of those who were with her were of opinion that she had intelligence with the Lords, especially such as were informed of the many indignities put upon her by the Earl of Bothwell since their marriage. * * * Thus part of his own company detested him; other part of them believed that her Majesty would fain have been quit of him but through shame to be the doer of the deed directly herself.' * * * "*I must do Bothwell the justice to say that, from all the accounts extant, his challenges were not mere bravado, but that he was almost insanely anxious to meet Morton in single combat. Bothwell was a man of great physical courage* [" gifted with superhuman daring"—Lamartine], *which is more than can be said for the adversary whom he selected*, who was very glad to accept of Lord Lindsay of the Byres as his substitute; but a duel under such circumstances would have been ridiculous. Mary wanted to be rid of Bothwell, and signified as much to the Lords who came in obedience to her summons; but, with that noble spirit which was always her characteristic, she refused to make any terms with the confederated nobles until Bothwell's retreat was secured. Then, and not till then, she took an everlasting farewell [utterly false and unsusceptible of proof] of the man who, instigated by others, *worse traitors than himself*, had achieved her ruin. Her [fiendishly treacherous] reception in the camp of the confederates does not fall within the scope of the poem." Aytoun's "*Bothwell*."

militia and some 200 regular musketeers. The traitor lords confronted him with a superior number of comparatively trustworthy troops. Le Croc, the French Ambassador, a competent judge, admits that Bothwell with his motley array displayed admirable generalship. Le Croc had so little friendly feeling for Bothwell that he refused to be present at his marriage to the Queen. Consequently any commendation from him is the highest praise, and can be relied upon. Had Bothwell attacked at once, now that the little armies were looking each other in the face, it is most likely that he would have been victorious. Unfortunately Mary insisted upon negotiations; hours were wasted; her "following" without food as without discipline, became tired with waiting, degenerated into an armed mob, took possession of some wagons loaded with wine, drank freely upon empty stomachs, got drunk, and were soon beyond control. The last envoy of the confederate lords, Kirkaldy of Grange, deluded Mary with his specious reputation for chivalry, and she determined to trust him, to her ruin. Bothwell, with his common sense, saw through the trickery and ordered a musketeer to shoot him. If ever a wise end could justify violent means, Bothwell was right. He wanted to kill Melville under similar circumstances, and he was wise also in that case, as it turned out. Mary interposed, saved Kirkaldy, blasted her own life and character, as well as that of Bothwell, and ruined both. It is sometimes best to violate the laws of propriety when those in the right are dealing with others altogether in the wrong.

Rapin is very clear on these points. Mary always ruined her own cause by obstinacy and precipitation. Bothwell's error in taking the field at this time, arose from courage and consciousness of right. The meeting and parting at Carberry Hill has never as yet, *as a whole,* been clearly stated or fairly told.

Bothwell's worst enemies admit that he was very anxious to meet Morton at Carberry Hill. The miscreant would not fight. Lindsay offered to take his place, but the Queen forbade the combat. Bothwell certainly had a right to choose his opponent, and the husband of a Queen was justified in selecting as his antagonist the chief among his foes, particularly when that chief was the arch-traitor both to himself and to his wife, one in whose blood he had threatened to wash his hands if he had the opportunity.

If Bothwell had not perfectly understood Kirkaldy, it might have been a dishonorable act to shoot a parliamentary acting under a flag of truce. But, will any military man deny that, if an envoy is using his immunity from peril or prison to deceive, a general who grasps the situation, who knows that the success of the operation will depend on the triumph of the deception, and that it is likely to succeed through the ignorance and weakness of a coadjutor—can, in such a case, any military man deny the right of a commander to dispose, summarily, of an individual seeking to betray under a flag of truce, and thus, by shooting the intriguer, frustrate the intended treachery? "Fraud vitiates every contract," says the law. Bothwell knew Kirkaldy of old, saw through and through the man, felt he was no better than a traitor, and the event proved that Bothwell's judgment was correct. O wonderful "Book of books" and exponent of common sense, the Bible! what marvelous revelations it discovers of the workings of the human heart. Hebrews (XII., 17) says of Esau, "He found no place for repentance, though he sought it carefully with tears." Kirkaldy afterwards, carried away by the demoniac fascination of Mary's charms,* repented of his conduct towards the Queen, and became her champion, and Morton, become Regent, of whom he was the tool in this Sabbath-betrayal on Carberry Hill, got hold of him after he surrendered to the English, and, soldier as he undoubtedly was, denied him a soldier's death, and hung him like a felon.

---

* "Oh, the horrid little monster that I am. Why can't I help it? *I verily believe I shall flirt in my shroud, and, if I were canonized, my first miracle would be, like St. Philomena's, to make my own relics presentable.*—" Hopes and Fears," by the author of the "Heir of Redclyffe."

AUTHORITIES IN THE AUTHOR'S POSSESSION.

Anecdotes of Distinguished Persons. Vol. I. London, 1798.
Aytoun, W. E. Bothwell. Edinburgh, 1856.
Balmanno, Mrs. Pen and Pencil. New York, 1858.
Bekker, Dr. Ernst. Maria Stuart—Darley—Bothwell. Giessen, 1881.
Benger, Miss. Mary, Queen of Scots. 2 vols. London, 1823.

Boulding, J. Grimsett. Mary, Queen of Scots. A Tragedy. London, n. d.
Brown, James H. Scenes in Scotland. Glasgow, 1833.
Buchanan, George. Detection of Mary, Queen of Scots. London, 1721.
Buchanan's History of Scotland. 2 vols. London, 1733.
Buckingham, L. S. F. Mary Stuart. 2 vols. London, 1844.
Burton, John H. History of Scotland. 8 vols. Edinburgh, 1873.
Burton, John, H. The Scot Abroad. New Ed. Edinburgh, 1881.
Campbell, Hugh. Case of Queens Mary and Elizabeth. London, 1825.
Chalmers, George. Mary, Queen of Scots. 2 vols. Philadelphia, 1822.
Cunningham, A. Mary, Queen of Scots. London, 1838.
Cyclopædia of Biblical Literature. Vol. V. New York, 1875.
Dargaud, J. M. Marie Stuart. 2 vols. Paris, 1850.
Ebner-Eschenbach. Marie, Freifrau. Aphorisms. Trans. by Mrs. Wister.
Eminent Scotsmen. (Society of Ancient Scots.) London, 1821.
Froude, James A. History of England. 12 vols. New York, 1875.
Gaedeke, Arnold. Maria Stuart. Heidelberg, 1879.
Gauthier, Jules. Marie Stuart. 3 vols. Paris, 1869.
Grant, James. Bothwell. London, n. d.
Grant, James. Mary of Lorraine. London, n. d.
Harpers' Monthly. Mary, Queen of Scots. February, 1873.
Hosack, John. Mary, Queen of Scots, and her Accusers. 2d. ed. 2 vols. Edinburgh, 1870.
Irving, Joseph. Eminent Scotsmen. Paisley, 1881.
King and the Commons; Cavalier and Puritan Songs. Edited by Morley. New York, 1869.
Labanoff, Prince Alex. Lettres de Marie Stuart. 7 vols. Londres, 1844.
La Collection des Portraits de Marie Stuart. St. Petersbourg, 1856.
Lamartine, Alphonse de. Mary Stuart. Boston, 1881.
Leader, J. D. Mary, Queen of Scots, in Captivity. Sheffield, 1880.
Letters of Mary, Queen of Scots. Agnes Strickland. 3 vols. London, 1843.
Life of the Regent Moray. Edinburgh, 1828.
Lingard, John. History of England. Vol. V. Paris, 1840.
MacLeod, Donald. Mary, Queen of Scots. New York, 1857.
Marie, Queen of Scots. From the Latin. n. d.
Meline, James F. Mary, Queen of Scots. New York, 1872.
Melville, J. G. Whyte. Queen's Maries. London, n. d.
Mignet, M. Marie Stuart. 2 vols. Paris, 1854.
Mignet, M. Mary Stuart. 2 vols. Translation of preceding.

Opitz, Theodor. Maria Stuart. 2 vols. Freiburg, 1879.
Petit, M. Marie Stuart. 2 vols. 4to.
Petrick, Dr. Phil. A. Zur Geschichte des Grafen Bothwell. St. Petersbourg, 1874.
Petrick, Dr. Phil. A. Briefe der Königin Maria Stuart an Bothwell und deren Unechtheit. St. Petersbourg, 1873.
Portraits of Illustrious Personages. London, n. d.
Schiller, Frederick. Mary Stuart. London, 1854.
Schiern, Frederick. Life of Bothwell. Edinburgh, 1880.
Scribner's Monthly. Mrs. Oliphant's Mary, Queen of Scots.
Scottish Biographical Dictionary. (Scoto-Brittanicus.) Edinburgh, 1822.
Scott, Sir Walter. Scotland. Vol. II. Philadelphia, 1830.
Scott, Sir Walter. Monastery and Abbot. Philadelphia, 1852.
Smith, Rev. James. The Coming Man. 2 vols. London, 1873.
Strickland, Agnes. Mary, Queen of Scots. 2 vols. Bohn, London, 1873.
Stuart, John. Lost Chapter in History of Queen Mary Recovered. Edinburgh. 1874.
Swarbreck, S. D. Sketches in Scotland. Folio. London, 1839.
Swinburne. Chastelard. New York, 1866.
Swinburne. Bothwell. 2 vols. London, 1875.
Swinburne. Mary Stuart. New York, 1881.
Teulet, M. Lettres de Marie Stuart. Paris, 1859. 8vo.
Townend, William. Descendants of the Stuarts. London, 1858.
Turnbull, William. Letters of Mary, Queen of Scots. London, 1845.
Tyng, Rev. S. H. Recollections of England. London, 1847.
Von Raumer, Frederick. Queen Elizabeth and Mary, Queen of Scots. London, 1836.
Von Raumer, Frederick. History of the 16th and 17th Centuries. 2 vols. London, 1835.
Von Raumer, Frederick. England during the 16th, 17th and 18th Centuries. 2 vols. London, 1837.
Wiesener, L. Maria Stuart et Bothwell. Paris, 1863.
Yonge, C. M. Unknown to History. New York, 1882.

Besides a number of other well-known standard historical and biographical works on Mary Stuart, John Knox, the Regent Murray, &c., &c., in the different public libraries in the city of New York, and various biographical sketches in German, French and English, published in Europe and America.

OMISSION. Note to page 175 *supra*, second paragraph.—In "Bothwell; a Vindication," page 11, was furnished a copy of a Love Letter, penned in 1492; and in the present work, page 175–'7, *supra*, the copy of another Love Letter, written about 1700. Here, subjoined, is the copy of a Royal Love Letter, indited in 1613, by the "Foremost man of all this Modern World," GUSTAF ADOLF, to his sweetheart, the lovely EBBA BRAHE, at the age of nineteen, a *chere amie*, out of whose possession he was basely tricked. The three are worthy of comparison.

"STOCKHOLM, 5th April, 1613.
"MOST NOBLE DAMSEL, ADORED OF MY HEART,
  WHOM I LOVE MOST IN THIS WORLD:
"I have received your loving letter, by which you tell me you have submitted to the good pleasure of your father, at my request, with which I must content myself. Praying God to bend in grace your heart, that you think always on me, and remember the faithful love I bear you; and that you may never be persuaded that I think of another than you. Oh, may you pray God, as well as I, that He may let us live to see the day which may bring me the soft consolation and to you the joy. To his guidance—the Holy and Almighty—I commend you, faithful and tender; and myself to your breast, so noble and faithful.—I, to my dying day, oh, cherished maiden of my heart, your faithful and attached kinsman. G. A. R."

Horace Marryat's "One Year in Sweden," Vol. I., page 392.

Bothwell's Book-Stamp.

Decay.

"THE WORD! Do you remember, Meister? I told you then, that you had found the right one.   *   *   But you look like a happy man, and to what do you owe it? *To the Word*, the only right word: 'Art!'"

He let her finish the sentence, then answered gravely:

"There is still a loftier word, noble lady! Whoever owns it is rich indeed. He will no longer wander—seek in doubt." "And this is?" she asked incredulously, with a smile of superior knowledge.

"I have found it," he answered firmly. "It is 'LOVE!'"

Sophonisba bent her head, saying softly and sadly, "Yes, yes; Love!"

GEORGE EBER's "*A Word, only a Word*," page 348.

> "*But, mortal pleasure, what art thou in truth?*
> *THE TORRENT'S SMOOTHNESS ERE IT DASH BELOW.*"
> CAMPBELL.

"Discarding modern historians, who in too many instances do not seem to entertain the slightest scruple in dealing with the memory of the dead."   *   *   *   "*I am not ashamed to own that I have a deep regard for the memory of* [BOTHWELL] *Lord Dundee—a regard founded on the firm belief in his public and private virtues, his high and chivalrous honor, and his unshaken loyalty to his sovereign.* But those feelings, however strong, would never lead me to vindicate an action of wanton and barbarous cruelty, or even attempt to lessen the stigma by a frivolous or dishonest excuse. No cause was ever effectually served by mean evasion, any more than it can be promoted by unblushing exaggeration or by gross perversion of facts."

WM. E. AYTOUN, "*Regarding John Graham, of Claverhouse, Viscount of Dundee.*"

"Women are the priestesses of Predestination."   D'ISRAELI's "*Coningsby.*"

"The man who [like Bothwell] anticipates his century is always persecuted when living and is always pilfered [robbed of his credit] when dead." D'ISRAELI's "*Vivian Gray.*"

> "*With him his Fortune played as with a ball,*
> *She first has tossed him up, and now she lets him fall.*"
> *Verses on Medallion of* COUNT GRIFFENFELD, *Royal Library, Copenhagen.*

"He will surely violently turn and toss thee like a BALL *into a large country* [or as in the margin, 'the captivity of a man']: there shalt thou die, and there the chariots of thy glory shall be the shame of thy lord's house. And I will drive thee from thy station, and from thy state shall he pull thee down." [What could be more apposite to the end of Bothwell than these verses.]   ISAIAH, xxii., 18, 19.

"The black earth yawns, the mortal disappears."
TENNYSON's "*Ode on the Death of the Duke of Wellington.*"

O anticipate, for the purpose of making a point, Bothwell's enemies depict him—the Hereditary Lord High Admiral of his native realm, born in one of the grandest ancestral strongholds and castellated mansions in Clydesdale; the theme of the historian, the poet and the minstrel; celebrated in the words of a ditty known during the Crusades, from the Atlantic to the Dead Sea,

"Bothwell Bank thou bloomest fair"—

Bothwell Castle on the Clyde.

as dying a maniac in chains, in a loathsome Danish cell. This statement is founded on malice, forgery and ignorance. Notwithstanding all the efforts of individuals and governments, of learning and industry, a screen, as impenetrable as the "Veil of Isis," fell over the last years of "the great" "Scotland's proudest Earl." His principal advocate, Petrick, says, "*Then suddenly* —(referring to the autumn of 1571)—ALL IS SILENT! a great gap of four years occurs:—for what reason?" There is a solution and a plausible one. For six years the Danish government "had been tormented by the demands of Queen Elizabeth [of England] and the [successive] Regents of Scotland for the deliverance of Bothwell into their hands." Worn out with communications, reclamations and declamations, Frederic II. " allowed the report of Bothwell's death to be circulated, and so put an end to all the worry on the subject." This accounts for the doubts as to whether Bothwell died in 1575, according to Petrick, or in 1577 or 1578, according to Schiern and others. One sad fact is certain. He realized the words of the Prophet, Isaiah, xv., 9-10, in regard to the once mighty Belshazzar, "Thou shalt not be joined with them [thy forefathers and thy peers] in burial." Belted Earl and husband of a queen, his corpse rests in an unknown grave and foreign land. Bothwell, from the fall of 1567 until his decease—whenever it occurred—was "a prisoner of Hope" in the hands of Frederic II., King of Denmark. This monarch was a curious character. He was at once the protector of Bothwell and his custodian—whether at the last a severe or a lenient jailor nothing is definitely known. Falsehoods on the subject have been propagated industriously, but nothing trustworthy. That Frederic allowed him, for years, pocket money, respectful attendance, company and correspondence, and sufficient means to dress in accordance with his rank and enjoy good cheer is certain. In November, 1567, the king styles Bothwell "Our particular Favorite" (Shiern, 332). In January, 1568, Bothwell was living in Copenhagen, without anxieties for the future. When transferred to Malmo, it was still a sort of honorable confinement. His apartment was stately for the time. Even after this,

Malmo-huus.

down to 1571, velvet and silk were furnished for his attire, and his residence in Malmo, except as to duress, was anything but derogatory. He was purely a prisoner of State and of consideration. It was not until the 16th of June, 1573, that he was transferred to Dragsholm. Even then, it is very doubtful if his confinement was as strict as represented. It is questionable if his treatment in Zealand was more rigorous or galling than that of Mary in England. According to inspiration, Jeremiah was promised again and again, as the recompense for his own unmerited sufferings, undergone in obedience to his call, that his life should be spared. "Thy life shall be as a prey unto thee; because thou hast put thy trust in me, saith the Lord." If life is a boon, and if the wise king was justified in saying, "A living dog is better than a dead lion"—in that while there is Life there is Hope—Bothwell was certainly better off in comfort and safety in Denmark than either one of his enemies perishing in their prime and power by violent ends—deaths* culminating in horror with the burning alive at the stake of the Scottish Lion King at Arms; sacrificed thus on his return to Scotland from his mission to Denmark to solicit the extradition of Bothwell, because on the voyage home he had learned too much of the villainy of Murray and his associates. A moral lesson is conveyed by a time-table presenting the miserable and often horrible manner in which those who persecuted Bothwell went to their last account. It is very comfort-

---

* It is more than remarkable how every one, of greater or lesser note, who persisted in aspiring to the hand of Mary, came to grief. The most extraordinary instance is that of Erik, King of Sweden, who, on hearsay evidence, became completely enamored of her, and made expensive preparations for a voyage to Scotland to prosecute his suit in person. But the fate of her other admirers came to him, and he ended his life, after many weary woeful years of imprisonment in a vile dungeon, by poison in a plate of pea-soup.

ing to his friends and admirers to learn this. The author has derived the greatest satisfaction from the investigation of each successive terrible and untimely catastrophe.

Extracts from Marryat's "Jutland and the Danish Isles" [Vol. I., 408-19], appended as a Note to subsequent pages, will serve to present a mingling of fact and fable in regard to Bothwell's last imprisonment and sepulture, which is about as true as tradition* generally is—that is to say, there is a basis of fact, but the superstructure is almost all fable.

---

* Scarcely any man living has had opportunities more ample than the author to become acquainted with the untrustworthiness of popular tradition. In tracing back the history of a neighborhood it was painful to observe the discrepancies manifested in the recollections of the "oldest inhabitant" in contiguous localities. "MEMORY IS ATTENTION," and it is seldom that individuals pay attention to anything that is not of immediate personal interest to themselves. All the passions and all the weaknesses influence memory. People hear what their elders gabble, then talk the matter over and garble it to suit themselves, and transmit a tissue in which truth is like the Bean in a huge "Twelfth Cake." The bean is there, but a hundred slices may be cut before one reveals its presence. The author once sought out a road which, about seventy years since, was a main route between two frequented settlements, one a little port. A number had heard of it, a dozen pointed out depressions which indicated where it must have been located, but only one man could trace it. Why? In his youth he had worked upon it. No one but the author had ever thought it worthy of inquiry. The informant is extremely aged, the investigator is over sixty; in a few years both will have passed away, and after them everything in regard to the case in question will be mere surmise. So it is as to the last days of Bothwell. Horace Marryat advances as a proof that the corpse, which he claims to be Bothwell's, was really so—"a pearl embroidered cushion [pillow], a mark of rank," among the dead of the sixteenth century, "was found in the Scottish earl's

' In permitting Bothwell to leave her at Carberry Hill—
when the winning cards were still in her hands and retreat
to Dunbar was by no means hopeless, nor even uncertain
(Wiesener, 408)*—with reinforcements coming up, which

coffin." Even this is apocryphal—mere report, as worthless as tradition ever turns out to be. As "belted Earl," as mighty Magnate, as Hereditary Lord High Admiral of a realm, as Lieutenant General and military *Alter Ego* of a sovereign, as her husband, he was "the observed of all observers!"

"'Tis 'great' to hear the passer by say, There he goes! That's he!" Greatness in a measure is proved when "the world is singling you out and indicating you." As a prisoner, in a foreign land, in a remote castle, on a sea-surrounded islet, Bothwell was buried alive, forgotten.

* That Bothwell, with his acknowledged ability, could have effected a retreat to Dunbar, a fortress impregnable to everything the Rebel Lords could have brought, or kept, together against it, which in itself alone would have insured ultimate success, is demonstrable by a hundred parallel operations. (*Declaration of the Earl of Bothwell, addressed to the King of Denmark.* Agnes Strickland's "Letters of Mary Queen of Scots," II., 324) All it required was military ability, coolness and intrepidity. He possessed all three (see pages 48-'9, *supra*). The Queen's Body Guard, of Hackbutteers, the men-at-arms of David Home of Wedderburn and of John of Blackadder, Bothwell's own Borderers and the three falconets (light field artillery) with their "constables," would have been amply sufficient to cover a withdrawal of less than twenty miles, especially after impending night set in. The effect upon a fight, at this date, of a few trained musketeers, was almost incalculable. With a few efficient cavalry in support they could have turned this "Black" Sabbath into a bright Sunday. Witness the victory won, in a disadvantageous position on the Gelt, near Naworth Castle, in Cumberland, England, 19th February, 1570, by Lord Hunsdon over Lord Dacre. The latter had 5,000 certainly as good troops as the "Bonded" Lords; the former 1,500, but among these were the trained "Berwick harquebussmen." The volleys of the latter staggered and demoralized the bold Dacre Borderers, horse and foot, and then Hunsdon fell on them with a

would have assured a victory to Mary, this determination of the Queen to separate her fortunes from her husband has always, and in some degree, justly been brought for-

---

squadron of horse—such as those under Wedderburn and Blackadder at Carberry Hill—and the rebel armament "went to water." To show the effect of coolness coupled with capacity, recall an incident in the life of Sir Andrew Murray of BOTHWELL, son of the favorite colleague of Wallace, Regent of Scotland. "He was in the Highlands, in 1336, with a small body of followers, when the King of England came upon him with an army of twenty thousand. The Regent heard the news, but, being then about to hear mass, did not permit his devotions to be interrupted. When the mass was ended, the people around him pressed him to order a retreat: 'There is no haste,' said Murray, composedly. At length his horse was brought out, he was about to mount, and all expected that the retreat was to commence. But the Regent observed that a strap of his armor had given way, and this interposed new delays. He sent for a particular coffer, out of which he took a piece of skin, and cut and formed with his own hand, and with much deliberation, the strap which he wanted. By this time, the English were drawing very near, and, as they were so many in number, some of the Scottish knights afterwards told the historian who narrates the incident, that no space of time ever seemed so long to them as that which Sir Andrew employed in cutting that thong of leather. Now, if this had been done in a mere vaunting or bragging manner, it would have been the behaviour of a vain-glorious fool. But Sir Andrew Murray had already fixed upon the mode of his retreat, and he knew that every symptom of coolness and deliberation which he might show would render his men steady and composed in their turn, from beholding the confidence of their leader. He at length gave the word, and, putting himself at the head of his followers, made a most masterly retreat, during which the English, notwithstanding their numbers, were unable to obtain any advantage over him, so well did the Regent avail himself of the nature of the ground."

A parallel to this is the British General Crawford's coolness, during the Peninsular War, under Wellington, in Spain, in quietly

ward as an argument that she had ceased to love him, if she ever did care passionately for him.* Here once more Mary's principal biographer and advocate can be cited against herself and client, admitting (II., 83–'4) that the Queen could be "ungrateful and unreasonable," subject to "strange infatuations;" "had taken her resolution"— devoid of common sense, and blind and deaf to the les-

---
stopping his retreat to trice up and flog delinquents in face of the superior forces of the pursuing French, pressing hard upon his rear guard, and so close upon him that spent shots sometimes fell among those present at the punishment. Sir Henry Clinton, the Royal Commander against the Colonies, 1777-82, owed his rise and rank to his successful retreat with a comparative handfull, in the face of the French, during the "Seven Years' War" in Germany; and the same was the case with the noble Fraser, killed, under Burgoyne, in the Battle of Bemis Heights or Second Saratoga, 7th October, 1777. Had he survived, and if Burgoyne had listened to his advice, the wrecks of the invading force might have been able to withdraw into Canada, under the cover of the famous Light Infantry, which Fraser knew how to handle so admirably. The military murder by Morgan's sharpshooters forbade the experiment. Lord Clive, one of the greatest born-generals who ever illustrated the Annals of War, gained all his successes in India—such as Arcot, Arnee, Cowcrepauk, Seviavaram, Plassey, &c.— victories which laid the basis of the vast dominion of Great Britain in that Asian peninsula—against greater odds than Bothwell had to contend with, even after his Militia—Temporary or Feudal Levies—had failed him and flunked.

*Mary "was impulsive, hot-headed, warm-hearted, and in her virtues and her faults essentially a woman. *She fell over head and ears in love with Bothwell*, and, as is often the case when this occurs to a woman, allowed her individuality to be absorbed in his, and became for a time a mere tool in his hands. With the exception of this episode, she conducted herself very properly." ("Mary and Elizabeth," in *Truth*, London, Thursday, 11th January, 1883.)

sons of experience—"before she asked advice." If she had only shown a small portion of the energy she displayed eight months before, when, in the rough autumn weather, through a difficult country, and dangerous population, she rode on horseback fifty miles, thither from Jedburgh and back to visit her lover, previously wounded in her service, in Hermitage Castle—his headquarters as Warden of the

Hermitage Castle.

Marches, (see article "Jedburgh Abbey," *Saturday Review*, 30th September, 1882, page 439), Carberry Hill would have been a decisive triumph, instead of a disastrous and disgraceful catastrophe. It was simply the effect of cause; the inevitable quantities uniting in the product: *Ate* and Fate! If readers would study the most flattering stories of her friends in the light of reason, not feeling, they would find enough therein, to condemn their heroine and absolve Bothwell. Froude's (VII., 369) exposition of her character is masterly, and its correctness is established more and more by comparison and investigation. If this stood alone there would be difficulty in meeting it.*

Rarely, perhaps, has any woman combined in herself so many noticeable qualities as Mary Stuart; with a feminine insight into men and things and human life, she had cultivated herself to that high perfection in which accomplishments were no longer advantitious ornaments, but were wrought into her organic constitution. Though luxurious in her ordinary habits, she could share in the hard field-life of the huntsman or the soldier with graceful cheerfulness; she had vigor, energy, tenacity of purpose, with perfect and never-failing self-possession (?) and, as the one indispensable foundation for the effective use of all other qualities, she had indomitable courage. She wanted none either of the faculties necessary to conceive a great purpose, or of the abilities necessary to execute it, except, perhaps, only this—that while she made politics the game of her life, it was

---

* To show how fallible, after all, Agnes Strickland—the accepted biographer *par excellence* of Mary, Queen of Scots—proves herself to be, page 119, Note 1, Vol. III., of her "Letters of Mary. Queen of Scots," she states that Bothwell was the author [of the French translation] of the *Latin Libel* (upon Mary) of Buchanan, styled his "*Detectio*." Such a mistake is not only wicked, inexcusable and absurd, but not more so than many of the epithets Miss Strickland applies to Bothwell and her inconsistent remarks upon him. When this "*Detectio*" appeared, Bothwell was already a captive in Denmark, and no one charges him, after that period, with any reflection upon his ill-fated but false consort.

a game only [like the battles of Pyrrhus], though played for a high stake. *In the deeper and nobler emotions she had neither share nor sympathy.* Here lay the vital difference of character between the Queen of Scots and her great rival, and here was the secret of the difference of their fortunes. In intellectual gifts Mary Stuart was at least Elizabeth's equal; and Anne Boleyn's daughter, as she said herself, was "no angel." But Elizabeth could feel like a man an unselfish interest in a great cause; Mary Stuart *was ever her own centre of hope, fear or interest. She thought of nothing, cared for nothing, except as linked with the gratification of some ambition, some desire, some humor of her own,* and thus Elizabeth was able to overcome temptations before which Mary fell. * * While her sister of England was trifling with an affection for which foolish is too light an epithet, Mary Stuart, when scarcely more than a girl, was about to throw herself alone into the midst of the most turbulent people in Europe, fresh emerged out of revolution, and loitering in the very rear of civilization; she going among them to use her charms as a spell to win them back to the Catholic Church, to weave the fibres of a conspiracy from the Orkneys to the Lands End; prepared to wait, to control herself, to hide her purpose till the moment came to strike, yet with a purpose fixed as the stars to trample down the Reformation, and to seat herself at last on Elizabeth's throne.

"Whatever policy," said Randolph of her, "is in all the chief and best-practiced heads in France, whatever craft, falsehood or deceit is in all the subtle brains of Scotland, is either fresh in this woman's memory or she can fette it with a wet finger." (Froude, VII., 369.)

She was deluded by Kirkaldy, as she had often been before by Murray; but her first act, after she discovered the awful mistake she had made in disregarding her husband's counsels, was to write to him, and send him a purse or sum of gold. She again wrote to him from Lochleven; she refused to separate her fortunes from his; her thoughts dwelt constantly upon him; and the very night of her escape from Lochleven, "while the men were stretching their aching legs, Mary Stuart was writing letters." To whom? To her uncle, the Cardinal of Lorraine, in Paris, for assistance, and to her lover and husband, Bothwell. She sent the Laird of Ricarton, a kinsman of Bothwell, to raise the Hepburns, united to the "great Earl" by family and feudal ties, and make a dash on Dunbar to secure a port for the arrival of himself and of succor from France, and, when that port of entry was secured, to go on to Bothwell and tell him that she was free. Bothwell himself wrote to Frederic that he was on his way to Scotland, to raise men and money, when he was "treacherously captured" in Carmo-sund. Ricarton did "go on," and found Bothwell in his confinement at Malmo. Another account says, as soon as she breathed the air of freedom, she despatched a messenger to find Bothwell, wherever he might be, and announce the happy tidings of her release, and summon him to her side, whence he never should have been permitted, for her security and honor, to depart. Agnes Strickland, color blind as to every shade which could relieve or glorify the portrait of Bothwell, says that on her flight from Langside, Lord

Herries wanted Mary to take refuge in Earlston Castle, a stronghold belonging to Bothwell; that Mary became greatly agitated, burst into tears, and refused, "as if fearing to encounter her evil genius in his form, and prefering to brave any other peril than that of meeting him again." This is a puerile idea, and unworthy anything but the pen of a woman fighting to rehabilitate one of her sex, and, in so doing, so bitterly prejudiced as to forget the very characteristics of a such peculiar specimen of her sex as Mary. Consistent with their nature, it is likely Mary's love for Bothwell was so strong in her bosom, that she could not bear to tread the halls without him that once she had trodden with him in happier days. There is no greater "suffering"—exclaims Dante—"than to recall past happiness amid present wretchedness." Finally, to demonstrate the fallacy, if not wickedness, of all this misrepresentation of Mary's feelings for Bothwell to screen and excuse the Queen, even as late as the spring of 1571, when she was at Sheffield, she was in correspondence with him in Malmo, and had written, herself, to Frederic II., entreating him not to listen to the pursuasion of the Scottish envoy, Buchanan, laboring with so much enmity and earnestness against her husband. The correspondence must have been patent, for Buchanan told Cecil that, "if he took the trouble, he might intercept some of her letters."

That Lord Boyd, in 1569, obtained Bothwell's consent to the dissolution of his marriage, to enable Mary **to marry**

Norfolk, shows that the intercourse between the Earl and Queen, by letter and messenger, was still permitted. The fact is, Frederic's whole treatment of Bothwell was regulated by the probabilities of Mary's restoration to her throne. It was not until her case seemed desperate that Bothwell was finally immured, if he was ever actually thrown into a dungeon, which is very questionable.

What became of Bothwell after they parted, forever on earth, at Carberry Hill, Sunday, 15th June, 1567, is soon told. He returned unmolested to Dunbar, and remained there for several weeks undisturbed, although he did not confine himself to the fortress, but cruised about in the Frith of Forth, even penetrating beyond Edinburgh to the neighborhood of Linlithgow, to hold a meeting with Lord Claude Hamilton. Of his political projects at this time no record remains. Confiding the defence of Dunbar to his kinsman, Sir Patrick Whitlaw, he sailed thence, in the beginning of July, with two light vessels, and steered northward to visit his brother-in-law, Huntley, at Strathbogie Castle, about ten miles south-by-west of Banff, to the eastward of the Moray Frith. His intention was, doubtless, to raise forces in the northeast and renew the struggle. The Queen had many friends in that quarter; adherents who did join her after her escape from Lochleven, next year, 1568, and fought for her at Langside. Thence he proceeded to Spynie Castle, just north of Elgin, the residence of his aged great-uncle, Patrick Hepburn, Bishop of Murray, by whom he was brought up. Here a project was entertained to murder Bothwell, and a proposition to this effect was made to the English ambassador, Sir Nicholas Throckmorton, at Edinburgh. Whether the offer was rejected from policy or morality is not clearly shown. Some difficulty occurred, and Bothwell is charged with having slain one of his illegitimate cousins, who, in conjunction with two Rokebys, English spies incited by greed, were plotting against him. The latter even offered to kill the Bishop as well as the Earl. Throckmorton seems to have objected to such a summary proceeding, because no advantage could be derived from the crime in favor of England and Elizabeth.

Bothwell now determined to visit his dukedom of the Orkneys, and sailed for the chief town of the group, Kirkwall. The opinion of those who have investigated the matter with most attention is that Bothwell—after his failure to enlist the active co-operation of his brother-in-law, Huntley—intended to proceed to the Orkneys, gather what strength he could, and then, by the way of Sweden, proceed to France to arouse the sympathies of Charles IX.—who, personally, was very friendly to him, and had confidence in the Earl based on his service as "Chamberlain" at one time, and as "Captain of the Royal Scottish Body Guard," at another,—and derive from France, not only "the sinews of war," money, but actual military assistance. Fate, however, traversed all Bothwell's bold projects, and, at Kirkwall, he was received with the treachery he had always experienced from those he had benefited. His castellan, Gilbert Balfour, brother of Sir James Balfour, who had betrayed him after his marriage, and delivered up Edinburgh Castle to the Rebels—both accomplices in the murder of Darnley—turned the cannons of the place upon his feudal lord and benefactor. In consequence of this, Bothwell remained only two days in the port of Kirkwall, and then sailed northward to the Shetlands. Here he met with better treatment. The Bailiff, Olaf Sinclair, was a kinsman of the Earl's (now Duke) mother, Jane Sinclair. Olaf received him kindly, and the people furnished him supplies—a gratuity which was afterwards made the excuse for an onerous tax. Meanwhile, 19th August, Kirkaldy of Grange, Murray of Tullibardine and the Bishop of Orkney, who had married Mary to Bothwell, sailed from Dundee with four ships of war, the best in Scotland, which, in addition to the seamen, carried four hundred picked arquebusiers (musketeers) as marines. The three commanders had authority to bring Bothwell, if taken, to a summary trial, and execute him. On the 25th August, 1567, the four pursuing ships sailed into Bressay Sound, on the shore of which stands Lerwick, the principal town of the Shetland group. At this date, Bothwell's squadron consisted of four small vessels, two of which he had brought from Dunbar, and two Hanseatic armed Pinks, "two-masted lesser war ships," which he had hired at Sumburgh Head. One of these was named the "Pelican." Unconscious of danger, Bothwell's ships lay at anchor, and a large portion of their crews were on shore. Bothwell, himself, at the time was a guest of the Bailiff, Olaf Sinclair. Those in command who had remained on board, cut their cables and put to sea, and made their way to Unst, the most northerly of the Shetlands. In his pursuit, Kircaldy ran his flagship, the "Unicorn," on a rock, and it went down. Bothwell, meanwhile, made his way by land to the Yell Sound, and thence by water to Unst, where he rejoined his ships. Thence he sent back one vessel to pick up his men who had been left on shore. With the other three he was overtaken, in the last days of August, by Kircaldy with his three remaining ships of war. A hard fight ensued, which lasted for many hours. In the course of it the mainmast of Bothwell's best ship was carried away by a cannon shot, and the south-west wind swelling into a fierce gale put an end to the conflict by dispersing the combatants. The Earl was driven with two of his vessels out into the North Atlantic, and one was captured. Running south-east-by-east before the quartering gale, Bothwell soon traversed the 250 miles of ocean which separated the Shetlands from Norway, and first made the Island of Carmoe, twenty miles north-west of Stavanger, and was piloted into the quiet waters of Carm or Carmoe Sound. The ships had scarcely cast anchor when the Dano-Norwegian ship-of-war "Bjornen," Captain Christern Aalborg, made its appearance. By this Aalborg, Bothwell was "treacherously captured," and carried into the port of Bergen. There his case was investigated by a commission or jury, composed of four-and-twenty principal men of the town, of which the foreman was Dr. Jens Skelderup, Bishop of Bergen. (Gaedcke, 396.) By them he was fully acquitted of the charge of "piracy," with which his enemies had and have so consistently and falsely branded him. There is not the slightest basis for such a charge. This was about 2d September, 1567. After this, the Governor of Bergen Castle showed Bothwell great honor, and gave him a magnificent banquet. The Earl always mentions this governor with favor, and styles him "that good lord Erik Rosenkrands." Nevertheless, however courteously treated, Bothwell was, in fact, a prisoner, and when Captain Aalborg sailed from Bergen, 30th September, for Copenhagen, he carried Bothwell and some of his people with him. In the author's "Vindication" of Bothwell, he has furnished the dry details of the Earl's detention in Denmark, of which the following is the summary: The king, Frederic II., would not consent to the extradition of Bothwell at the urgent requests either of the usurping Scottish government or of Queen Elizabeth, nor would he let him go free. Comparing lesser things with grander, it was exactly the case of "The great Apostle" and the Roman Governor—"and Felix, willing to show the Jews a pleasure, left Paul bound." Frederic II. and Bothwell never met, but corresponded. In a letter, dated 18th November, 1567, the King designated Bothwell as "Our particular Favorite," and the Earl is syled in the correspondence, "the Scottish King," On receiving Bothwell's statement, Frederic allowed him to remain at Copenhagen, supplying him with apparel suitable to his rank and liberal entertainment.

In January, 1568, when the pressure of the Scotch regency became stronger, Bothwell was transferred to Malmo Castle*—then in Denmark, now in Sweden—on the

---

* "MALMO.—Soon church-towers arise in the distance, shipping, and a harbor; to the right stands a grim old castle, with staircase—gable and high-pitched roof, encircled by moat and bastion—once the prison of Scotland's proudest earl, the bad and reckless Bothwell. [See engraving, Malmo-huus, page 216.]

"An ancient plan of Malmöhus is preserved in the archives of the Radhus, by refering to which we discover the '*corps de logis*' to be the original palace of King Frederik II.'s time; the remaining buildings were added by Christian IV., as is testified by his cypher, entwined with that of his queen, Anna Catherine, A. K. 1608. * * But, before searching out his prison, we must first turn to the story of Bothwell himself, according to the records (some sixty-eight in number) which still exist in the Royal Archives of Copenhagen. In the autumn of the year, 1567, Bothwell arrived at Copenhagen, where we find him, about the latter end of December, a prisoner in the *king's palace*.

"Frederik was at that time absent from the capital, hunting at Frederiksborg, from whence he issued the following order to Biörn Kaas, the Seneschal of Malmö:

"Frederik, &c. Be it known to you that we have ordered our well-beloved Peter Oxe, our man, councillor and marshal of the kingdom of Denmark, to send the Scottish earl, who resides in the castle of Copenhagen, over to our castle of Malmö, where he is to remain for some

northern shore of the Sound, about opposite Copenhagen.
As the greater part of this castle was subsequently destroyed by fire, or "submerged in the stormy waves,"

time. We request of you, therefore, to have prepared that same vaulted room in the castle where the Marshal, Eyler Hardenberg, had his apartment, and to cover over with mason-work the private place in the same chamber; and, where the iron bars of the windows may not be sufficiently strong and well guarded, that you will have them repaired; and when he arrives, that you will put him into the said chamber, give him beds and *good entertainment*, as Peter Oxe will further direct and advise you; and that you will, above all things, keep a strong guard, and hold in good security the said earl, as you may best devise, that he may not escape. Such is our will.

"Written at Frederiksborg, 28th December, 1567." * *

"We entered the square court of the castle, and * * inquired whether there still existed any 'vaulted rooms' in the building of King Frederik II. time. In reply, we were informed that there were two large vaulted chambers on the ground floor, to one of which was attached a small square cabinet, scooped out in the thickness of the castle wall, towards the moat side. An exterior flight of steps led us to the entry of the chamber in which there is every reason to suppose that Bothwell passed some five years—may be the most tranquil of his unquiet life. It is a lofty, oblong, vaulted room, some thirty feet in length, lighted by strongly-barred windows looking on the court. On opening the door of the square closet, the floor was still covered over with mason-work of a blackish stone, well-worn, and polished by the friction of ages—that long narrow pavement so generally used in buildings of the sixteenth century. We quitted the castle perfectly satisfied that we had found the 'vaulted chamber' we had come in search of—the state-room of early days, in which the husband of Scotland's queen, Frederik II.'s own kinswoman, was ordered to receive '*good treatment*.' On the head of Bothwell, as on that of Mary, rested a fearful accusation—that of murder—an accusation which Frederik II. was reluctant to credit, as he writes word in his letter to the infant James, then eighteen months old, in answer to an epistle penned by the hand

there is no certainty as to what portion was assigned as an abode for "the most distinguished state prisoner of Frederic II." It is supposed that he was located in a

---

of Murray. The Danish sovereign refused to receive Bothwell into his presence; but, though he ordered him to be kept *a prisoner, he wished him to enjoy all the comforts and luxuries due to his rank and position,* EVERYTHING SAVE LIBERTY, 'until his case could have better consideration.' Of the doings of Bothwell during his residence at Malmöhus, we know but little. Two days after his arrival (30th December, 1567 [10th January, 1568?]) Peter Oxe writes from Copenhagen to the king to say that the Scottish earl desires to obtain a loan of 200 specie (£40), and to ask whether or not he shall advance it on the king's account; and later, in a MS. register of expenses in the Royal Archives, is preserved a statement, dated 2d March, A. D. 1569, which runs as follows: 'Likewise delivered to Bion Kaas, our man, councillor, and seneschal, at our castle of Malmo; according to order from our high steward aforesaid, English velvet and silk for 75 sp. 6 sk. (£15), of which we have made a present to the Scottish earl, who is imprisoned there.' It was during his imprisonment in Malmöhus that Bothwell composed that narrative of the leading events which terminated in his flight from Scotland, in 1567, as well as of his subsequent adventures, known by the title of 'Les Affaires du Comte de Boduel,' forwarded by him to the Danish sovereign. The MS., entitled 'Les Affaires du Comte de Boduel,' now in the library of Stockholm, is a copy of the original in the handwriting of Dantzay, followed up by his own correspondence with the French king. Bothwell concludes his narrative in the following words: 'Cet ecrit une je prye estre delivré à sa Majesté a fin qu'elle congnosse l'intention et finale volouté de la Royne Madame Marie qui estoit tellelment que je deborois demander a la Majesté de Dannemarch comme allie et confederé de ladite Royne ayde faveur et adsistance tant de gens de guerre que de navires pour la delivrer de la captivité ou elle est.' Lucky had it been for Frederik II. had Bothwell never set his foot on Danish ground, for never was potentate more tormented. First came monthly demands: vehement, and later even violent, from the Earl of Murray, for the handing over of

spacious apartment previously assigned to the governor—
a large, oblong, vaulted hall, with windows to the south
looking out upon the grand panorama of the Sound, re-

---

the earl's person to his custody for capital punishment, *with even hints
of a little previous wholesome torture*, such as boot, maiden, or something worse. Our Virgin Queen, too, dictated four letters on the subject to the Danish King, written in a pretty Italian hand, supposed to
be that of Ascham, to not one of which did Frederik (wise man) deign
a reply, at which neglect Elizabeth expressed herself much wounded,
though in one of them, by way of a sop, she adds with her own royal
pen, " Vestra bona soror et consanguinea." But *she got no Bothwell*
all the same. Then Catherine de Medicis was sure to write, at least
once a month, to her envoy, Charles de Dantzay, 'to insist that Bothwell should *not* be given over to the Scotch.' As to Frederik himself,
worried out of his senses, he was not at all inclined to deliver up
his prisoner, and that for certain reasons of his own ; for Bothwell,
in a letter dated 13th January (1568), had offered, if the king would
procure 'la deliverance de Madame Marie la Reyne sa Princesse,' to
cede to him the Orkney and Shetland Isles, a regretted appanage, long
since severed from the Danish crown.*

"As matters stood, therefore, it was perhaps as well to bear the
worry, and see what might turn up later. So he unburdens his mind
by writing to the German princes, his relations, explaining to them
what he has done, why he has so acted, and asking their advice; albeit,
at the same time determined to follow his own inclination, whatever
their answer might be. In the meantime Bothwell goes on drinking,
carousing and receiving the visits of his Scotch friends, *snapping his
fingers at Queen Elizabeth and the Scottish peers*, until the 16th of June
(1573), when he is suddenly removed to the castle of Draxholm, in the

---

* " Pour les frais qui y pourroyent estre faicts que je fisse offre à
ladite Majesté de vandre les Isles d'Orquenay et de Schetland libres et
quittes sans aucune empeschement à la couronne de Dannemarch et
de Norwegue comme ils avoyent cydevant quelque tems esté.

" Presenté à Helsingbourg au S. Peter Oxe et S. Jehan Fris Chan-
celier, le 16th Janvier, 1568."

motely to the west on the Island Hven, the residence of Tycho Brahe; nearer, on the Island of Saltholm opposite, and Amager beyond, in fact, the whole interesting and

---

island of Zealand. On the 28th of June following, Dantzay writes to his master, the King of France: 'Le Roy de Danemarck avoit iusques à pũt assez bien entretenu le Conte Baudouel, mais depuis peu de jours il l'a faut mettre en une fort maulvaise et estroite prison.' In addition to the testimony of Dantzay, the following entry has been lately discovered in a MS. of Karem Brahe, preserved in the library of Odense: 'In the year 1573, on the 16th of June, was the Scottish earl placed at Draxholm.' Scarce had the prisoner been removed when, on the 26th day of the same month, arrives a letter from the new Regent, Morton, demanding the deliverance of 'Damnatæ memoriæ parricidam nostram,' as he terms Bothwell, which, considering he had been himself a party to the murder of Darnley, is strong language, and with this epistle terminates the correspondence, for on the 24th of November following, Dantzay, after first announcing 'Au Roy—Sr Peter Oxe mourut le 24 jour d'Octobre,' continues, 'le Comte de Baudouel, Ecossais, est aussi decedé,' and this report of the Earl's death was believed by Mary herself, and generally credited throughout the whole of Europe, at the very time he was languishing in a damp unwholesome prison (?) of the Castle of Draxholm. It may be inferred that Frederik had been persuaded by his new Minister, Walkendorf, a man not over-scrupulous as to truth, to announce the death of his illustrious prisoner as the best answer to all the reiterated demands for his person, and thus putting an end to the vexed affair for ever. From this date we hear no more of the Earl, until the record of his death on the 14th April, 1578 (?), and his subsequent interment in the church of Faarveile.   *   *   What was the cause of this sudden change in the treatment of the Scottish earl, so well entertained by the King of Denmark for the space of five years? The Protestants, and those who were hostile to Queen Mary's cause, will tell you that from the year 1572, after the massacre of St. Bartholomew, the feelings of the Lutheran ruler of the realm underwent a change towards his Roman Catholic kinswoman, and that Bothwell to him was naught save the husband of Mary. The Roman

lively environs of the Danish capital not farther distant than from ten to twenty miles. Meanwhile the King took care that his food and clothes should be rich and ample. "He

Catholics on their side assert, and that strenuously, the story of his confession to be true, in which he 'malade à l'extremite au chateau de Malmay, declared la Royne innocente de la ditte mort—lui seul ses parens et quelque noblesse autours d'icelle.' The confession of Bothwell, printed by Drummond of Hawthornden, 1625, has disappeared, as well as the other copies known to have existed formerly(?). The Danish archives lend no aid to the solution of the mystery. Frederik may have forwarded the original to Queen Elizabeth, the paper she 'kept quiet,' but *up to the present time the proofs are wanting, and all is doubt and obscurity.* How Malcolm Laing can assert these names are apparently fictitious is surprising. In olden times Malmö, before orthography was settled, was written Malmöye, Malmöge as well as Malmay: all these terminations being different dialects of the word *o* or *ey* island Malm, sand (Mœso-Gothic)—*ay* (island) being the real signification of the name. The Skane nobles were men of note and position, possessors of the lands and castles alluded to, lansmen and governors of fortresses and districts. The spelling of their names in Queen Mary's letter differs from that of the documents preserved in the Scottish College at Paris, but this is not to be wondered at. I myself, in the 19th century, after two years' familiarity with the Danish language, should be sadly at a loss to write them down correctly from dictation. Though old Otto Brahe, father of the illustrious Tycho, was at that time gathered to his ancestors, yet the province of Skane was peopled by his descendants. But argue as you may—well or ill—until the missing document be forthcoming all will be vexation of spirit—so let the matter rest, and each man hold to his own opinion.

"There is nothing more to relate, so let us bid adieu to the vaulted chamber in the degraded fortress of old Malmo-huus, once a prison, far too good and spacious for the most restless adventurer of his age, the husband of Queen Mary—James Erle Boithuille."—"One Year in Sweden," Vol. I., pages 3-20, by Horace Marryat. From the de Peyster Collection, in the New York Society Library.

was detained there [Malmo] as a State prisoner, indeed, but led a luxurious life, and was treated far better than he deserved, being allowed the liberty of shooting and other recreations, while the King of Denmark ordered and paid for velvet dresses and other costly array for his use." When those "Titans of fraud" and crime, the Scottish authorities, empowered Colonel (*Obrist* or *Oberst*) and Captain John Clark, a Scottish mercenary—nominally commanding, in 1564, 200 Scottish cavalry soldiers in the service of Denmark—to demand the extradition of Bothwell, Bothwell turned the tables upon Clark by showing that when the Danish government sent Clark over to Scotland, in 1567, to enlist troops for its service, this agent was induced to expend the money entrusted to him for that special purpose for the benefit of the "Bonded" Lords in rebellion against Queen Mary and Bothwell, and actually marshalled the soldiers, mustered in to serve Frederic, to fight against the Queen at Carberry Hill. Clark was sent before a court-martial, and, in spite of the remonstrances of Elizabeth and Murray, was found guilty, consigned to the same castle, Dragsholm, that eventually received Bothwell within its dragon ward, and died there, a prisoner, before his intended victim.

After this affair of Clark (1568-70), Frederic II. relaxed the restraint on the Earl, and he was allowed full liberty within the precincts of the castle; nay more, he "was allowed no small liberty in Malmo," dressing in velvet and silk, and leading a tranquil, and by no means an unhappy life. In fact, except that he was not free (Wiesener, 505), "his life was that of a brilliant lord;" an existence far happier, perhaps, and certainly more comfortable than that of the majority of potentates at this era. At a later date, it is said, Captain Clark became reconciled with Bothwell in Dragsholm, and together they drowned their cares and ennui in wine. This kind of living killed Clark in July, 1575, and seriously injured the health of Bothwell.

Dissolution.

All upon a summer sea
Sailing in an argosy—
  Rebecs, lutes and viols sounding,
  While the ship o'er wavelets bounding,
Skims the surface of the sea.
   *   *   *   *   *
Stealing down a gloomy river,
Where dull water-grasses quiver,
  From a barque come sounds of sorrow,
  Never ceasing with the morrow—
Mournful barque upon the river.
   *   *   *   *   *
Sullen clouds obscure the moon,
Darkness cometh all too soon!
  Black the clouds and black the river,
  Black the barque, and oh! the shiver
As it sinks beneath the moon!—*The Argosy*.

ACT V. SCENE LAST. (ABBREVIATED.)

CARBERRY HILL. A knoll, whence the prospect extends to the westward and northward, looking over the nearer lines of the Queen's forces, and towards those, beyond, of the Confederate Lords. In the immediate rear stand three pieces of artillery, pointed at the latter, with a few "Constables" in charge : of whom one, assigned to each gun, at intervals waves his linstock to keep the slow-match alight and ready for immediate use. Near these are groups of royal regular Hackbutteers, belonging to the Queen's body-guard, at ease, and parties of Border noblemen and their retainers, Jackmen, evidently as if just dismounted, and leaning on their long spears. In the front centre are Mary Stuart and Bothwell ; and, to the right, but withdrawn a space, Kirkaldy of Grange. Behind the Queen is Captain Blackadder, one of Bothwell's subordinates, watching what is occurring in the enemy's ranks, and his remarks serve as an explanation or *Chorus*.]

    BLACKADDER. [*To Bothwell.*]
Hasten, my Lord, your colloquy : the foe
Are striving to outflank us. Look, their horse
To close the road to Dunbar, headlong spur.
If fight 's the word, now is the time to fight,
Lest we both lose advantage of the sun
Full in their faces ; our position too ;
And worst, if beaten, our retreat 's cut off.

MARY. [Continuing a conversation which had been going
on before the scene opened.]
I am resolv'd to trust Kirkaldy—
BOTHWELL.   Ah!
What glamour blinds thee, love? Thou know'st him not:
The hireling spy and England's traitrous tool.
He but deceives thee, with his specious tale;
His boasted chivalry is mere lacker.
Beneath the semblance of the golden truth
Is falsehood's foul and cheap-jack metal. Think
Ere you commit your fortune to such crew.

Bothwell breaks off suddenly, rushes to a Hackbutteer and, by signs and words inaudible to the spectators, directs him to shoot Kirkaldy, who, shading his eyes against the declining sun, is looking in a different direction towards his own friends. Mary, moved by Bothwell's charges, seems lost for a moment in deep thought; then suddenly perceives Bothwell's intention and throws herself between the musketeer and his aim.]

MARY. What would'st thou do?
BOTHWELL.   Slay the deceiving villain
By whom you are infatuated.
MARY.   James,
He 's under safeguard of my queenly word,
And, though he were the very knave thou say'st,
He must not die by an assassin shot.
BOTHWELL. [With difficulty restraining himself, and
    making a gesture to the musketeer to " recover
    arms," returns to the Queen's side.]
My love, my queen, my sweetheart and my life,
Thy noble nature and thy native sense
Are both the victims of this knave's device.
Is it not better, here upon this field,
To strike one blow for honor and thy crown
Than thus abase thyself to traitors—yield
Thy freedom, and perchance thy life, to those
Who never yet have kept a single Bond
Beyond the signing, had their purposes
But borne their fruit perfidious. Hast thou not
Prov'd me, as never yet woman prov'd man
Or had the chance to do 't? Have I not shown,
By ev'ry thought, word, act, since manhood's dawn,
That Truth and Bothwell were synonymous?
" KIIP TREST!" my motto—emblem of my life.
Was I not faithful to my mother; then
With equal truth did I not turn to thee;
Until thy love, enkindled at my own,
Or my big love, inflam'd by thy bright eyes,
Converted me from loyalty to love?
Have I e'er fail'd thee? Have I not been truth,
Love, faith, devotion: *all* thy sex can ask?
And yet thou dost not trust me; but prefer'st
The specious promise of a hireling tongue!
MARY. I am resolv'd to trust the Bonded Lords;
Not, that I have lost faith in thee, mine own,
But cause 't would seem as if by Fate impell'd,
This is the wisest course and fits the time.
A brief, sad parting and a better meeting
May bring again a long and halcyon term.

BOTHWELL. No, no! No, no! I tell thee, No! 'T would seem
As if, on board a stout still lusty frigate,
Because 't is slightly shatter'd by a squall,
Thou would'st abandon ship and practic'd captain,
To trust a pirate's skiff to save from storm
That lowers, but has not burst. Oh! Mary,
Dost thou love me?
MARY. My acts are the best answer.
I have gone through too much for thee to doubt it.
Oh, what have I not done to prove my love? [*Wringing her hands.*]
Oh, what have I not suffer'd to be thine?
BOTHWELL. Then, by the tie united us when twain,
And by the two church rites that made us one,
I do conjure thee, let me fight this day:
Not like a felon bid me steal away.
Never before has Bothwell quit the field,
But all victorious or upon his shield.

[Bothwell takes Mary's hand in his, and they stand thus, grasping each others hands, for some minutes; then clasp each other in a sad but fierce embrace. He glues his lips to hers, then suddenly releases her, and, gazing, seems to discern that neither kisses nor caresses have changed her resolution. His eyes question her.]

MARY. [*Suddenly.*] I am resolv'd to keep my word to Grange.
BOTHWELL. Oh, love! my life!
MARY. [*With a sad smile.*] Alas! we here must part;
Part for a time, assur'd of future meeting.
BOTHWELL. Wilt thou be true to me, and keep thy promise,
So often seal'd with kisses, e'en beside
The dead man's corse; to ne'er even in thought,
Nor word, nor bond, nor deed, annul nor weaken it;
Be my own Mary, till the whelming sea
Or the cold earth put seal to either life?
MARY. I promise. Go! Before it is too late,
Take horse for Dunbar, ere the foeman's horse
Cut in and make escape impossible.
BOTHWELL. [*With desperation.*] Will you not fight,
or let us fight?
MARY. Too late!

[Bothwell seizes her in his arms and kisses her wildly; but, seeing that even in this supreme moment she makes a motion for Kirkaldy to approach, he suddenly releases her and strides to the left of the stage; then turns, and perceives that Kirkaldy has drawn nearer to the Queen. Some one in the rear has given a signal to the enemy, and without, to the right, arise shouts, fanfares of trumpets and triumphant flams of drums.]

BOTHWELL. [*To those without.*] Ho! To horse! To horse!
MARY. [*Giving her hand to Kirkaldy.*] Come, Sir, let us go!

[These two last exclamations are simultaneous as the curtain falls. Rude, loud, triumphant music accompanies its descent, which gradually changes into softer and mournful notes, as the curtain again rises upon a double scene.]

FOTHERINGAY.	DRAGSHOLM.
Mary, with her head on the block, and the executioner standing over her with upraised axe.	Bothwell, lying dead upon the floor of his dungeon at Adelsborg.

[Curtain falls again to sad music, which gradually changes into a symphony, as it rises on the reunion of Mary and Bothwell.]

" JAMES HEPBURN, Earl of Bothwell," *an unpublished Tragedy.*

UNE 16th, 1573, why does not appear, Bothwell was privately transferred to the Castle of Dragsholm* (Dragon's Island), now Adelsborg. Dragsholm appears to be an isthmus (island ?) between Seiro Bay and the La(o)mme Fiorde, one of the arms of the Ise-Fiorde, on the northwest coast of Zealand, fifty-eight miles west of Copenhagen, off the road between the seaport towns of Holbek,

* Leaving the highroad from Copenhagen to Holbek, "before long the imposing Chateau of [Dragsholm, now] Adelsborg [the last place of confinement for Bothwell] appeared in sight, well placed among the surrounding woods, * * * in a private demesne. * * * As we approach the borders of the [tranquil] fiorde, on a little promontory jutting out into the sea, stands a whitewashed gabled church, and its spire of ancient date, simple and unadorned, but made to paint, the village Church of Faareveile, within whose walls repose [what are erroneously represented as] the mortal remains of the Earl of Bothwell, the so-called [the third and best beloved] husband of Mary Stuart, who died a prisoner, some say a maniac, within the walls of Draxholm, where he had been privately removed by the King of Denmark. * * The ancient castle of DRAXHOLM, or *Dragon's Island*, was, in former days, the property of the Bishop of Roeskilde: the huge mass of buildings are still something ecclesiastical in their appearance, surrounded by a moat, and of no architectural beauty. The great tower [represented] in the old engravings of Resen, was destroyed by the Swedes, in 1658; the chapel gutted during the War of the Counts, in 1533. It is the intention of [the present owner, 1860,] Baron Zeutphen Adeler to restore [it] to its former state. * * Before we proceed to visit the church of Faareveile, I may as well explain [in my way] how Bothwell came to end his days within the prison of the castle of Draxholm.

"It was in the year 1567 that sentence of death was passed by the Scottish Parliament on the Earl of Bothwell, at that time resident in

to the east, and Kallundsborg, to the west. Faareveile, where the body of Bothwell is said to have been deposited, is on, or near by, the shore of the L(a)omme Fiorde.

the Orkney Islands, having under his command a squadron of five light-armed vessels of war. * * * Bothwell's squadron, endeavoring, during a terrific storm, to escape from an armament sent in their pursuit [all mixed up, truth and error], two of his vessels managed to enter the harbor of Karmsund, in Norway. Bothwell here declared himself to be the husband of the Queen of Scots, and demanded to be conducted into the presence of the King of Denmark. Such is the account given by English historians. Now, however, that Bothwell is safe arrived in Norway, it is as well to consult the account given by the Danes themselves. In the '*Liber Bergensis Capituli*' we find the following notice:

"'September 2, A.D. 1568 [1567], came the King's ship "David," upon which Christian of Aalborg was head man; she had taken prisoner a Count [Earl] from Scotland, of the name of JACOB HEBROE *of Botwile*, who first was made Duke of the Orkneys and Shetland, and lately married the Queen of Scotland, and after he was suspected of having been in the counsel to blow up the King [Darnley]; they first accused the Queen, and then the Count, but he made his escape, and came to Norway, and was afterwards taken to Denmark by the king's ship "David [Bear]."' *The accusation of piracy made against the Scottish earl was never credited by Frederic II., or his advisers.* Bothwell had hired two [two-masted, lesser war-ships, called] pinks, when in Shetland, of Gerhard Hemlin the Bremois, for fifty silver dollars a month, commanded by David Wodt, a noted pirate [privateer, or letter of marque, for the terms were then synonymous and expressed by the same word], in which he arrived on the coast of Norway, in a miserable plight, his own vessel [flag ship] having returned to Shetland, with his valuables on board, to fetch his people [and valuables]. Erik Rosenkrantz, the Governor [of Bergen], thought necessary to summon a jury of the most respectable people of the town, 'twelve brewers of the bridge,' to enquire into the Earl's case, and how it was he had become associated with so well-known a pirate. Some of the crew affirmed they knew of

According to generally received accounts, Bothwell was plunged into a dungeon. This is mere surmise. Nothing is positively known.

— —

no other captain than one Wodt, to whom the pink belonged. The commission add, that this Hamburger (as Bothwell styles him in his narrative) was a well-known pirate.

"Still they suspected the Earl was about to go over to Sweden, a country at war with Denmark ; they accordingly recommend that he should take an oath that he would keep peace towards his Danish Majesty's subjects, as well as towards all those who brought goods to his Majesty's dominions. On this account only [a fear that the Earl was about to serve the Swedes, and not for piracy] Erik Rosenkrantz sends him a prisoner to Copenhagen. This was, no doubt, the origin of the accusation of 'piracy' made by the Earl of Murray [an unrelenting, malignant, personal foe] against Bothwell by the mouth of the infant king [James VI.], aged eighteen months. *The Earl had come to raise men in the North to aid the royal* [Mary's and his own] *cause*. Indeed, so satisfactory was his examination on this point, it is mentioned in the '*Liber Bergensis*' that, two days after his examination—

"September 28th [1567], Erik Rosenkrantz gave to the Earl and his noblemen a magnificent banquet : and, again, 'the Earl repaired to the Castle, and Erik received him with great honor.' * * * *

"On the 30th September, comes our last notice : 'The Earl was conducted to a ship and led prisoner to Denmark, that is Malmo-huus. This assertion is not quite correct ; as Bothwell remained in Copenhagen until the 30th of December [until 10th January, 1568, if not later], when he was consigned to the custody of Biorn Kaas, Governor of Malmo-huus, together with his companion, Captain Clarke. *Here he remained, well treated, with a liberal allowance from the King of Denmark*, indulging in potations with his comrade, which later brought him to death's door. Many were the requests from the Queen of England and the Scottish Lords to Frederick, demanding that the Earl should be handed over to their custody, to which the Danish Sovereign always replied by a refusal. If they chose to proceed against him they were are at liberty so to do, but judged he must be by Danish

Even Agnes Strickland is forced to admit that the popular tradition of Bothwell's madness is entirely without foundation, and that when at Dragsholm he was treated much

laws. It is related how, after a season, being brought to a state of weakness from the effects of a dangerous illness, his conscience tormented by anguish and remorse [utterly false], he made, in the presence of several witnesses, a confession of his share of Darnley's assassination, exonerating Queen Mary from any participation or knowledge of his crime. Mary, in a letter to her Ambassador on the subject, writes the names of those before whom the attestation was made, to be: Otto Braw, of the Castle of Eleembre; Paris Braw, of Vascu; Monsieur Gullensterna, of the Castle of Fulkenster; Baron Cowes, of Malinga Castle; so Miss Strickland gives them. I have this morning consulted a Danish *nobilier* to see whether I can, among the manors once in possession of these families, find any names similar to those here given. The spelling is obscure, but really not worse than that of a foreigner of the 19th century, if he attempted to write down the names by ear.

"Otto Braw, of the Castle of Eleembre, stands for Otto Brahe, of the Castle of Helsingborg, of which he was governor—father of Tycho Brahe. He died, however, in 1571. [It does not stand to reason that a corse was admitted as a subscribing witness, except in a blood-and-thunder drama, such as the Old Bowery 'Dead Hand.'] His son, Steen, was at that time alive, and resided near Malmo—indeed, the whole province of Skaane teemed with his family, *lehnsmend* and governors, high in authority. Paris Braw, of Vascu, I take to be Brahe, of Vidskovle, a chateau near Christianstad; Gullensterna of Fulkenster, Gyldenstierne of Fuletofte, probably Axel, son of Mogens Gyldenstierne, Stadtholder of Malmo, and himself a Governor; while for Baron Cowes, of Malinge, read Biorn Kaas, Governor of Malmo-huus, whose son, Jorgen, was possessor of Meilgard, in Jutland.

"In the copy of Bothwell's confession, preserved in the Scotch College in Paris, these names are again differently written. The Swedes, to whom Skaane now belongs, possess again an orthography different

better than he deserved; perhaps not worse than Mary was by Elizabeth. Schiern has demonstrated with greater clearness the *utter falsity* of the CONFESSION attributed to

---

from the Danes. You will not find them written in two books alike. After a lapse of fifty years, nothing can be more puzzling.

"It was in the year 1573, after the confession, that Bothwell was removed to Draxholm, and treated as a criminal; *though of that no documentary evidence exists.* * * * M. de Dantzay ['The French ambassador] writes word to Charles IX. that the King of Denmark, up to the present time, had well treated the Earl of Bothwell, but a few days since had caused him to be put 'en une fort maulvaise et estroite prison.' [This may simply refer to the strength of the Dragon Island keep and its loneliness, characteristics which would affect the judgment and language of a Frenchman accustomed to court life and long residence in a refined capital.] In the month of November, the same year [1573], he again announces, 'le Comte de Baudouel, Ecossais, est aussi décédé.' Bothwell, however, did not die till April 19th, 1578. [Not so, 1575:—1578 is disproved by the very narrator further on.] According to the chaplain of Draxholm, Frederic, tormented by the demands of Queen Elizabeth and the Scotch Regents for his deliverance into their hands, *allowed the report of his death to be circulated, and so put an end to all the worry on the subject.*

"In the chronicle of Frederic II.'s reign, Resen, under the year 1578, after stating that Frederic II. caused the dead body of his father to be removed from Odense to Rosiklde, continues: 'At that very time the Scottish Earl Bothwell also died, after a long imprisonment at Draxholm, and was buried at Faareveile.' That the Scottish Queen, in her damp prison of Fotheringay, receiving her intelligence in secret, should have been misinformed as to the christian names of the Danish noblemen who were summoned to the sick-bed of Bothwell, is not surprising;—such a confusion, too, as exists in these ancient geneologies; such an intermarrying between the families of Kaas, Gyldenstierne, and Brahe; such a changing and exchanging of manors by sale, by dowry, by gifte, *maal and morgen gaffue* (marriage settlement)—my head,

Bothwell. In all the authentic papers known to have been written by him, he insists upon his innocence, and with equal force alleges the guilt of Murray and Morton, and

before we had finished our researches, became a very chaos. [It was, the story shows it.]

" The [supposed] prison of Bothwell is now the wine-cellar of the castle, and the iron ring, to which he is reported to have been attached a maniac [which is false], stands inserted in the wall, between two shelves of the wine-bins—on one lies crusty Port, in the lower Château Lafitte. What a tantalizing sight for his wine-loving spectre, should he by chance revisit the seat of his former prison! *Bothwell died at Draxholm two years after his removal thither* [1573, consequently 1575, *not* 1578], and was interred in the parish church of Faareveile. * * * On the iron-bound door [of the church] appears the dragon, titular patron, I suppose, of the place. The interior is simple, of good architecture, with pulpit and altar-piece of Christian IV.'s date, and in sound repair. * * * They raise a folding trap [since definitely closed] in the chancel; a ladder leads to the vault below; on the right lies a simple wooden coffin, encased in an outer one for protection; the lid is removed, a sheet withdrawn, uncovered within which lies the mummy-corpse [this is altogether without proof and apocryphal] of Scotland's proudest Earl. The coffin in earlier times reposed in a vault of the chapel of the Adeler family, but was removed by the baron to its present place for the convenience of those who desire to visit it without intruding on the dormitory of the family. It had always, for centuries, been known as the tomb of 'Grev. Bodvell" by sacristan and peasant. When the wooden coffin was first opened, the body was found enveloped in the finest linen, the head reposing on a pillow of satin (?) THERE WAS NO INSCRIPTION.

Now, I am no enthusiast, and take matters quietly enough, but I defy any impartial *Englishman* [a nationality most inimical to Bothwell living and dead] to gaze on this body without at once declaring it to be that of an ugly Scotchman. [? ! ? ! ? ! Ridiculous assertion, and no proof whatever, as Schiern demonstrates.] It is that of a man about the middle height—and to judge by his hair, red mixed with

their associates. Even at Draxholm, it is stated that Bothwell "nevertheless, got permission to go hunting." It is supposed that Frederic transferred the Earl from Malmo to Dragsholm to relieve himself from the annoyances of the applications made by the successive Regents of Scotland and the Queen of England. In her endeavors to injure Bothwell with Frederic II. and retaliate upon the Earl in his distress for his life-long patriotic refusals of her invitations to imitate Murray, Morton, Kirkaldy and others, and become her tool, spy, and, like Murray, her "fawning spaniel," traitor to his country, she descended to the meanness of styling Darnley as "King," whereas she had hitherto refused him that title, both while living and when dead,

---

grey, of about fifty years of age. The forehead is not expansive; the form of the head wide behind, denoting bad qualities, of which Bothwell, as we all know [how, by misrepresentation ? yes !] possessed plenty ; high check-bones ; remarkably prominent, long, hooked nose, somewhat depressed towards the end (this may have been the effect of emaciation); wide mouth ; *hands and feet small, well shaped, those of a high-bred man.* I have examined the records of the Scottish Parliament, caused researches to be made at the British Museum—the copy of his 'Hue and Cry' is not forthcoming ; *no description of Bothwell exists* [great error], save that of Brantome, who saw [is supposed to have seen] him on his visit to Paris, where he first met Mary, during the lifetime of King Francis. * * Having first severed a lock of his red and silver hair as a souvenir, we let close the coffin-lid. * * Bothwell's life was a troubled one ; but, had he selected a site in all Christendom for quiet and repose in death, he could have found none more peaceful, more soft and calm, than the village church of Faarveile." (HORACE MARRYATT's "Jutland and the Danish Isles ;" pp. 408-19. de Peyster Alcove, N. Y. Society Library.)

styling him in her correspondence "the dead gentleman," "*le mort gentilhomme*" (Buckingham, I., 363–'4). Now she invoked vengeance upon Bothwell, as the cruel assassin of his relative and sovereign. And here it may be pertinent to observe that Bothwell was of the noblest blue blood on all sides. He was as nearly related to Mary as he was to his divorced wife, Jane Huntley, as he was descended from Joanna, daughter of James I., King of Scotland, and also from Queen Joanna, or Jane Beaufort, wife of James I., by her second husband, Sir James Stewart, "the Black Knight of Lorn." That Bothwell was in any degree related to Darnley is not shown.

When and where did Bothwell die? Many say in Malmo-huus. Sheer ignorance! Shiern says 14th April,

Ma'mo-huus.

1578; Petrick in the beginning of November, 1575. Whether he died in 1575 or 1578 there is nothing positive known of the details of his life after 1571.*

Reader, have you ever met with "Historic Doubts,"

---

* He made no Confession, he left no Testament inculpating himself or exonerating Mary in connection with the Darnley killing, and everything of the kind attributed to him are manipulations or forgeries. The best authorities now unite in conceding this. "Mary Stuart received the intelligence of Bothwell's decease"—says Gaedeke, 410—"without being much moved at it; passionate natures like hers have ever been wanting in feeling." Just so! She was a heartless, although excitable woman. Now Bothwell, then Darnley; now Bothwell then Norfolk, and then the Axe. Anathema upon her, she was unworthy of a "REAL MAN."

Schiern, Petrick and others have shown that no amount of research can discover any data to enable the biographer or antiquarian to lift even the lowest corner of the veil of doubt and ignorance which hangs over the last years of Bothwell. Schiern (386) corroborates Petrick. "The Earl's coffin was brought from Dragsholm to the nearest church at Faareveile. This church, which stands away from the village, on the west bay of Isefjord, in a lonely and quiet spot, the haunt of gulls and sea-fowl, is said to be the last resting-place of him who was the third and best loved husband of Scotland's Queen.

"As tradition still points out in Dragsholm the room which was Bothwell's prison, so among the coffins in Faareveile church, it continues to indicate one, without any inscription or adornment, as the coffin of the famous Scotsman. To ascertain the truth of the legend, the coffin was opened on the 31st of May, 1858, but without any positive mark being seen that the corpse found in it was really Bothwell's."

Marryat asserts that, unmistakably, the body he saw was that of an ugly Scotchman. Schiern explodes such a silly argument and assertion by citing the fact that "Bothwell was not the only Scotchman that was buried in Faareveile Church," and added the question, "How much of the 'ugliness' alleged here ought to be ascribed to the fact of the

or any one of the careful treatises written to prove how unworthy of trust are generally received traditions and the majority of histories, so styled. Do you know? Can you answer at once, Who was Joab? The author has asked this question indiscriminately many hundreds of times, and, except from a constant Bible reader, scarcely ever got a correct answer, if any at all, and yet Joab was the grand and able general of a great king, the father of the wisest monarch that ever grasped a sceptre, and the story of Joab, David and Soloman is told in the Book read by all civilized people. Joab's dispositions and victory at Medeba constitute an example of a class of peculiar battles, of which the latest was our Chancellorsville. Who was Simon Stevin of Bruges? A Dutch mathematician, who was the first to throw light on the darkness which had brooded upon the world, for 1800 years, since Archimedes. Maurice of Nassau was the restorer of military discipline; Simon Stevin was his preceptor in military science, proper,

---

body having passed three hundred years in the grave, it is certainly not so easy to determine." Why was not this the body of Captain Clark? Marryat says that the corpse he saw was that of a man of middle size. This does not agree with the traditional full-length "columnar," "overtopping tall," portrait of Bothwell. The famous Prussian General, von Moltke, justly conceded that great men would not enjoy posthumous excellence and immortality without poets and historians. By impartial pens Bothwell was represented as a stalwart, columnar, martial figure, as a powerful and imposing military chief, whose resounding tread rang battleward.

castrematation and engineering. Who was John Cavalier? A little Protestant baker's boy, in a small town among the mountains of Languedoc, who, at the age of twenty, made an army, equipped with weapons, mostly curiosities preserved in old armories, until he wrested better from his foes. With some three thousand peasants whom he had drilled, he held at bay sixty thousand regulars—veterans, volunteers and militia—and was a match in succession for two Marshals of France, one of whom was the celebrated Villars, who declared that his youthful opponent had performed "actions worthy of Cæsar." He treated as equal with equal with this same Villars, who was a local *Alter Ego* of Louis XIV., and by keeping such a mass of the best French troops in check in southern France, Cavalier converted Marlborough's campaign, which culminated at Blenheim, 13th August, 1704, from a probability into a certainty, that burst at once the bubble of French invincibility. Bothwell belonged to this class of marvels. Henry Taylor, author of the wonderful dramatic poem, "Philip van Artevelde," tells us

"The world knows nothing of its greatest men."

"Such souls,
Whose sudden visitations daze the world,
Vanish like lightning, but they leave behind
A voice that in the distance far away
Wakens the slumbering ages."

Bothwell lived on, and died at Dragsholm (? 1575, '76 or '78) faithful to the motto of his house, "KIIP TREST!"

Dragsholm Castle.

Keep Trust! Be faithful!

"A gentleman of credit, noble, honest,—
As true as his own sword."

His devotion, boy and man, to Mary of Guise, Queen-Dowager and Regent of Scotland, was inviolate and inviolable, and when Queen Mary returned to Edinburgh she still found his loyalty so lofty and unchangeable, that "it seemed to partake of that devotion which shed a halo over the days of Chivalry." Bothwell committed the crime which, in this world, never receives any other than the enigmatic absolution accorded by Pope Pius III. to the murderers of Cardinal Beatoun, "REMITTIMUS IRREMISI-BILE." "*We pardon the deed which admits of no pardon.*" Bothwell's crime—such a deed—was FAILURE, and, despite his loyalty, bravery, ability, patriotism and manifold other gifts,

> "He left a name at which [his] world grew pale
> To point a moral, or adorn a tale."

Bothwell's culmination or transit realized the language of Macbeth, about to perish:

> "Life's but a walking shadow ; a poor player,
> That struts and frets his hour upon the stage,
> And then is heard no more : it is a tale
> Told by an idiot full of sound and fury,
> Signifying nothing."

Bothwell's Book-Stamp.

APPENDIX.

ARNOLD GAEDEKE (Giessen, 1879,) on the Authenticity of the Casket ("*Chatoullen*") Letters, &c. Translated from the original German.

The genuineness of these celebrated letters has so often been a subject of the most embittered controversy, and so many hypotheses of all sorts, made with such an expenditure of ability, have been advanced* concerning it, that a rehearsal of all the arguments brought out for and against it, appears superfluous, especially since, to the opponents of their authenticity, little peculiarities and immaterial circumstances count for more than the most obvious deductions. *The genuineness of the letters—in my opinion—if one excepts perfect verbal correctness,† no longer admits of a doubt.* The attempts of the majority of recent writers must, decidedly, be rejected.‡ and the rather should this be done, that as good as nothing new is brought forward by them, as a basis for their views. It is the old *hair-splitting*, as to date, style, &c., which is again raked up, and which we encounter about equally in all of them.

There is only the fierce attack on Crawford's deposition, with the reasons given for it, which is new, and, therefore, of some importance, for this a document lately discovered among the Hamilton Papers has furnished the material. This document is a letter which Darnley's father, the Earl of Lenox, it is said, directed to Crawford from Chiswick. In it he conjures him, for God's sake, to furnish further matter of accusation against the Queen, or else the worst result—that is to say, the acquittal of Mary Stuart—was to be feared at York. "By all possible methods, to search for more matters against her," writes Lenox to Crawford, June 11th, 1568. ("Hamilton Papers;" Hosack, I., 199.) ☞ It is well known that the adherents of Mary Stuart have falsified to an enormous extent, and the circumstances that they should have been found in the possession of the Hamiltons is moreover very striking.

However—granted the genuineness of this letter—we can in the extremest case only conclude from it that Crawford, who had been summoned to York as a witness, and was preparing his testimony before hand, may have obtained previous knowledge of the contents of the *Chatoullen* letters, and the contents of the Lenox letter shows nothing at all against their genuineness. The *Chatoullen* letters had been long before the Scottish Parliament. Besides this the anxiety of Lenox was natural. When he wrote the letter in question, Murray had not yet thrown aside his hesitating attitude, which the Duke of Norfolk evidently had caused him to take, and he held back with the principal article of accusation. The anxiety of Lenox was acutely shared by Queen Elizabeth and by the English Commissioners. It is also to be remembered that Throckmorton had already declared, in a report of 15th July, 1567, that there were in Scotland proofs, in Mary's own handwriting—and finally, it is further to be borne in mind, that

---

* The attempt of Wiesener has been very justly rejected by Maurenbrecher ("historische Zeitschrift," XIV., 521 ff.)

† The original letters and the original casket (Fassung) are no longer to be found. The letters were in the possession first of Morton, then of Gowrie, and, finally, came into the hands of *James VI., who, no doubt, destroyed them*. We have only the Scotch and Latin translation, as also the retranslation into French of 1572.

‡ The opinion of the correspondent of the *Augsburger Allgemeine Zeitung*, of the 5th May, 1878, appears very groundless and rash. In a criticism of the works of Chantelauze and Morris he is bold enough to assert, on the basis of the recent publications, "that the view founded on a shuffle can scarcely any longer enjoy general assent."

the, as yet, cherished idea, that, the falsity of one letter being proved, the fate of all the others is decided, does not answer in historical criticism.

The chief arguments for the genuineness of the *Chatoullen* [difficult to be dealt with ?] letters have, up to the present time, been the following :

1. The agreement of the first principal letter with the declarations of Crawford, to whom Darnley, immediately after his interview with the Queen, imparted what was said, in order that the former should give an account of it to his father.

2. The mention of Hiegate, &c., a circumstance which no falsifier could have invented. This Hiegate was a town-clerk of Glasgow, who was said to have made a declaration as to the intention of Darnley to obtain possession of the young prince, his son. The Queen wrote about the affair to Archbishop Beatoun on the 20th January, 1567, and for many years no one knew how to explain the passage concerning it.

3. The peculiar form of the letter, which breaks off in the middle, from want of paper, &c., and is afterwards finished.

4. The confidential letter of the Earl of Lenox to his wife, in which the finding of the *Chatoullen* letters is discussed.

5. The unanimous decision of the English Commissioners, among whom was the Duke of Norfolk. No one held the letters to be falsified, there is nothing of the sort mentioned in the record.

6. The behavior of the Queen herself. Her commissioners declared, only on the 6th December, that all writings which could be brought forward by the rebels were calumnies and private communications, which could in no way be prejudicial to their mistress. Finally the Queen herself declared that Murray was, without doubt, in possession of papers of the highest importance.

To these proofs we are, in my opinion, now able to add a new and not inconsiderable argument. A passage of that first letter has remained up to this day (it has escaped even Froude) unconsidered, and this, simply, because it was not understood. We have, only within a few years, obtained the key to it through Teulet's publications. Just at the commencement of the conversation, we find a short question of Darnley's, whether the Queen had already prepared her "*état*," a question which she answers in the affirmative. We now know that this "*état*" was a List, prepared for inspection, of pensions and pensioners, and which was paid in France, out of the widows's-portion of the Queen, 40,000 Livres ; and that this list was prepared annually and forwarded to France, in order to serve as a *warrant* for the payments. The chief part of the recipients were Frenchmen, or servants living in France, as Beatoun, the ambassador, who received 3,060 Livres. The document of February, 1567, is in existence, signed by Mary Stuart and her secretary, Joseph Rizzio, brother of David, and, therefore, must have been prepared immediately before the Glasgow visit. (Estat des gaiges des dames, desmoiselles, gentilzhommes et outres officiers domestiques de la Royne d'Ecosse, Douairalre de France. Teulet II., 268.)

It is almost impossible that a falsifier should have hit upon this question, and very unlikely that the fact, in general, was known to many persons. Its being a short simple question is of consequence here ; if a falsifier had wished to make use of the circumstance, the passage would, without doubt, have been worded in an entirely different manner. But it is, most of all, of consequence, that in the Scottish Parliament, when the papers were laid before it, no one stood up for the Queen, although Huntley, Errol, and, above all, Herries were present. A circumstance which alone should be of sufficient weight to confute all the objections of apologists. The Parliament declared that "the process against the Queen was caused by her own offence," which was proved by various confidential letters, in her own hand, written to Bothwell before and after the murder of the King.*

---

* To be attributed to her own default, in so far as be divers her privie lettres written halely by her ann hand, and send be her to James, sometime Earl of Bothwell, chief

I will now turn to the objections which have been made by the other side. As regards the date of the letters, there is to be put into the scale that we have not the original letters, and that, in writing the translations, errors and faults in writing might easily occur. If there were a desire to falsify, it was easy either to omit the date entirely or to give it with the greatest exactness. I can find no contradiction in this regard. The Queen reached Glasgow on the 24th of January; the same night she wrote that long, famous letter to Bothwell, which she finished on the morning of the 25th. Paris set out at once, reached the capital on Saturday night, and brought the answer back to Glasgow on the morning of the 27th. The distances are not so great as to throw any doubt on this. Mary Stuart left Glasgow on the 27th, and arrived at the capital on the 28th. Paris, as a courier, accomplished the journey in still shorter time. Murray's Journal is in error when it makes Bothwell's first arrival in Edinburgh on the 28th, or, what is more likely, Bothwell, who stayed in the capital on the 25th and 26th, incognito, left the city with Paris, and returned on the 28th.

Hosack's grounds for the spuriousness of the letters have no significance. He directly denies Mary's passion for Bothwell (a thing which cannot be doubted), because she had "known him altogether too long." The audacity of Hosack's conclusions is generally wonderful. He likewise brings up Murray's will as a proof of Mary's innocence.

When Murray, after the murder of Darnley, betook himself to France, he made his will, and in it recommended his only daughter to the care of the Queen, in the most urgent manner. ("Morton Papers." Printed by the Bannatyne Club, I., 19.) At this time Murray had not the slightest knowledge of the *Chatoullen* letters; but, even if he had, he might still have commended his daughter to the care of his sister and sovereign, without thereby admitting the innocence of this last.

The "noisy" method and manner in which Darnley was killed, has also often been brought forward in favor of Mary Stuart. It certainly cannot be denied that the good sense of the Queen would at once cause her, in case she was initiated into the plans *of her lover*, to protest against this way of death, and, if one wishes to be just, it must further be admitted that, besides the declarations of Bothwell's servants—to which I attach but small importance—there is no piece of proof in existence that the Queen had a knowledge of all the details. ☞ This, however, diminishes her guilt in a very small degree : it does not even remove the character of treachery from her, since, that something was intended against her husband, Mary Stuart must have known as certainly as it is certain that she stood in a lover's relation with Bothwell. We possess the most indubitable proof of this.

Froude, an opponent, cannot conceal his wonder at the above. A murder by poison, he thinks, would, relatively, have but little injured her character. Aside from the fact that in Scotland such a thing was not usual, Bothwell knew perfectly well what he was about when he chose the "more noisy" mode of death. Already in possession of the *Chatoullen* letters, he then had the means of compelling the Queen to marry him. Exactly this noise-making, and otherwise entirely senseless mode of murder, is a proof, little considered, but very weighty for the genuineness of the letters. ☞ From the openness of the crime these letters first obtained their peculiar value. Hence sprang, after the marriage, the curious, heretofore incomprehensible, sadness and despair of the Queen, for whom there was no alternative from submitting to the will of Bothwell, although she foresaw the consequences and was badly treated by her lover.

It is, moreover, frequently maintained, of late, that the style of the letters is too inelegant and unpolished for the Queen to have written them, and that the Sonnets are too poor to pass for the work of so good a poetess ; that Mary's letters are refined, elegant, harmonious; these the opposite, "coarse, awkward and the merest patchwork," as

---

executer of the said horrible murther, as well before the committing thereof as thereafter. "Anent the retention of our Sovreane Lords Motheris Person Act, 1567, c. 19, Act Parl. III., 27." Burton, IV., p. 438. Scribner & Welford's edit., IV., 264–'5 (3).

Skelton calls them [passion, mixed with conscious guilt, does not produce fine composition].

The Sonnets, however, are by no means so bad, particularly when one compares them with those poems of the Queen on her first husband; in addition the form and [sound of the words?] as they now appear (are) probably not the original ones. Finally we possess very few really intimate and confidential letters written by the Queen. But these (last named) letters, as, for instance, the one to the Duke of Norfolk, whom Mary had never seen, betray in their style a remarkable similarity to the style of the *Chatoullen* letters, as Burton has elegantly and strikingly shown (Labanoff, III., p. 4, 11, 18); and this fact is in a much higher degree true of the well known letter which Mary Stuart wrote under passionate excitement to Elizabeth, in which she repels the calumnies of the Countess of Shrewsbury.

Furthermore, a forger would certainly not have introduced this degree of passionateness into the letters, it lay in the character of the Queen; also, he would never have put in the numberless trifles, from doing which, it is the custom for any one to be on their guard in a forgery. Petit maintains, since other grounds of proof fail him, that the Sonnette, in which the words, "I put my son in thy hands" occur, is alone a sufficient proof of spuriousness, because the young Prince had never been in Bothwell's hands. Yet it does not read. "I have put," and it is only intended to imply that Mary with her marriage expected to leave the safety of herself and of her son trustfully in the hands of Bothwell.

Very remarkable, also, is the view of the same author, to the effect that Bothwell would, had he been in possession of the letters, infallibly have shown them to the Lords at the Ainslie Tavern, and not less remarkable, finally, that Bothwell would have destroyed the letters after the marriage, since it was for his interest to annihilate the written proofs of his guilt. They were articles of proof for Mary's guilt; for that of Bothwell there were certainly other and far more weighty ones.

It must be explained, also, that the report of de Silvas to Philip II., of 21st July, 1567, has, as Petit reviews it, been torn out of its proper connection. Elizabeth was, in the highest degree, enraged at Lethington, and the other Lords. In respect to the letters she had not yet a satisfactory understanding. Thus she could speak to de Silvas in no other way.

It is remarkable that Skelton does not completely reject the genuineness of the *Chatoullen* letters, and this shows that he had not been able to get rid of the impression of their testing by the English Commissioners, in Westminster. He thinks that they, in part, really are from the hand of the Queen, but he excepts the two dated from Glasgow and Sterling. The others, he thinks, are from Mary's hand, yet written to Darnley, and taken by the opponents of the Queen, *i. e.*, in this case the falsifiers, from her papers, "in order to intermingle truth and falsehood, and give to the falsified parts the appearance of genuineness." He directly accuses Lethington as the falsifier, he expressly exempts Murray, for the letters were tampered with during his absence from Scotland. The accusing of Lethington is the more senseless since he (Lethington), from direct political reasons, had made the greatest efforts to prevent Murray's accusation and the production of the letters.

The conversation which Murray had with the Spanish Ambassador, de Silva, in London, on his return journey from France, is brought up by Hosack as a vindication. From what was said, however, it can only be concluded that Murray, then, had no precise knowledge in regard to the *Chatoullen* letters. But Hosack immediately concludes that another letter had been first falsified, and at a later time changed.

On the other hand, as regards direct participation in and privity to the murder of her husband by Mary Stuart, people have, up to the present time, gone somewhat too far. That Mignet should, at once, give full faith to the declarations of Bothwell's servants, which they made before their executions, has always been wonderful to me. The probability is very apparent that the accessory's accessories strove to cover themselves under the Queen's participation and approval of it.

It is, too, a decisive weight in the scale, that the chief actor, Hubert, called French Paris, did not make the compromising statements against the Queen until the second day of the examination; on the first day he, on the contrary, only described Bothwell's arrangements and activity. The conclusion is almost self-evident that his last declarations were pressed from him by the opponents of the Queen through hints of escape. Among these, especially belong the story of the costly coverlet, which the Queen caused to be brought away, shortly before the explosion. As to the (particulars) of Hubert's examination and the review of it, we know nothing. Haste was made to have him executed when he was, in the middle of June, 1569, brought to Scotland from Copenhagen by Captain Clark. As being in accordance with these points, the pretended Will of Bothwell is also brought forward by these recent authors. It has very recently been proved, in the most convincing manner, to be a forgery, although not unskilfully done, after very careful examination by Fred. Schiern, in Copenhagen.

As a new and important proof of the innocence of Mary Stuart, Hosack finally also cites an unquestionably very interesting letter from the Earl of Sussex to Cecil. This letter, however, on closer examination, contains entirely different things from what Hosack would make us believe. Sussex only says, in this letter: "It will be difficult to find ground for an accusation against the Queen, for if her opponents brought forward the letters, she might simply deny these, and justly accuse many among them of having themselves wished for the murder. So there might be better proofs." Thus, now, to draw the conclusion that Sussex considered the letters as falsified is an unhistorical and illogical proceeding, especially as Sussex, at that time, had in no way seen them. This letter is dated 22d October, 1568. That remarkable account of a contemporary (Dr. Thomas Wilson), concerning a confidential conversation, which he says he had with the Bishop of Ross, in relation to the imprisoned Queen, is also worthy of little credit as to its contents, and of doubtful meaning. The Bishop, and thus the representative of Mary Stuart, according to this conversation, not only allows the guilt of his mistress, but accuses her, most unambiguously, of killing, by poison, her first husband, the Dauphin. If Lesly really made this declaration, he appears as one of the most contemptible characters of that time, and Wilson's exclamation, "Lord, what a people, what an ambassador!" seems to be justifiable. We know too little of the personality of Wilson, and of the relations of the two men to each other, to be able to pass a clear judgment in the case.   *   *   *

I come, finally, to the declaration of Crawford. Burton, very properly, emphasizes the weight which his testimony possesses, under any circumstances. It possessed more clearness than any statement of facts which the Lords handed in. Crawford was known as a quiet honorable man, an excellent soldier, who, at a later period, performed distinguished service. Crawford, on his oath, declared what was read to him was true and accurate, "although it was, perhaps, not in the very words." He declared that Lenox, disquieted in regard to the unexpected visit of the Queen, had begged him to take notice of all that passed. And that the King, immediately afterwards, had communicated to him the particulars of the conversation, in order that he might inform his father of them. The commissioners of Mary declined, at Westminster, to hear Crawford orally on the subject. Hosack considers it entirely impossible that any interview could be rehearsed by two eye-witnesses with such similar expressions, and instances two reports of a modern legal speech. The question, however, is here, over some few very definite questions and answers; and, besides, as already mentioned, it is not impossible that Crawford had obtained a look at the Queen's letters before he prepared his testimony. Those letters of Lenox and Wood, which asked from Crawford details in regard to the sojourn of the Queen in Glasgow, in regard to her arrival, suite, conversation, whether she sent off letters and parcels, and had received returns, only show that Lenox was gathering all the materials he could, as, indeed, Murray in like manner, without doubt, caused his *Book of Articles* to be carefully prepared.

𝔉𝔦𝔦𝔭 𝔗𝔯𝔢𝔰𝔱.

www.ingramcontent.com/pod-product-compliance
Lightning Source LLC
Chambersburg PA
CBHW032146230426
43672CB00011B/2470